SECRET LIVES

OF

GREAT COMPOSERS

Library of Congress Cataloging in Publication Number: 2009922322

ISBN: 978-1-59474-402-0

Printed in China

Typeset in Helvetica and Trade Gothic

Designed by Doogie Horner
Illustrations by Mario Zucca
Production management by John J. McGurk

10 9 8 7

Quirk Books
215 Church Street
Philadelphia, PA 19106
www.quirkbooks.com

SECRET LIVES

OF

GREAT COMPOSERS

WHAT YOUR TEACHERS NEVER
TOLD YOU ABOUT THE WORLD'S
MUSICAL MASTERS

QUIRK BOOKS
PHILADELPHIA

BY ELIZABETH LUNDAY

ILLUSTRATED BY MARIO ZUCCA

CONTENTS

INTRODUCTION

You've checked your coat, handed in your ticket, and settled into your seat for an evening at the concert hall or opera house. You open the glossy printed program and turn to the notes to get some sense of the cultural enlightenment the evening has in store. Reading that erudite text, it is easy to come away with the idea that all composers pursued lives of moral rectitude and personal honor, one worthy of the refined attention about to be given their masterpieces.

Er, not so much. The idea of the "outrageous musician" is much older than rock and roll. Trashing hotel rooms? Beethoven could wreck a suite like nobody's business. Scandalizing audiences with sexual shenanigans? Liszt had passionate "fans" from Brussels to Budapest. Demanding concessions from concert promoters? They don't get much weirder than Wagner.

In fact, a lot of composers led truly outrageous lives. Mozart had a potty mouth, Schumann had syphilis, and Bernstein had an ego bigger than New York City. Bach wrote *The Well-Tempered Clavier* while locked up in the clink, Wagner cranked out *Lohengrin* while on the run from creditors, and Puccini crafted *Madama Butterfly* while trying to keep his wife from hunting down his (latest) mistress.

None of those details will turn up in that dull and well-intentioned concert program. So you have this book instead.

For *Secret Lives of Great Composers*, I hunted down the most outrageous and outlandish stories about some of the most remarkable composers of Western culture. This book won't tell you what to listen for in the fourth movement of some symphony or other, but it will tell you who tried to murder his ex-fiancée while dressed drag, who became a world authority on mushroom identification, and who shared compositional credits with his pet rabbit.

Of course, I had room for only a limited number of composers, so don't be hurt because I left out Holst, Offenbach, or Rimsky-Korsakov. This book isn't about musical significance, and I'm not judging quality. And please don't let the dirt on your favorite composer get in the way of your enjoyment of the music. Beautiful melodies, haunting chords, and glorious choruses can—and have—been composed by truly outrageous people, and the impact of the music is in no way lessened by a composer's oddities or aberrancies.

That said, the conductor has taken the stage, the lights have dimmed, and the conductor has raised the baton. You might want hold on to your seat—it's going to be a bumpy ride.

ANTONIO VIVALDI

MARCH 4, 1678–JULY 28, 1741

ASTROLOGICAL SIGN:
PISCES

NATIONALITY:
ITALIAN

MUSICAL STYLE:
BAROQUE

STANDOUT WORK:
THE FOUR SEASONS (1723)

WHERE YOU'VE HEARD IT:
IN UMPTEEN-MILLION MOVIES AND TV SHOWS, FROM *THE SOPRANOS* TO *THE SIMPSONS, SUPERMAN RETURNS* TO *A VIEW TO A KILL*

"I'VE BEEN A MAESTRO . . . FOR THIRTY YEARS AND ALWAYS WITHOUT ANY SCANDALS."

QUOTABLE

*I*n his day, Antonio Lucio Vivaldi was known far and wide as "the Red Priest" for his distinctive red hair and early training as a clergyman, but music lovers today know him best for the omnipresent strains of *The Four Seasons* piped everywhere from elevators to movie theaters.

Born into a family of meager means, Vivaldi had as little control over his future priestly occupation as he had over his hair color. When he was a child his parents decided he should enter the clergy, but this career path certainly wasn't his choice. His interests were always and only music. Fortunately for him, the priesthood never much got in his way. A convenient asthma condition excused him from priestly duties but somehow never interfered with his directing concertos or putting on operas.

Nor did the priesthood prove a stumbling block for other, fleshier interests, if the gossip around Venice is to be believed. The scandal of Vivaldi's life was his attachment to a soprano singer better known for her attentiveness to her "vocal coach" than for her singing talent. In the end, Vivaldi's loyalty to his student/lover would drive him from the country where he had enjoyed a successful career and into penury and eventually to his death in a strange land.

Reluctantly Religious

Vivaldi entered the world in a precarious state—apparently born premature, church records note he was baptized at home, "being in danger of death." He pulled through, although he remained sickly all his life. The eldest in a family of three sisters and two brothers, Vivaldi studied violin with his father, Giovanni Battista Vivaldi, who had started off as a barber but ended up as a professional musician in a local orchestra.

But life as a violinist back then promised even less financial security than it does today, and the impoverished family decided their oldest son should enter the priesthood. How Vivaldi felt about this decision we don't know, although he certainly took his own sweet time—a full ten years— training for the cloth. Nor did he seem to enthusiastically embrace his new duties. Apparently he presided at church services for only a year when "tightness in the chest" forced him to give up saying the Mass. It should be noted that this "tightness," today believed to be asthma, never posed a problem while he was conducting.

Girls, Girls, Girls!

By his twenties, Vivaldi had built a reputation as an accomplished performer and composer, and in 1703 he became a music teacher at the Ospedale della Pietà. The Pietà was an orphanage for girls, many of whom were the illegitimate daughters of the city's wealthy and powerful men. With ample support, much of it provided by conscience-stricken parents, the Pietà included an excellent choir and orchestra that was one of the main attractions of Venice. Tourists from across Europe came to gawk at young girls who not only played such ladylike instruments as the flute but also pounded away at manly kettledrums.

Presumably Vivaldi's priestly status made him a safe choice for instructing so many young women. In addition to serving as music director, he churned out some four hundred concertos for the Pietà orchestra over the next thirty-five years (although the twentieth-century composer Stravinsky once claimed Vivaldi actually wrote one concerto four hundred times). Among these is Vivaldi's most-remembered work, *The Four Seasons*. Composed in 1725 and based on four sonnets apparently written by the composer himself, *The Four Seasons* is Vivaldi at his best: charming, imaginative, inventive, and undemanding. Audiences loved it from the start— King Louis XV of France was a particular fan, so much so that his courtiers put on a special performance of the "Spring" movement just to keep him happy.

But What I Really Want to Do Is Direct

As much as Vivaldi seems to have thrived while writing for the Pietà, he had set his sights on a larger goal: composing for the opera. Opera had been invented in 1607 by the Italian composer Claudio Monteverdi in an attempt to re-create the musical style of the Greeks, who had incorporated music, dance, and acting into their dramas. The sights and spectacles of this new form of musical diversion immediately took off, particularly in Italy.

Vivaldi traveled around Italy, putting on his operas to enormous acclaim. His output was simply astounding: Between 1713 and 1739, he wrote nearly fifty operas, averaging almost two per year. The whole of *Tito Manlio* was written in five days. Audiences flocked to his productions, even if their appreciation at times seemed only half-hearted. "The new opera at San Grisostomo was more successful than the previous one . . . but the composition is so detestable and the music so sad that I slept through one act," wrote one

Venetian opera-goer to a friend in 1727. (The more things change, the more things stay the same, it appears.)

Lovely *La Giró*

The Red Priest eventually found a suitable consolation for underappreciative audiences: the soprano soloist Anna Tessieri Giró, known as *la Giró,* who made her performance debut in 1725. At some point, she moved into Father Vivaldi's house, joined eventually by her sister Paolina, who acted as a nurse for Vivaldi, whose health had become precarious due to his recurring asthma.

Everyone assumed Anna and Vivaldi were lovers; a few even claimed sister Paolina joined in the fun. Most people seemed not to mind—except for the Cardinal of Ferrara, who wasn't most people. In 1737, Vivaldi was in the midst of organizing an opera in Ferrara when the cardinal abruptly forbade him from conducting and Anna from singing. Outraged, Vivaldi protested that the cardinal had "put a stain on these poor women" and that he had as yet never been associated with any scandals. But the cardinal wouldn't budge, so the opera went on without Vivaldi and Anna. As one would expect, it flopped.

To Everything There Is a Season

In fact, a lot of Vivaldi's operas were suddenly flopping. Modern times and tastes had shifted away from the Red Priest. However, his name still had cachet north of the Alps, so the sixty-two-year-old composer left Italy sometime in 1740. His destination was Vienna, home of Emperor Charles VI, who was an old admirer of Vivaldi's music. Anna and Paolina in tow, he set out, only to have the emperor drop dead that fall after eating a plate of poisonous mushrooms.

The new royal family had more on their minds than the troubles of one Italian composer—namely, war with Prussia—and Vivaldi was forced to sell his composition manuscripts to make ends meet. In the summer of 1741, he fell ill of "internal inflammation" and died on July 28. His funeral service was held at St. Stephen's Cathedral, where a young Joseph Haydn was a singer in the boys' choir.

Vivaldi left behind hundreds of concerti, sonatas, and sinfonias—253 concerti for violins and strings alone—but little had been published during his lifetime. It was only in the 1920s that a huge portion of Vivaldi's compositions were discovered and entered the repertoire.

Today you're much more likely to hear his concertos—particularly the ubiquitous *Four Seasons*—than his operas, despite the fact that during his lifetime it was his operas that brought him fame. This is partly due to the nature of the scores, which are often incomplete and require extensive additions and revisions, and partly to their completely outlandish plots. Nevertheless, Vivaldi operas are enjoying a revival, with the first new productions of his works since the early 1700s recently appearing on stages from New York to Rotterdam.

SINGERS A CUT ABOVE

Another reason baroque operas such as Vivaldi's are seldom performed today is that they relied on a particularly strange (even barbaric) practice of the era: the use of singers known as *castrati*.

Castrati were men who had shown promise as boy sopranos; to preserve their exquisite high voices, they were castrated before reaching puberty. At the time, it was considered unseemly for women to parade themselves on stage, although why eunuchs performing in their stead was more "seemly" is unclear.

Castrati voices, which combined the high tones of women with the lung power of men, were so much the accepted standard that even after women were no longer barred from performing, castrati continued to take the stage. Italy produced the most castrati, despite that the operation was illegal in all of the peninsula's city-states. As an end run around the law, the boys were claimed to have suffered bizarre farming accidents or unusual cases of the mumps. Successful castrati could demand the most outrageous fees. The most famous insisted on singing their favorite arias in every opera, even if the arias were written by different composers and had nothing to do with the action at hand. (These pieces became known as "suitcase arias," since the performers took them with them wherever they went.)

For more than a century, starting in the mid-1600s, every opera that *was* an opera included at least one castrato. But by the mid-1700s, as some four thousand boys were castrated annually in Italy, the practice began to lose acceptance. In the nineteenth century, fewer and fewer castrati were created each year. The last castrato was Alessandro Moreschi, who died in 1922; having lived to the age of voice recording, Moreschi can still be heard singing in his unnaturally high voice.

ORANGE YOU GLAD TIMES HAVE CHANGED?

From the poorest to the richest, everyone went to the opera in Venice. But of course the fabulous upper crust would never allow themselves to mingle with the lower classes. Aristocrats sat in private boxes on the upper levels, where they passed the time playing cards and dining on lavish meals. (Back then everyone talked during the opera—insistence on reverent silence is a recent phenomenon.) Apparently, a favorite game during long recitatives was to drop orange peels on the peasants below, as well as to spit on them.

TOURISTS GAWKED AT VIVALDI'S ORCHESTRA OF YOUNG ORPHAN GIRLS WHO PLAYED EVERY INSTRUMENT FROM THE FLUTE TO THE KETTLEDRUMS.

HE'S THE POETRY MAN

As well as composing the music for *The Four Seasons*, Vivaldi also wrote sonnets to accompany the four movements. The poetry, frankly, lacks flair, but it is evocative, particularly when read along with the music. "Autumn," for example, "Celebrates the peasant, with songs and dances, / The pleasure of a bountiful harvest." "Winter" includes the lines, "We tread the icy path slowly and cautiously, for fear of tripping and falling. / Then turn abruptly, slip, crash on the ground and, rising, hasten on across the ice lest it cracks up."

Along with the poems, Vivaldi also wrote unconventional instructions for musicians. The second movement of "Spring" is to be played like a "barking dog," the first movement of "Summer" should evoke "languor caused by the heat," and the second movement of "Autumn" is to remind audiences of "drunkards [who] have fallen asleep."

Modern-day musicologists say all this extra-musical material makes *The Four Seasons* the first tone poem. Audiences have responded by making the work the most popular classical recording of all time, according to *Classic CD* magazine.

GEORGE FRIDERIC HANDEL

FEBRUARY 23, 1685–APRIL 14, 1759

ASTROLOGICAL SIGN:
PISCES

NATIONALITY:
GERMAN; LATER AN ENGLISH CITIZEN

MUSICAL STYLE:
BAROQUE

STANDOUT WORK:
MESSIAH (1741)

WHERE YOU'VE HEARD IT:
ON THE RADIO, IN SHOPPING MALLS, AND IN CHURCHES EVERY
CHRISTMAS AND EASTER

"I SHOULD BE SORRY IF I ONLY ENTERTAINED
THEM. I WISHED TO MAKE THEM BETTER."

QUOTABLE

George Frideric Handel is known primarily for one work, and even more for one part of that work: the "Hallelujah" chorus from the *Messiah*. A favorite of church choirs and TV advertising producers alike, "Hallelujah" has come to represent triumph and joy.

Yet *Messiah* wasn't particularly the triumph Handel had hungered for. He considered himself first and foremost a composer of operas, not religious music. But years of success and fame as an opera impresario came crashing to a halt when English audiences lost interest in his lavish productions. He cast about for something to compose other than operas, settling on oratorios such as *Messiah* only because he had no choice. So the next time you see an audience surging to its feet at the exultant opening chords, remember that Handel would much rather you were listening to one of his operas.

Papa, Can You Hear Me?

Handel's father was a respected barber-surgeon who considered music an uncertain and ignoble field. Unfortunately for him, his son George showed such an early and intense interest in playing and composing that the elder Handel was forced to bar all musical instruments from the house. His wife, however, believed in her son's talent and managed to sneak a small harpsichord into their attic.

One year, the elder Handel took George along on a trip to the court of the Duke of Saxe-Weisenfels. After chapel service, the boy snuck into the choir loft and began to play the organ. The duke asked who was at the instrument, and upon being told it was the child of the visiting doctor, he asked to meet them both. The good doctor immediately denounced his son's passion for music and declared his intention for George to be a lawyer. The duke replied that it would be a shame to stifle what was apparently a God-given gift. And so, bowing to royal pressure and, perhaps, the inevitable, Handel's father allowed him to receive musical training.

But Papa still had a say in things, and in 1702 the seventeen-year-old enrolled at the university in Halle to study law. When his father died the next year, however, all bets were off, and George moved to Hamburg to play harpsichord in the opera house. Exposure to opera transformed him. He presented his first two operas in Hamburg in 1705 to great acclaim and then headed south to Italy in 1706. His career took a temporary detour in 1707 when the pope briefly banned operatic performances; but Handel took to writing religious music instead, a strategy that would also serve him well in later years.

How to Appease Kings and Influence Singers

As Handel's fame grew, he attracted the attention of George, the elector of Hanover. George hired Handel as his *Kapellmeister* (choir master) in 1710, but the composer had no intention of hanging around stuffy, provincial Hanover. Within days, he took advantage of a loophole in his contract and was headed for cosmopolitan, opera-loving England. In London, he produced elaborate, extravagant operas. One of the most lavish was *Rinaldo*, which involves not only thunder, lightning, and fireworks but also live sparrows released on stage. (The effects were hampered, however, by the wealthy audience members who, as was the custom, were seated on the stage: In addition to chatting with one another and taking snuff, they felt at liberty to walk around the set. One operagoer complained that it was disconcerting to see gentlemen wandering through what was supposed to be the middle of the ocean.)

Handel eventually returned to Germany to appease his irritated boss, but within a year he was back in England. A stay of a few months then stretched into years, but before the elector could show his pique, Queen Anne died, and Elector George became King George I of England. Far from punishing his recalcitrant composer, the king commissioned multiple works, including "The Water Music," an instrumental concerto played for a royal party held on barges in the middle of the Thames.

Handel continued his operatic efforts, despite the sometimes difficult job of managing his performers. He had particular difficulty with sopranos, who argued with him over the length, complexity, and style of their solos; when one refused to sing a particular piece, Handel lifted her in the air and threatened to throw her out the window. On another occasion two rival sopranos grew so jealous of each other that, to appease them, Handel had to compose two arias of exactly equal length, right down to the number of notes. The public took sides in the dispute, and at one performance in 1727 the audience's hissing and catcalls turned into shouts and obscenities. The night ended with the two singers in a hair-pulling brawl right onstage.

The Coming of the *Messiah*

By the 1730s, English tastes in music began to shift: Most significantly for Handel, audiences grew tired of hearing operas in foreign languages. He persisted in his work, but the opera season of 1737 ended in failure, and Handel himself experienced a total physical collapse. Indeed, his illness was so severe that friends feared he would never recover. He did, but only to be confronted with the question of what to do about his failing career. It is at this point that he perhaps recalled those long-ago days in Rome, when a papal ban had led him to compose religious music.

An oratorio is a religious choral work; in the eighteenth century, oratorios followed the same format as operas, but without scenery, costumes, or all that onstage strutting. Handel set to work on the oratorios *Saul, Samson,* and *Joshua* to significant acclaim, despite some carping from religious types who felt the pieces transformed sacred scripture into entertainment. Handel, a church-going Lutheran his entire life, argued that he wasn't in the business of idle diversions but rather of Christian education, saying of his audience, "I should be sorry if I only entertained them. I wished to make them better."

Handel's best-known oratorio—in fact, his most famous composition—got its start in 1741 when the Lord Lieutenant of Ireland requested an oratorio to be performed in Dublin for the benefit of several charities. Handel created *Messiah*, which tells the story of the life of Christ from birth through crucifixion and resurrection. The composer's fame preceded him to Dublin, and the demand for tickets was so high that the promoters urged women to forego wearing hoops in their skirts so the hall could hold more people. From opening night, *Messiah* was a hit.

Burning Down the House

Handel continued to compose important works for English royalty. In 1749, he received a commission to commemorate the conclusion of the War of the Austrian Succession (not a war you hear a lot about anymore). The *Music for the Royal Fireworks* debuted at a public dress rehearsal so popular it attracted an audience of 12,000 and caused a three-hour traffic jam on London Bridge. The main event took place about a week later in Green Park. The plan had been for a massive fireworks display to take place as soon as the concert ended, but the evening faltered first when it rained and then when the pyrotechnics were disappointing. To top it off, an errant rocket set fire to the musician's pavilion, which promptly burned to the ground.

The early 1750s saw the composer in decline. He gradually lost his sight, becoming fully blind by 1752. Numerous treatments were attempted on his eyes, including surgery from the wandering self-proclaimed "opthalmiater" John Taylor, who had operated, with similar lack of success, on Johann Sebastian Bach. After several years of illness, Handel died on April 14, 1759, at age seventy-four, and is buried in Westminster Abbey.

Handelian Heritage

Handel's music has never fallen out of favor, particularly in England; Victorian-era nationalists embraced him as a truly English musician, despite his German birth. Huge musical festivals each year were dedicated to his oratorios; the largest, in 1859, included an orchestra of 500, a choir of 5,000, and an audience of 87,769.

Germans tried to reclaim Handel as their own in the 1920s and '30s. The Nazi Party got in on the act, although they were frustrated that many oratorios, taken from the Old Testament, reflected too positively on Jews. Several works were "aryanized" with new librettos that replaced Jewish heroes with German ones. *Israel in Egypt*, for example, became *Mongolensturm (Mongol Fury)*. With the end of World War II, these bastardized versions were thankfully forgotten.

Despite all the hoopla, Handel probably would be disappointed to see that his oratorios were getting all the attention instead of his operas. This began to change in the post–World War II period, and today Handel's operas are produced regularly to critical if not always popular acclaim. Nevertheless, no other musical work in English has achieved the near ubiquity of *Messiah*.

WHEN ONE OF HIS SOPRANOS REFUSED TO SING A PIECE, HANDEL LIFTED HER IN THE AIR AND THREATENED TO THROW HER OUT THE WINDOW.

NO SUCH THING AS LOVE AT FIRST SIGHT

When Handel traveled to Ireland for the premiere of *Messiah*, he had to rely on unfamiliar singers, most of whom were not professionals. One bass named Janson, trained as a printer, had been recommended as a good singer with the ability to sight-read even the most complicated works.

At the rehearsal, however, Janson could only muddle through the pages. An enraged Handel swore at the printer in four languages and then shouted,

"You scoundrel! Did you not tell me you could sing at sight?"

"Yes, sir," replied Janson, "and so I can, but not at *first* sight."

DUELING HARPSICHORDISTS

In 1704, when Handel became harpsichordist for the Hamburg orchestra, he befriended a young musician named Johann Mattheson. Something of a showoff, Mattheson at age twenty-three produced operas for which he wrote the score, conducted the orchestra, played the harpsichord, and sang solos.

One performance, however, ended with a near-fatal encounter. Mattheson's opera *Cleopatra* was on stage, with the composer himself singing the part of Antonius. Since Antonius kills himself a good half-hour before the end of the opera, Mattheson liked to slip down to the orchestra pit and take over at the harpsichord. However, at this performance, Handel refused to give up his seat at the instrument. An outraged Mattheson challenged Handel to a duel, and the two came to blows outside the stage door. Mattheson nearly did in his rival when he landed a blow on Handel's chest—except that either a large metal coat button (one story) or the opera score stashed in Handel's coat pocket (another story) stopped the blade.

Mattheson liked to brag in later years that he taught Handel everything he knew about composing, a claim that should be taken with a big shaker of salt. Unlike Handel, who became an international celebrity, Mattheson never left his native Germany and is now largely forgotten.

BACH BLOCKER

Born only weeks apart in the same country, one might think that the composers Handel and Bach would have been friends. In fact, the two never met, despite Bach's earnest efforts on multiple occasions. Handel seemed less inclined to meet his compatriot—not surprisingly, from his perspective: Handel was the favorite composer of the king of England, and Bach was a rural nobody. Handel would never have predicted future generations would rate the church organist higher than the king's composer.

MESSIAH MYTHS

A number of legends have grown up around the composition of *Messiah*. First, while Handel did compose the oratorio in less than three weeks, it's misleading to think of him as working in a white-heat of divinely inspired passion, as is widely reported. Handel always worked quickly, and three weeks is nowhere near his record: He composed the opera *Faramondo* in nine days. (He speeded things up by reusing music from previous scores, never hesitating to plagiarize himself—or even, critics claim, others.)

Second, the story that a servant found him writing with tears pouring down his face as he said, "I did think I did see all Heaven before me, and the great God himself," has absolutely no factual basis and sounds completely out of character for the notoriously terse composer.

Finally, it has become tradition for the audience to stand during the singing of the "Hallelujah" chorus, supposedly because King George II stood up the first time he heard it. Several theories have been advanced for the king's standing, from the profound (he was honoring Christ as King of Kings) to the medical (his gout acted up and he stood to relieve the discomfort) to the ridiculous (he had dozed off and the triumphant chords shocked him into standing). There's absolutely no contemporary evidence for any of this, but standing during "Hallelujah" has become the musical equivalent of the seventh-inning stretch. If you don't want odd looks at the concert hall, you'd better stand.

JOHANN SEBASTIAN BACH

MARCH 21, 1685–JULY 28, 1750

ASTROLOGICAL SIGN:
ARIES

NATIONALITY:
GERMAN

MUSICAL STYLE:
BAROQUE

STANDOUT WORK:
THE GOLDBERG VARIATIONS (1742)

WHERE YOU'VE HEARD IT:
AS DR. HANNIBAL LECTER COMMITS TWO GRUESOME MURDERS IN
THE SILENCE OF THE LAMBS

"THERE'S NOTHING REMARKABLE ABOUT IT. ALL
ONE HAS TO DO IS HIT THE RIGHT KEYS AT THE
RIGHT TIME AND THE INSTRUMENT PLAYS
ITSELF."

QUOTABLE

Perhaps it's not surprising that Johann Sebastian Bach's father was a musician—sons often took up the professions of their fathers in rural German villages. But it *is* remarkable that Bach's grandfather, great-grandfather, numerous uncles, cousins, second cousins, and nephews were also musicians. So tight a grip did the family have on the local musical trade that when a vacancy occurred in a court orchestra in 1693, an urgent summons went out not for a violinist or organist, but for "a Bach."

Bach in turn passed on a musical career to four sons, one son-in-law, and one grandson. He also passed on to future generations an absolutely astounding volume of music. Bach wrote a new cantata every week for years. That's on top of the concertos, canons, sinfonias, sonatas, preludes, and partitas he cranked out in spare moments. This is the guy who wrote the sixteen-piece "The Art of the Fugue" for the sheer intellectual exercise.

Bach's was not a life of drama and excess; he never went on tour, performed before huge crowds, or even left his corner of southern Germany. Admittedly, he found the time to marry two women and father twenty children, but on the whole his days consisted of a steady round of teaching, conducting, and composing.

I've Got a Great Idea: Let's Name Him Johann!

As inevitable as a musical career was the name "Johann" for the young Johann Sebastian, born in 1685 in the small German town of Eisenach. His father, great-grandfather, seven uncles, and four of his five brothers carried the name, along with a sister, Johanna, and another brother christened, oddly, Johannes.

Bach's peaceful and contented childhood ended in 1694 when his mother, Elisabeth, died unexpectedly; his father followed her to the grave less than a year later. Sebastian was sent to live with his older brother Johann (natch) Christoph in the town of Ohrdruf. J. C. was a noted organist who had studied with Johann Pachelbel (of the famous Canon in D Major).

The brothers' relationship was not without conflict. J. S. longed to study a collection of music that J. C. had been given by Pachelbel, but J. C. kept the highly valuable hand-copied score locked in a cabinet. However, J. S. figured out a way to slip his hand through a grille in the cabinet door to sneak out the manuscript. Every night he would lift his brother's music and surreptitiously copy the score by moonlight. This went on for six months until J. C. realized what was going on and not only locked away the score more securely but also took away Bach's copy.

Grumpy Young Man

In 1702, Bach got his first job, as organist for the town of Arnstadt. He was required to direct a choir and orchestra with many members older than he— a sometimes difficult task. One twenty-three-year-old instrumentalist started a scuffle with the eighteen-year-old Bach in the market square because Bach had called him a *Zipplefagottist* ("nanny-goat bassoonist").

Bach eventually moved on to Arnstadt, then Mülhausen, then Weimar, always working as an organist and conductor. Along the way, he married Maria Barbara Bach, his second cousin, with whom he later had seven children. He also earned a reputation as a temperamental prima donna. He pulled such stunts as asking for four weeks' leave and not returning for four months; he once threw his wig at an organist and told the man he would be better off as a cobbler. When offered a prestigious job at the court of Anhalt-Cöthen in 1717, he made such a fuss back in Weimar about receiving an early dismissal that offended officials threw him into jail for nearly four weeks. Never one to mope, he used the spare time to compose part one of *The Well-Tempered Clavier.*

Kickin' It with Counterpoint

It was at Cöthen that Bach came into his own as a composer. His preferred style was counterpoint, a form of music that dominated the Baroque period. In counterpoint, rather than supporting one melody with harmony, two or more melodies are played over and against one another. (If you've ever seen the musical *The Music Man*, you've heard counterpoint. The two songs "Lida Rose" and "Will I Ever Tell You?" have completely different melodies but are sung together.) Counterpoint evolved a complex set of theories as well as strictly defined compositional forms. Bach mastered it all, combining mathematical rigor with breathtaking inventiveness.

Bach's life in Cöthen was dealt a blow when he returned from a short trip and found that, in his absence, his wife had died suddenly. Again, never the moping type, within a year he had become smitten with a soprano soloist seventeen years his junior named Anna Magdalena Wilcke. After giving her a prominent position in the court choir, he upped her salary to three times that of the instrumentalists and then married her. When the Anhalt-Cöthen court hit a budget crisis, the Bachs decided it was time to move on.

Ambien? Sominex? No, Variations!

They landed in Leipzig, where Bach took the position of cantor at St. Thomas's church. This began the most productive period of his life. He churned out a new cantata *once a week*, eventually completing five full cycles of church music—that is, vocal music for every Sunday of the year. He also composed the *St. Matthew Passion*, *St. John Passion,* and the *Christmas Oratorio.*

Another commission supposedly came from Count Hermann von Keyserling, who suffered from chronic insomnia. Keyserling wanted his pianist, a former Bach student named Johann Gottlieb Goldberg, to have something special to play to put his boss to sleep, so Bach supplied him with *The Goldberg Variations.*

It's a nice story—and most likely entirely apocryphal. Goldberg was only fourteen years old at the time the anecdote would have taken place, and the *Variations* aren't exactly what you would call relaxing. It's more likely that Bach intended the work as an exercise in counterpoint and that Goldberg was one of its first performers. Experts describe *The Goldberg Variations* as Bach's greatest masterpiece for keyboard.

Deaths Anticipated and Real

Bach remained in Leipzig the rest of his life, although his prodigious output eventually slowed. He couldn't stop himself from quarreling with his bosses—one feud over who got to pick the hymns for Sunday services dragged on for three years. In 1749, the Leipzig city council started auditioning for his successor, even though Bach was still alive and kicking—and rather displeased to have his demise so eagerly anticipated.

By then, Bach was an anachronism, and counterpoint's precision and rigor were considered hopelessly passé. But the stubborn composer dug in. In *The Art of the Fugue,* he explored the possibilities of a single melodic line, even weaving himself into his music by creating a theme based on the notes "B-A-C-H" (in German musical notation, "H" is B major and "B" is B-flat).

The "BACH" fugue breaks off abruptly: The story goes that in the middle of writing it, Bach dropped dead. The truth is more complicated. Starting in the late 1740s, the composer's eyesight began to fail. In the spring of

1750, he turned to the "famed oculist" (a.k.a. certifiable quack) Dr. John Taylor to operate on his eyes. Taylor was no more successful with Bach than he had been with Handel; a brief reprieve of full sight was quickly followed by complete blindness. Seemingly drained of all energy, Bach struggled on for a few weeks and then suffered a stroke. He died on July 28.

I Can't Believe It's Not Butter!

Bach's music seemed likely to die along with him. Very little had been printed in his lifetime; the rest was squirreled away in church libraries. What saved him from obscurity was the gift of a manuscript copy of the *St. Matthew Passion* to Felix Mendelssohn for his fourteenth birthday. His grandmother obtained the original from Mendelssohn's piano teacher, Carl Friedrich Zelter, who claimed he had found the score some years earlier in a cheese shop, where it was being used to wrap butter. Most music historians think Zelter was full of it and that he had inherited the music from a former student of Bach's.

Whatever the case, the young Mendelssohn was immediately transfixed and, in 1829, the nineteen-year-old arranged for its performance in Berlin. He couldn't resist interfering with the music, cutting it from three to two hours, substituting a piano for the organ, and generally downplaying the Baroque-ness of the score. Bach would have been appalled by the lush and Romantic *Passion* that Mendelssohn performed, but Berlin audiences were wowed. Immediately the hunt was on for more hidden Bach gems, and ever since, Bach has been a staple of concert halls worldwide. Not bad for a guy who never left his provincial corner of Germany.

BACH COMPOSED THE FIRST PART OF *THE WELL-TEMPERED CLAVIER* WHILE IMPRISONED.

THAT'S A LOT OF BACHS

Bach eventually had twenty children by his two wives, although only ten survived to adulthood. Of his six sons, only one didn't become a professional musician—Gottfried Heinrich, who seems to have been developmentally disabled.

Another son, Gottfried Bernhard, showed great promise. Bach pulled

strings to get Gottfried a job as organist at Mülhausen, but within a few months he had to return in embarrassment to pay off Gottfried's debts. A second job in Sangerhausen ended even more badly when Gottfried vanished, leaving behind still more debts. The family had no word of Gottfried for more than a year, and then news arrived that he had died while enrolled as a law student at the University of Jena.

Fortunately, Bach's four other sons were made of sturdier stuff. Wilhelm Friedemann, Carl Philipp Emanuel, Johann Christoph Friedrich, and Johann Christian all composed music, although works by W. F. and J. C. F. are rarely played today. C. P. E. and J. C. were both widely known during their lifetimes and considered more important than their father, a situation entirely reversed today.

BAA-BACH'S BLACK SHEEP?

A final Bach to remember is P. D. Q., claimed to have been the twenty-first of Bach's children. In fact, P. D. Q. is the invention of musical satirist Peter Schickele and part of a long-running gag that has Schickele periodically "find" compositions of P. D. Q. and present them along with a heavy dose of musicological nonsense.

Schickele divides P. D. Q.'s life into three periods: the Initial Plunge, the Soused Period, and Contrition. Better at stealing other people's music than composing his own, P. D. Q. wrote works that are a pastiche of this and that—Baroque counterpoint, Romantic melodies, Renaissance madrigals, bluegrass, and even rap. Favorites include the "1712 Overture," *Oedipus Tex*, *The Short-Tempered Clavier*, and the *Grande Serenade for an Awful Lot of Winds & Percussion*.

GOULD'S GOLDBERG

One of the most famous twentieth-century interpreters of Bach was the Canadian pianist Glenn Gould. Born in 1932 in Toronto, Gould showed remarkable early talent, and by age fifteen was a professional soloist. For the next twenty years, he toured North America and Europe, impressing audiences with his amazing technical ability and eccentricities alike. He habitually shambled onstage dressed in layers to ward off drafts. Avoiding looking at the audience, he swayed and bobbed as he played, invariably accompanying his music with an off-pitch hum.

Gould claimed he could never sleep on an unfamiliar mattress and gave up touring in 1964. Many orchestras were relieved. He exhausted conductors with his insistence on unconventional musical interpretations, his rejection of almost any piano provided to him, and his endless adjustments to his specially constructed piano chair. He also canceled appearances at the drop of the hat. Gould devoted himself to studio work and began recording Bach's keyboard compositions, including not one but two versions of The Goldberg Variations. In most recordings, his hum can be heard over the piano, despite the heroic efforts of recording engineers to remove it. No matter—Gould played Bach like no one else, and fans around the world hailed his recordings as the definitive interpretations of the master's work.

Gould was a notorious hypochondriac. He once sued Steinway and Sons when a store manager patted him on the back a little too vigorously. He called it assault and claimed he had suffered permanent damage to his shoulder and spine. However, the pianist celebrated his fiftieth birthday in surprisingly good health. So everyone was shocked when, a few days later, he suffered a stroke. He lapsed into a coma and died on October 4, 1982. His recordings, particularly his two versions of *The Goldberg Variations*, remain hugely popular.

FRANZ JOSEPH HAYDN

MARCH 31, 1732–MAY 31, 1809

ASTROLOGICAL SIGN:
ARIES

NATIONALITY:
AUSTRIAN

MUSICAL STYLE:
CLASSICAL

STANDOUT WORK:
STRING QUARTET IN D MINOR

WHERE YOU'VE HEARD IT:
IN THE BACKGROUND OF NUMEROUS WEDDING SCENES IN FILMS,
INCLUDING *WEDDING CRASHERS*

"I WAS CUT OFF FROM THE WORLD. THERE WAS
NO ONE TO CONFUSE OR TORMENT ME, AND I
WAS FORCED TO BECOME ORIGINAL."

QUOTABL

For thirty years, Joseph Haydn was a servant. Admittedly, he was a high-class servant, but a servant nonetheless who received daily orders—just like a cook.

Although life as a musical servant meant a lot of bowing and scraping and an extreme amount of brownnosing, it had its advantages. For decades, Haydn had a ready audience for his compositions, a quality orchestra at his disposal, and time to explore his musical inclinations.

And whereas Haydn was happy when he could finally become his own man, he recognized the value of those years of servitude. They helped him become one of the most original—and influential—composers of his era.

Poverty and Prodigy

Haydn was born to a wheelwright in the peasant village of Rohrau in Austria, near the Hungarian border. Mathias, his father, had taught himself to play the harp, and he wiled away the long winter nights strumming folk tunes. As a tiny boy, Mathias's second son, Joseph, joined in with a beautiful soprano voice. His parents noticed that he beat time with remarkable accuracy. But Rohrau could offer little to a bright, musical child, and so when Haydn was only six years old he was sent to live with an older schoolteacher cousin in Hainburg.

Two years in Hainburg broadened Haydn's education, but greater horizons beckoned when the *Kapellmeister* (choirmaster) of the Cathedral of St. Stephen in Vienna traveled through Hainburg and heard the boy sing. Soon the eight-year-old Haydn was established in the cathedral's boys choir.

Unfortunately, boy sopranos have a short shelf-life. The worried teenager actually considered preserving his voice by joining the ranks of the *castrati*, but his father caught wind of the plan and rushed to Vienna to stop him. When Haydn's voice broke, the choir director promptly fired him. The sixteen-year-old found himself on the street with three shirts, a ragged coat, and the entirety of his musical knowledge.

Frau Haydn's Baking Secret

A fortunate encounter with a friend saved Haydn from sleeping on the street. In time, he was able to rent his own place in Vienna, a miserable sixth-floor room with neither stove nor window; but he had scrounged enough to buy himself a piano, and so had all he needed.

In time, Haydn began to attract the attention of prominent music lovers by playing in local orchestras and occasionally getting his own music performed, and in 1759 he landed a position as music director to one Count Morzin. Finally, the young man had enough money to get married. He had fallen in love with Theresa Keller, the daughter of a wig-maker, but her parents were insistent that Theresa become a nun. Nevertheless, the Kellers knew good husband material when they saw it, so somehow they convinced Haydn to marry Theresa's sister Maria Anna instead.

Whatever high hopes accompanied this union were quickly dashed. Maria Anna was older than her husband and possessed a shrewish temper, but her worst fault—in her husband's mind—was her utter lack of interest in music. "She doesn't care a straw whether her husband is an artist or a cobbler," Haydn complained. The couple had no children, and within a few years the relationship disintegrated into a series of jealous scenes and spiteful quarrels. Supposedly, Frau Haydn used her husband's manuscript scores as linings for her pastry.

AS A VIRGINAL YOUNG MAN, HAYDN BECAME TOO FLUSTERED TO PLAY THE HARPSICHORD AT THE SIGHT OF A FLIRTY COUNTESS'S DÉCOLLETAGE.

Counting on the Count

Despite his marital difficulties, Haydn was thriving professionally. In 1761, he was appointed Vice-Kapellmeister to Prince Paul Eszterházy, a wealthy and powerful Hungarian nobleman. In exchange for conducting and managing the talented Eszterházy orchestra and choir and composing music for both everyday use and special occasions, Haydn was given an excellent salary, comfortable housing, and a handsome clothing allowance. So pleased was the Eszterházy family by Haydn's work, they kept him on when Prince Paul died and was succeeded by his brother Nikolaus, who eventually named Haydn full Kapellmeister.

Despite the fancy title, however, he was a servant—a fact made clear by his contract, which called for him to report to the prince's antechamber every day to receive orders. Haydn spent a lot of his time soothing the egos of the prince and his courtiers, and his letters contain the effusive brown-nosing ("I

kiss the hem of your robe!") apparently required from subordinates. One of his major tasks was to intervene between the orchestra members and the court; his kindness and generosity toward the musicians earned him the nickname "Papa" Haydn.

Each spring the court traveled to rural Eszterháza, Prince Nikolaus's isolated estate, where they remained until late fall. Winter stays in Vienna were painfully short. As a result, Haydn spent thirty years isolated from the musical mainstream. Alone, he was forced to innovate. Because he lacked the brilliant intuitiveness of Mozart or the theoretical rigor of Bach, his advances were incremental rather than brilliant leaps. But over time, Haydn became a remarkable composer, one who refined the form of the symphony into what we know today. He essentially created the string quartet, establishing the defined structures for these works, which composers have been experimenting with ever since. Whereas many of his works were written simply to suit the tastes of his patrons—he wrote numerous trios featuring Prince Nikolaus's favorite instrument, the now obsolete baryton, as well as operettas for the marionette theater at the Eszterháza estate—he also composed pieces applauded for their clarity, elegance, and upbeat mood.

Free at Last

Nearly thirty years of virtual exile ended in 1790 when Prince Nikolaus died. He was succeeded by his unmusical son, Prince Anton. Haydn was finally free to pursue his own professional interests. (He felt equally free to pursue his own romantic interests; he and Maria Anna continued to live separately, and Haydn had a string of discreet affairs.) He embarked on a series of triumphant tours of England and Italy, conducting and performing his own compositions, and took the stage repeatedly in Vienna.

Prince Anton died in 1795 and was succeeded by Nikolaus II, who sought to restore the musical glories of the Eszterházy nobility. Since this Nikolaus didn't intend to live shut away in the country like his predecessor, Haydn returned to service with complaisance if not enthusiasm. These later years saw Haydn working on cantatas such as *The Creation* and *The Seasons*, today recognized as his best works for their inventiveness and beauty. By the turn of the century, Haydn had become tired and ill. His last years were marked by the savageries of Austria's war with Napoleonic France. French forces began heavy bombardment of Vienna on May 12, 1809, and cannon balls fell within yards of Haydn's house. The city soon capitulated, but the

French placed a guard of honor on Haydn's doorstep. He died on May 31, shortly after midnight.

THE STRANGE MISADVENTURES OF HAYDN'S HEAD

With the war still raging at his death, Haydn was buried rather hastily in Vienna. In 1814, however, Prince Nikolaus II applied for permission to move the body to the Eszterházy estate in Eisenstadt. The body was exhumed, but as officials opened the casket, they were shocked to discover that the corpse had no head.

An immediate headhunt was launched. It turned out two amateur enthusiasts of the now-debunked nineteenth-century science of phrenology (which purported to determine personality traits by analyzing the bumps on one's skull) had bribed the gravedigger to remove it. The two would-be phrenologists, named Rosenbaum and Peters, had encased the skull in a specially made black box.

When the body arrived in Eisenstadt without its head, the prince was outraged. He ordered police to search Peters's house but later learned that Rosenbaum's wife had buried it in the straw of her mattress and then pretended to be asleep during the search. The prince bribed the Rosenbaums, and, in exchange for a big check, they handed over what they purported to be the proper skull.

The Haydn skull ended up a museum in Vienna, where it remained until 1954, when Prince Paul Eszterházy finally reunited it with the composer's body in a grave in the Austrian town of Burgenland. After 131 years, Haydn was again in one piece.

LITTLE DRUMMER BOY

Haydn's cousin and guardian Johann Mathias Franck was responsible for providing the band for public festivals and church processions in Hainburg, and when his drummer died suddenly, he was in a real fix. Franck immediately taught Haydn, his seven-year-old ward with the precocious musical talent, to play. The problem was, the drum was much too heavy for the young boy to carry. Thinking quickly, Franck found a local hunchback willing to strap the drum to his back, so the young Haydn happily marched through the streets of Hainburg pounding away as the hunchback walked in front of him.

BEST FRIENDS FOREVER

Haydn met Mozart in Vienna in 1781, and the two quickly became close friends, despite the twenty-four-year disparity in their ages. Each recognized true musical brilliance within the other. Mozart claimed he learned the art of writing string quartets from Haydn, and Haydn once told Mozart's father, "I tell you before God as an honest man that your son is the greatest composer known to me."

Sadly, Mozart died while Haydn was on an extended stay in London. At first Haydn refused to believe the news, hoping it was a false rumor. When word of the death was confirmed, he fell into deep mourning. As late as 1807, when a friend mentioned Mozart's name, Haydn burst into tears. "Forgive me," he said, "I must ever, ever weep when I hear the name of my Mozart."

THE COMPOSER'S COMPOSURE

In 1759, when Haydn received his first major appointment as music director to Count Morzin, he was still a young man, one whose busy schedule and high morals had left him unacquainted with the pleasures of the flesh.

One day, as he sat playing the harpsichord, the lovely Countess Morzin leaned over to the see the score Haydn was reading, providing the virginal composer with a generous view of her décolletage. Haydn became so flustered that he abruptly stopped playing. When the countess asked him what was the matter, he exclaimed, "But your Grace, who would not be undone at such a sight?"

SURPRISE!

Haydn had a distinctively playful musical sense of humor. When composing a symphony for the orchestra of the Eszterháza court, he devised a subtle way to express the players' frustration at being kept far from their families each time the prince delayed their departure from his remote estate. Haydn's "Farewell" Symphony directed each musician to fall silent in turn at its conclusion, instead of winding up to a grand finale. As they finished, each quietly blew out his candle and tiptoed out. At the end, only the first violins remained. The prince got the message: The day after the first performance of the ""Farewell" Symphony, he gave orders to pack up.

A second symphony was designed especially for London audiences, which, Haydn noticed, had the unfortunate habit of drifting off during slow movements. He composed the *andante,* or slow portion, of his next symphony with the greatest sweetness and tranquility, eventually dropping into near silence. The quiet is then shattered suddenly by a massive shout of music and pounding on the kettledrum. At the piece's premiere, audience members nearly leapt out of their chairs—and thus the "Surprise" Symphony was born.

A HATE-HATE RELATIONSHIP

Although Haydn's long estrangement from his wife was well known to his friends, they were sometimes surprised at the level of mutual animosity. Once a friend noticed a big pile of unopened letters sitting on Haydn's desk. "Oh, those are from my wife," the composer said. "She writes me monthly, and I answer her monthly. But I do not open her letters, and I'm quite sure that she does not open mine."

WOLFGANG AMADEUS MOZART

JANUARY 27, 1756–DECEMBER 5, 1791

ASTROLOGICAL SIGN:
AQUARIUS

NATIONALITY:
AUSTRIAN

MUSICAL STYLE:
CLASSICAL

STANDOUT WORKS:
SERENADE NO. 13 FOR STRINGS IN G MAJOR (1787) (A.K.A. "EINE KLEINE NACHTMUSIK"

WHERE YOU'VE HEARD IT:
IN *ACE VENTURA: PET DETECTIVE*, *ALIEN*, *BATMAN*, *CHARLIE'S ANGELS*, *DADDY DAY CARE*, AND *THERE'S SOMETHING ABOUT MARY*

"THE ONE WHO DOESN'T WANT ME CAN KISS MY ASS."

QUOTABL

*T*he life story of Wolfgang Amadeus Mozart is one of the best known in classical music, yet much of what we think we know about him simply isn't true. Yes, he was a child prodigy, but a compositional genius as a preteen? Not exactly. Yes, he died far too young and in debt, but a despised failure? Hardly. Even the oft-told tale of his burial in a common grave is false.

But if the life of Mozart isn't what we think we know, the truth is in many ways far more compelling.

Daddy Dearest

To understand the man, one must first understand his father, Leopold. A bookbinder's son, Leopold gained exposure to the royal courts as a violinist and developed a burning ambition to better himself. Leopold hoped his compositional skills would vault him to the status he desired, but they only got him so far as a gig with the prince-archbishop of Salzburg.

He went on to marry Anna Maria Pertl, who bore him seven children, although only two survived infancy: a girl named Maria Anna, known as Nannerl, and a boy three years her junior, named Johann Chrysostom Wolfgang Gottlieb. "Gottlieb," German for "lover of God" or "god-love," would be translated into Latin as "Amadeus," given the free-form linguistic customs of the times. (So even Mozart's given name isn't quite what you may have thought.)

Leopold started teaching Nannerl how to play the clavier when she was six, but it was three-year-old Wolfgang who toddled over to the keyboard and started picking out chords. By four he had blazed through Nannerl's music books, and soon he was sawing away at a violin far too big for him. Leopold rejoiced to find that nature had provided a path to the good life in the form of his precocious son.

When Wolfgang was six, the family visited the Hapsburg imperial court, where the adorable child alternated between dazzling audiences at the keyboard and climbing onto royal laps. Trips around Germany and Austria were followed by years in France, England, and Italy. In London, Wolfgang improvised alongside Johann Christian Bach; in Italy, he received honors from the pope. Occasional snipes that Leopold was exploiting his son could easily be ignored. Money poured in, the family dressed in silks and brocades, and evenings were spent in the company of the social elite.

The only problem? Child prodigies refuse to remain children. The adorable boy transformed into a gawky, pock-faced adolescent whose skills were impressive but not unprecedented. Invitations dried up.

Love Hurts

Forced to return to Salzburg in 1773, Leopold got his son a job at court. The Mozart family, by now accustomed to more worldly amusements, were bored by their new lives, but at least Wolfgang had time to compose. (He had been publishing music since he was a child, but these were as much Leopold's compositions as Wolfgang's; eager to get his son's name in print, Leopold had extensively corrected these early efforts.) By his late teens, Wolfgang began to demonstrate his astonishing talent as a composer by whipping out five remarkable violin concertos and numerous piano concertos including the E-flat Concerto of 1777, a technical masterpiece and favorite of soloists to this day.

OCCASIONAL SNIPES THAT LEOPOLD MOZART WAS EXPLOITING HIS SON FOR COLD, HARD CASH WERE EASILY IGNORED.

That year, Wolfgang decided he'd had enough of Salzburg. Leopold suggested that they embark on another Grand Tour, but a new prince-archbishop had come to power, one who had no intention of letting the pair gallivant across the continent on his dime. Wolfgang requested release from his duties, and the archbishop summarily fired both father and son. A flurry of brown-nosing letters won Leopold his job back, but it was made clear that the tours with his son were over.

And so Wolfgang set out to find his fortune. Accompanied by his mother, Maria Anna (at his father's insistence), the twenty-one-year-old former boy genius headed first for Mannheim, Germany, where he met the lovely soprano Aloysia Weber and tumbled into love. The starry-eyed youth was sternly scolded by dear old dad in a deluge of angry letters—with all of Europe at his feet, he wanted to throw his life away on a soprano!

His father's harangues and his own uncertain finances forced Wolfgang and his mother to set out for Paris, but he garnered little attention there and even less income. Maria Anna, meanwhile, found herself isolated and ill in

a strange city. She took to bed but refused to see a French doctor. When she died on July 3, 1778, it took five days for her grief-stricken son to steel himself to send home the news. He left Paris within weeks.

His first stop was Munich, where Aloysia Weber had taken a position with the opera. Mozart begged the now successful singer to marry him, but she refused. Mozart sat himself down at the first available piano and regaled her with the following brilliant composition: "The one who doesn't want me can kiss my ass."

Speaking of Asses . . .

Back in despised Salzburg, Wolfgang spent several grim months squirming under the eyes of his father. He was then summoned to Vienna, where the archbishop was in residence. Mozart jumped at the chance to visit the capital—Vienna had all the musical opportunities Salzburg lacked. But life at the archbishop's residence exposed him to a succession of indignities, including having to eat at the servant's table: "At least," he snapped, "I have the honor of sitting ahead of the cooks." Matters disintegrated when the archbishop planned to return to Salzburg. Mozart had no intention of going back and requested paid leave to remain in Vienna. The outraged archbishop exploded, calling Mozart a scoundrel, a rascal, and a miserable fool.

Leopold wrote frantic letters attempting to restore peace, but his efforts were undermined by his son. Mozart ultimately alienated all his supporters at court, and his final visit to the archbishop's residence ended with Mozart being literally booted out of the house.

Fortunately, the Weber family—excepting the now-married Aloysia—had moved to Vienna and opened a boarding house. Mozart moved right in—and fell in love once again, this time with Constanze, Aloysia's younger sister. Ignoring his father's hysterical rants, Mozart married her in the fall of 1782. Constanze became pregnant almost immediately, and their first child, a boy, was born in 1783. Five pregnancies followed, although only two sons survived infancy.

Mozart struggled to survive as a freelance composer. While producing chamber music and symphonies, he focused primarily on opera (*The Marriage of Figaro* premiered in 1786, *Don Giovanni* in 1787, and *Così fan tutti* in 1790). Despite some success, his complete lack of financial sense lead to questionable decisions, and the family found themselves deep in debt. Constanze's health also began to suffer after her pregnancies, and she spent months at costly spas.

Upon Leopold Mozart's death in 1787, none of Wolfgang's efforts to build a more adult father-son relationship had succeeded: To Leopold, Wolfgang's life as an adult was an affront to his paternal tutelage. The will left everything to Nannerl, despite the family's small fortune having been earned by Wolfgang on those long-ago tours.

Requiem for a Heavyweight

The clouds finally lifted in 1791: Mozart's grief over his father's death subsided, Constanze regained her health, and the family began repaying its debts. His career reached an all-time high with the premiere of *The Magic Flute,* the epitome of light opera: It is melodramatic, funny, and contains dazzling displays of musicianship, including the famous "Queen of the Night" aria.

But Mozart's other major composition that year had strange and sinister origins. One day a messenger arrived at Mozart's home with a request for a requiem mass. The messenger refused to identify his employer and insisted all attempts to discover his name would prove futile. Years later, Constanze remembered her husband saying that he intended the project to be his "masterpiece and swan song." This seems highly improbable—Mozart was only thirty-five at the time, and there seemed no reason to believe he wouldn't have decades of work ahead. Nevertheless, the composer fell ill. In November, he took to bed with swelling in his arms and legs and fits of vomiting. (It's now believed he had rheumatic fever.) Mozart died less than two weeks later, on December 5, 1791. Despite melodramatic tales of Mozart's body being unceremoniously dumped into an anonymous, common grave, he was in fact buried in a single, unmarked plot. The lack of a tombstone was not unusual: At that time, all burial sites in Vienna were leased for ten years, and then the ground was plowed and readied for new occupants.

Meanwhile, the *Requiem* sat unfinished. Constanze, a widow with two small children, desperately needed money, but unless she could find a way to (a) have it finished and (b) pass it off as Mozart's, she wouldn't receive the balance of the fee. She turned to Franz Zaver Süssmayr, one of Mozart's students, who used remaining notes and sketches to finish the work. Constanze soon handed the score, complete with a forged signature, to the mysterious messenger.

So who was the anonymous commissioner? It turns out the secret wasn't so much sinister as sordid. An eccentric count named Franz von Walsegg had a nasty habit of secretly commissioning works from famous musicians and passing them off as his own. He intended to present Mozart's *Requiem* as his personal commemoration of his recently deceased wife. Instead it became a monument to its own composer—a man whose genius was cut tragically short.

MERCY FOR . . .

Way back in 1638, shortly after Gregorio Allegri composed his *Miserere*, Vatican authorities decided the choral work was so magnificent that all reproduction of the score was forbidden, as was performance of the work outside the Sistine Chapel. Any musician who broke the ban faced excommunication.

That didn't stop the adolescent Mozart. When the twelve-year-old arrived in Rome in 1770 with his father, one of their first visits was to the Sistine Chapel, where they heard the *Miserere*. Wolfgang immediately returned to his room and wrote the score from memory. After a second, confirmatory trip to the chapel, Mozart played *Miserere* for the pope and demonstrated his score. Fortunately, the pope was more impressed than annoyed by the precocious musical feat.

FECAL MATTERS

Mozart's music has a kind of elegance that might lead you to think the composer was a refined individual with sophisticated tastes. Not so much. Mozart retained a puerile sense of humor his entire life. He frequently concluded his letters with the kindly injunction, "Shit into your bed until it creaks." Or take this letter he wrote in 1778 to his cousin:

> Be sure to come, otherwise it's a shit; then I shall, in my own high person, compliment you, put a seal on your ass, kiss your hand, shoot off the rear gun, embrace you, clean you behind and in front, pay to the last penny whatever I owe you, and sound out a solid fart, and perhaps let something drop.

ROCK ME, AMADEUS!

Mozart and his wife had an intense sexual relationship that endured through their years of marriage and the birth of six children—as expressed in this letter from the late 1780s:

> Get your dear and lovely nest ready and most prettily, for my little fellow indeed deserves it. He has behaved very well and desires only to possess your beautiful [word crossed out]. Picture to yourself the little rogue who, even as I write, creeps up onto the table and looks up at me questioningly. On guard, I give him a smart slap . . . but the rascal only burns yet more and can hardly be controlled.

FACT OR FICTION?

The dramatic swings of fortune and ultimate tragic ending of Mozart's life have inspired numerous retellings, none more impressive than the stage play (1979) and later movie (1984) *Amadeus*. The Broadway production won the Tony award in 1981 for best play, and the movie won eight Oscars in 1985 including best actor, best director, and best picture.

The unfortunate result has been a lot of confusion between fact and fiction, most damningly in the play's portrayal of Antonio Salieri. Although not a genius on the level of Mozart (few are), Salieri was a talented composer who remains respected to this day. Far from being enemies, he and Mozart admired each other and even collaborated on a now-lost cantata. The rumors that Salieri conspired to murder Mozart were begun many years after the fact, primarily by nineteenth-century nationalists who sought to glorify the Austrian Mozart by painting the Italian Salieri as an evil, manipulative villain.

So enjoy *Amadeus,* but remember: It's *fiction*.

Child Prodigies

For reasons little understood by science, children as young as four or five years old sometimes demonstrate astonishing musical talent beyond the ability of many adults. Mozart is the prototypical child prodigy, but other famous composers also began as prodigies, including Chopin, Liszt, and Mendelssohn. Many contemporary world-class musicians began as child wonders, including pianist and conductor Daniel Barenboim and cellist Yo-Yo Ma.

But life is not always easy for these wunderkinds. Gangly, pimply adolescents tend to lack the charm of precocious children, and audience standards are higher for performers who abruptly cease to be unique. In reaction, some former prodigies decide to abandon performing in favor of a more normal existence. Pianist Marnen Laibow-Koser, for example, gave up a promising career to attend college, take up Web design, and learn Klingon. Others go through a period of self-doubt and then make a comeback with even greater success, such as violinist Julian Rachlin, who stopped performing in 1994 when he turned twenty but returned to the stage in 1997 and now tours widely.

Not all prodigies are so lucky. Violinist Josef Hassid had a nervous breakdown at age eighteen, was diagnosed with schizophrenia at twenty, and died of a botched lobotomy at twenty-six. Pianist Terence Judd debuted with the London Philharmonic at twelve but committed suicide at twenty-two. Other stories are more sordid than tragic: Pianist Ervin Nyiregyhazi was schlepped around Europe to perform at only six years old, soloed at Buckingham Palace at eight, and was a celebrity in both Europe and the United States in his teens. However, within a few years, the "new Liszt" had earned a reputation as an arrogant, temperamental prima donna with debilitating stage fright. He acquired ten wives along with an addiction to alcohol, but often lacked a piano, which was hard to haul to his flophouse.

Word to the wise: If your preschooler shows miraculous musical talent, think twice before pushing him or her to be a prodigy.

LUDWIG VAN BEETHOVEN

DECEMBER 16, 1770–MARCH 26, 1827

ASTROLOGICAL SIGN:
SAGITTARIUS

NATIONALITY:
AUSTRIAN

MUSICAL STYLE:
CLASSICAL

STANDOUT WORK:
THE "ODE TO JOY" FROM THE NINTH SYMPHONY (1824)

WHERE YOU'VE HEARD IT:
IN *A CLOCKWORK ORANGE* WHEN PSYCHOPATH ALEX DELARGE IS UNDERGOING VIOLENCE-AVERSION THERAPY

"MUSIC IS THE WINE WHICH INSPIRES ONE TO NEW GENERATIVE PROCESSES, AND I AM BACCHUS WHO PRESSES OUT THIS GLORIOUS WINE FOR MANKIND AND MAKES THEM SPIRITU-ALLY DRUNK."

QUOTABLE

*L*udwig van Beethoven transformed classical music into something bigger, bolder, and more extravagant than ever before. And the most remarkable thing about his accomplishment is that he did so when he was deaf as a post.

Beethoven was only twenty-six years old when he started losing his hearing, but he went on to compose for more than thirty years. There's no other achievement like it in the annals of human artistry. It's as if Michelangelo went blind but still painted the Sistine Chapel.

Unfortunately, going deaf did nothing to cure Beethoven's violent temper. As his hearing failed, his rages became uncontrollable and his outbursts more irrational. And still, the more bizarre his behavior, the more exalted his music became.

Why Can't You Be More Like Wolfgang?

Beethoven was born into a family of musicians in the German city of Bonn. His father, Johann, a tenor soloist at the local court and a budding alcoholic, greeted with indifference the birth of his son in 1770 and paid little attention to the child until he realized the small boy had an instinctive gift for music. The example of Mozart's early success was not lost on him, and Johann decided his own fame rested on the tiny shoulders of his son.

But whereas Leopold Mozart was a manipulative jerk, Johann Beethoven was a cruel, violent boor. Neighbors never forgot the sight of tiny Ludwig weeping over the piano keys. Time away from the keyboard was spent poring over lessons in music theory or practicing the violin. Rare were the days Ludwig wasn't locked in the cellar or flogged.

Johann's methods were brutal, but they bought results: By age ten, Ludwig possessed an encyclopedic knowledge of musical theory as well as virtuosic skills at the keyboard. But since he never had much time for schoolwork, his spelling was atrocious and his grasp of arithmetic shaky—he never mastered multiplication or division. (There is also some evidence that he was dyslexic.) At age eleven he left school permanently.

Mastering the Master

Johann never succeeded in transforming his son into a popular prodigy, but Ludwig's talent brought him to the attention of local aristocrats, and in 1787 patrons sent him to Vienna to study with Mozart. The giddy seventeen-year-old was introduced to the master, but before any lessons could take place, word reached Vienna that Beethoven's mother was critically ill.

The young musician headed home, arriving just in time to witness his mother's death. There would be no immediate return to Vienna; his two younger brothers needed supervision, and Father Johann was worse than useless. Within a few years, the elder Beethoven had become so unstable that he was pensioned off at half-salary, with the other half paid to Ludwig for the care of his brothers.

It wasn't until 1792 that Beethoven was able to return to Vienna, where, with the assistance of a wealthy sponsor, he took up lessons with Joseph Haydn. Here he was disappointed, however: Beethoven found Haydn unwilling to drill him as rigorously as he liked, and Haydn thought the twenty-two-year-old was arrogant. Not that Beethoven needed much more training. In 1795, he debuted with his Second Piano Concerto; by 1800, his First Symphony was presented. Vienna had found its newest superstar.

The Many Disgusting Habits of a Highly Successful Composer

It was at this time that Beethoven's friends began to notice he was avoiding social gatherings, Haydn commented that he never came to call anymore, and a visitor to Beethoven's apartment thought it odd his piano was out of tune. Beethoven knew very well what was wrong: He had lost his hearing. The decline was gradual, but eventually no amount of shouting penetrated his ears.

Beethoven had other health problems as well, including abdominal cramps, recurrent diarrhea, and frequent headaches. So miserable was the composer that he considered suicide. The only thing that stopped him was his fervent belief in his art. In the fall of 1802, while staying in the small town of Heiligenstadt, he wrote a moving description of the artistic resolve that kept him alive: "It seemed to be impossible to leave the world until I brought forth all that I felt was within me," he wrote in what has become known as the Heiligenstadt Testament. Constructed as a letter to his brothers, the document remained sealed in his desk for the rest of his life.

His new resolve left Beethoven bursting with renewed energy and ideas. The Third or "Eroica" Symphony (originally dedicated to Napoleon Bonaparte—until the general decided to invade Beethoven's Austria) was so revolutionary that the orchestra repeatedly broke off in confusion during rehearsals and critics declared the piece "bizarre." Audiences also complained the work was too long; "I'd give a kreuzer [a silver coin] if it would stop," complained one concertgoer.

Beethoven's "bizarreness" did not stop with his musical eccentricities. He composed best while walking and so became a familiar figure in the city as he wandered the streets, waving his arms and roaring out snatches of music, oblivious to the crowds of curious boys who followed him.

He never lived in one place very long; in Vienna he moved nearly forty times, and at one point was paying four different rents simultaneously. He was also a lousy tenant: A visitor to his apartment in 1809 found him living in "the dirtiest, most disorderly place imaginable." Every chair was covered with plates of half-eaten food and draped with discarded clothing. The piano and the desk beside it were deluged with half-completed, ink-smudged scores. And below the piano sat an unemptied chamber pot.

Nor was his physical appearance any more appealing—his wardrobe was so torn and dirty that appalled friends periodically replaced it for him. He had been dark-complexioned as a young man, but illness turned him sallow. His broad face was pockmarked and his gray hair stood on end.

ACCORDING TO ONE VISITOR, BEETHOVEN LIVED IN "THE DIRTIEST, MOST DISORDERLY PLACE IMAGINABLE"—FULL OF DISCARDED FOOD AND REEKING CHAMBER POTS.

It's little wonder members of the fairer sex weren't interested him, despite his fervent interest in them. Beethoven had a bad habit of falling in love with unavailable women—usually of a higher class and often married. His greatest love has achieved mythic status since her existence is known through another unmailed letter, this one addressed to the "Immortal Beloved." The addressee's identity has been widely disputed, but today most historians agree she was Antonie Brentano, wife of a Frankfurt banker. Delicate and refined, Antonie worshipped Beethoven ("He walks godlike among the mortals," she wrote) but remained faithful to her husband. If Beethoven found this painful, perhaps he derived some consolation from the fact that a doomed love is a whole lot more romantic than a wife who would expect him to put his dirty clothes in a hamper.

Futile Family Feud

Beethoven remained obsessed with the idea of family, even though he had alienated both of his brothers by violently opposing their marriages (he actually had their fiancées declared immoral in court). When his brother Caspar fell ill with tuberculosis, Beethoven fixated on gaining custody of Caspar's son Karl. He convinced Caspar to name him sole guardian, although Caspar later added a codicil making Beethoven's guardianship equal with that of his wife, Johanna.

When Caspar died in November 1815, Beethoven first accused Johanna of poisoning her husband and then snatched nine-year-old Karl from her care. His rants against Johanna became increasingly deranged: Johanna might not have been an ideal mother, but one might assume she wasn't really a "raging Medea" with "pestilential breath" whose sole intention was to "involve her child in the secrets of her own vulgar and evil surroundings." Poor Karl became a pawn in a series of legal attacks and counterattacks designed more to wound the other party than to promote the child's well-being. After five years of conflict, Beethoven, with all the power and money Johanna lacked, won the case.

It's difficult to believe that this bizarre, unhinged character was the same man who would, just four years later, write a triumphant hymn to universal brotherhood. His Ninth Symphony of 1824 concludes with a choral setting of Friedrich Schiller's poem "Ode to Joy" even as his own life was constricting in misery.

Beethoven's Last Movements

Poor Karl reached adulthood permanently and emotionally scarred. Beethoven barely let him out of his sight, and when Karl announced he wanted to enter the military, his guardian erupted in such screaming rages that their landlord evicted them. In the summer of 1826, Karl snapped under the strain and shot himself in the head. Amazingly, he survived—one bullet missed entirely and the other lodged in his skull without damaging his brain.

Karl left the hospital determined to forge his own life and immediately enlisted in the military. Friends described Beethoven as a broken man. A respite was granted by Beethoven's brother Johann, who invited the two to stay at his country house until Karl's service started. But summer stretched into fall. Johann's repeated hints having failed, he had to order his brother and nephew out of his house. A cold spell gripped the countryside as the two men journeyed in an open carriage and slept in an unheated inn.

By the time Beethoven reached Vienna, he had a high fever and pneumonia. He never fully recovered, lingering on in increasing misery for nearly three months. What happened next is highly debated. According to one account, the composer had been in a coma for forty-eight hours when, on March 26, 1827, in the midst of a massive thunderstorm, he suddenly opened his eyes as a flash of lightning illuminated the room. He lifted his right hand, clenched it into a fist, and fell back, dead.

A procession of more than ten thousand people followed the composer's coffin to its final resting place. Beethoven became an idol for the next generation of Romantic composers, who applauded not only his intense and expressive music but also his refusal to bow to common taste. And yet today, his themes and motifs are immediately recognizable even to those with absolutely no interest in classical music.

WATCH THE ROAR OF THE CROWD

By the premiere of the Ninth Symphony in 1824, Beethoven had been completely deaf for years. It was impossible for him to conduct this last masterpiece, but the maestro encouraged the composer to stand on the podium and set the tempo for all four movements.

The music filled the hall for more than an hour before reaching its triumphant conclusion. Concert-goers erupted with unbridled enthusiasm. The entire audience was on its feet clapping, shouting, weeping, and waving handkerchiefs.

Yet the composer heard nothing. He stood, his back to the crowd, peering down at the score. A young soloist named Caroline Unger gently took Beethoven's arm and turned him to see his adoring audience. It was one of the most poignant moments in the history of classical music: The ill and aging genius brought face to face with a celebration of music he no longer heard.

THE GENTLE ART OF MAKING ENEMIES

During Beethoven's lifetime, the aristocratic patronage system that had given composers their livelihoods ended, and the era of public concerts and music publishing began. Somehow Beethoven managed to antagonize the key players of both eras: wealthy noblemen and music publishers.

Beethoven once stood outside the palace of his patron Prince Joseph Franz Maximilian Lobkowitz shouting, "Lobkowitz is a donkey!" On another occasion he smashed a chair over the head of the wealthy nobleman Karl Alois, Prince Lichnowsky. When the prince understandably quit paying him a stipend, Beethoven had the nerve to be offended.

Music publishers and concert organizers fared no better. Beethoven was convinced people were out to get him and wrangled endlessly over terms and conditions. It didn't help that he had absolutely no concept of math; he covered the margins of letters and contracts with his frantic attempts at multiplication. Even more harmful to his financial security was his belief that such haggling was beneath him—"the human brain is not a salable commodity," he once wrote.

Because Beethoven always complained he had been cheated out of his last penny and lived in filth, most people believed he was desperately poor. On his deathbed, his pleas of poverty reached the Philharmonic Society in London, and the organization hastily collected £100 (about 1,000 Austrian florins) to send to him. After his death, when Beethoven's total estate was valued at 10,000 florins, the London Philharmonic Society was not amused.

THAT'S WHY THE COMPOSER IS A TRAMP

On one of Beethoven's long rural walks, he wandered into a small village. Local residents promptly called the police because they thought he was a tramp. He protested, but the officers hauled him off to jail. Finally, someone thought to ask the music director of a nearby town if he could identify the composer, which he did. Feeling guilty for imprisoning Austria's musical hero for vagrancy, villagers bought Beethoven a new set of clothes and sent him home.

TAKING THE FIFTH

Beethoven's Fifth Symphony premiered in 1808 but gained particular prominence during World War II. The British noticed that the famous opening theme (da-da-da-*dum*) has the same rhythm as the Morse Code "V" (dot-dot-dot-dash), so the symphony became a symbol of victory over fascism. The BBC began all of its broadcasts to occupied Europe with those four notes, symbolizing hope for victory to come.

BEETHOVEN'S HAIR AND HEAVY-METAL PHASE

Shortly after Beethoven breathed his last, his friend Johann Hummel and Hummel's student Ferdinand Hiller paid their last respects. In a gesture of homage, Hiller snipped some of the composer's hair. He treasured the lock the rest of his life, carefully preserving it under glass.

Nearly two hundred years later, those strands became a critical piece of evidence in determining Beethoven's cause of death. Scientists at the Energy Department's Argonne National Laboratory used the most powerful X-ray beam on the planet to examine six of them. They discovered lead levels one hundred times higher than normal. Such massive quantities were most likely responsible for Beethoven's constant nausea, diarrhea, and headaches, and caused his death by destroying his liver. It's unknown how he was exposed to such a high concentration of lead, although eating contaminated fish, drinking from lead-lined cups, and receiving lead-based medical treatments are all possible causes.

Lead poisoning, however, does not generally cause hearing loss, and most scientists believe his deafness had unrelated origins—possibly a condition called otosclerosis, which creates abnormal growth of bones in the ear.

GIOACHINO ROSSINI

FEBRUARY 29, 1792–NOVEMBER 13, 1868

ASTROLOGICAL SIGN:
PISCES

NATIONALITY:
ITALIAN

MUSICAL STYLE:
CLASSICAL

STANDOUT WORKS:
GUILLAME TELL (1829)

WHERE YOU'VE HEARD IT:
AS THE THEME SONG OF *THE LONE RANGER*, OF COURSE

"NOTHING PRIMES INSPIRATION MORE THAN
NECESSITY, WHETHER IT BE THE PRESENCE OF A
COPYIST WAITING FOR YOUR WORK, OR THE
PRODDING OF AN IMPRESARIO TEARING HIS
HAIR. IN MY TIME, ALL THE IMPRESARIOS OF
ITALY WERE BALD AT THIRTY."

QUOTABL

*T*he fame Gioachino Rossini achieved before age twenty-five amazed Europe. In Italy, he commanded the sort of star power reserved in later centuries for teen idols and boy-band singers. (Picture a young Justin Timberlake with a mastery of counterpoint.)

Everyone went to his operas, and everyone memorized his songs. Every Venetian gondolier, Bolognese businessman, and Roman pimp could belt out "Largo al factotum" from *The Barber of Seville*. Crowds followed him through the streets and attempted to cut off locks of his hair.

Then he quit. Gave it all up. Retired. The music world had never seen anything like it. For a man who made £30,000 on one tour of London, walking away seemed inconceivable. Even more inconceivable was the sight of the composer ten years later: a recluse, barely able to leave his bed, paralyzed by depression and tormented by insomnia. He had grown fat and bald.

The darling of Italian opera was transformed into a nervous wreck. The ultimate cause? A modern world he could not—or would not—understand.

Scoring It Big

The composer's father, Giuseppe Rossini, was an itinerant musician who settled in the Adriatic town of Pesaro and took up with a seamstress/soprano soloist named Anna Guidarini—although it was rumored she occasionally joined her sister in the local prostitution trade. In any case, the couple married in 1791 when Anna was five months pregnant with their son.

Gioachino's relatively uneventful childhood was disrupted when Napoleon invaded northern Italy. His father, Giuseppe, seems to have been overcome with revolutionary fervor, and his subsequent fortunes rose and fell along with the general's—in other words, he spent the next few years in and out of prison. Anna did her best to promote her son's obvious musical talent. Despite less-than-stellar instruction, by 1804 the twelve-year-old was singing at concerts. Crowds delighted in his pure, high voice, and, like Joseph Haydn before him, Rossini considered joining the ranks of the *castrati*. Giuseppe thought castrating his son was a great idea, but Anna put a stop to the scheme.

Rossini's fame really took off when, at age eighteen, he wrote his first opera (*La cambiale di matrimonio*) in Venice. The comedy was an immediate hit. Suddenly, Rossini was in demand at opera houses all over Italy. He became known for the speed at which he produced scores: a month, a few weeks, even (he claimed) eleven days. It helped that he didn't hesitate to lift melodies from one piece for use in another. He usually procrastinated until the last minute, driving impresarios crazy. Rossini later claimed that he was so behind in writing *La gazza ladra* that the stage manager put him under the guard of four burly stage hands until he finished the score.

How Many Barbers Does It Take to Make an Opera?

By 1815 Rossini was in Rome preparing for his most famous opera, *The Barber of Seville*. In later years, he claims to have whipped out the score in thirteen days. This is probably at least partially true, seeing as he merely recycled an overture he had used three times before.

The libretto was based on a famous play by Pierre Beaumarchais, the first part of his famous Figaro trilogy. Unfortunately, a popular Roman composer named Giovanni Paisiello had written an opera on the same story in 1782. Paisiello was an old man by then, but he still had committed fans, and they conspired to wreck the premiere of Rossini's opera. The opposition hissed and jeered every act, booing so loudly on the prima donna's entrance that the orchestra couldn't be heard. They also snuck a cat on stage. As the baritone soloist tried to chase it away, the audience barraged him with loud "meows."

Rossini was devastated and barricaded himself in his hotel room. He refused to emerge the second night, which, with all the Paisiello fans gone, was a triumph. The impresario hurried to the hotel to encourage Rossini to get dressed and go to the theater so the public could thank him. "Fuck the public!" shouted Rossini.

Music, Marriage, and Meeting the Maestro

By the early 1820s, Rossini was outgrowing comic opera—he was even outgrowing Italy. No longer was he satisfied to rush from one Italian town to another, cranking out score after score. For the first time, he wanted to be taken seriously as a composer. He also wanted to settle down. He had fallen in love with a talented soprano named Isabella Colbran in 1815; she was then the mistress of a Napolese opera impresario, who graciously gave way to Rossini. In 1822, Rossini and Colbran married.

What seemed like an opportunity to promote the more mature Rossini came the same year, when he was invited to Vienna. He leapt at the opportunity, excited to expose his work to new audiences and to meet the famous

Beethoven. Rossini was shocked to find the famed composer living in ragged clothes in a filthy apartment, but the two men had a long conversation. The German master praised *The Barber of Seville* but then told Rossini never to try to write anything but comic opera. "You do not possess sufficient musical knowledge to deal with real drama," Beethoven said. Rossini tried to laugh off this criticism, but in fact he was deeply wounded by the charge that he was incapable of composing serious music.

Depressed by Modernity

The next year saw Rossini on tour again to France and England. The trip started off well enough, but crossing the Channel aboard a new-fangled steam boat had terrified the composer. He took to bed for a week. None of the honors that followed—recognition from the king, long ovations at the opera, breathless reports in the papers—lessened the trauma. Rossini left England considerably richer but determined never to return.

The first signs of his debilitating depression were starting to appear. Despite settling in Paris and successfully producing the opera *Guillame Tell*, he talked only of retiring. He struggled to write less frothy music and created the oratorio *Stabat Mater* but seemed convinced that no one would take him—or it—seriously. Then in 1830 he announced he was giving it all up. The public was shocked: He was not even forty. But nothing could lure Rossini back to the stage.

Life with Isabella had grown increasingly intolerable. Her voiced had failed, and she had taken up gambling and drinking. Rossini turned to Olympe Pélissier, a rich and beautiful Parisian courtesan. Theirs wasn't a sexual relationship—a case of gonorrhea had rendered him impotent—but was the union of a devoted nurse and dependent patient. In 1837, Rossini was formally separated from Isabella, and he and Olympe settled together in Italy. When Isabella died in 1845, the couple married.

Nevertheless, the decade was wretched: The modern world terrified the composer. A railway journey left him in a state of collapse. Upstart composers like Wagner bewildered him. The political upheavals sweeping France and Italy mystified him. As one Italian city after another rebelled against Austrian rule, Rossini and Olympe wandered the country in search of a quiet retreat.

Rossini suffered from a bewildering array of physical complaints: lethargy, headaches, diarrhea, chronic inflammation of the urethra, and

hemorrhoids. He could hardly be dragged from bed, yet he complained of incessant insomnia. Even more debilitating was the depression that consumed him. He played the piano infrequently and always in a darkened room so no one could see him crying over the keys.

Better—and Worse

At Olympe's insistence, Rossini returned to Paris in 1855, where he began to emerge from his depression. He began receiving guests, exploring the city, and even composing. He never again attempted the serious music he had once longed to write, nor the witty operas that had made him famous, instead composing short, clever piano pieces he called *Péchés de vieillesse* ("Sins of My Old Age"). One piece titled *The Four Hors D'oeuvres* features movements named "Radishes," "Anchovies," "Gherkins," and "Butter"— combining Rossini's music with his newfound passion for gourmet dining.

By the late 1860s, however, the composer was physically ailing. He developed cancer of the rectum, the treatment of which caused more pain than the disease. At one point he begged his doctor to throw him out the window so he wouldn't suffer anymore. On Friday, November 13, 1868, he died with his wife by his side.

ONE OF ROSSINI'S OPERAS WAS SABOTAGED BY AN AUDIENCE OF JEERING FANS—THE CROWD EVEN RESORTED TO SNEAKING A CAT ONSTAGE.

A DRAFT-DODGING WOMANIZER

Rossini had a succession of affairs with opera singers, one of which brought unexpected benefits. The mezzo-soprano Maria Marcolini was the former mistress of Napoleon's brother Lucien Bonaparte. So when Napoleon mandated compulsory enlistment in the French army, Marcolini was able to pull strings to gain Rossini an exemption. This timely intervention spared the composer from joining the 90,000 Italian conscripts to the Grande Armée, most of whom died during the emperor's ill-fated invasion of Russia in 1812.

A STAND-UP KIND OF GUY

The story goes that a group of Rossini's friends wanted to erect a statue in his honor. When they approached him with the idea, the composer asked how much such a statue would cost. "About twenty-thousand liras," they replied. Rossini thought for a moment and then said, "Why don't you give me ten thousand liras and I'll stand on the pedestal myself?"

SETTLING A SCORE WITH WAGNER

In 1860, the guiding light of the new German opera, Richard Wagner, paid a call to Rossini, the faded star of the old Italian opera. The two had a gracious conversation, but Rossini thought Wagner's music self-indulgent and overbearing.

A friend recounted that he had once seen the score to Wagner's *Tannhäuser* upside down at Rossini's piano. The friend tried to turn the score around, but Rossini stopped him. "I already played it right side up but could making nothing of it," he said. "Then I tried it the other way and it sounds much better."

Rossini was also quoted as saying: "Mr. Wagner has beautiful moments, but bad quarters of an hour."

THE PETTY PRINCESS OF PESARO

In 1818, on a stay in his hometown of Pesaro, Rossini met Caroline of Brunswick, the estranged wife of the English Prince of Wales. The fifty-six-year-old princess lived in state with her much younger lover, Bartolomeo Bergami, and annoyed Pesaro society with her arrogance, ignorance, and vulgarity (much as she had annoyed her husband.)

Rossini refused invitations to the princess' salon and neglected to bow in her presence, a snub Caroline would not forget. A year later, when Rossini returned to Pesaro to stage *La gazza ladra*, Caroline and Bergami packed the audience with paid thugs who whistled, shouted, and waved knives and pistols during the performance. A terrified Rossini had to be smuggled out of the theater and fled the city in the middle of the night. He never performed in Pesaro again.

HECTOR BERLIOZ

DECEMBER 11, 1803–MARCH 8, 1869

ASTROLOGICAL SIGN:
SAGITTARIUS

NATIONALITY:
FRENCH

MUSICAL STYLE:
ROMANTIC

STANDOUT WORK:
SYMPHONIE FANTASTIQUE (1830)

WHERE YOU'VE HEARD IT:
AS JULIA ROBERT'S SADISTIC HUSBAND TORMENTS HER IN
SLEEPING WITH THE ENEMY

**"AT LEAST I HAVE THE MODESTY TO ADMIT THAT
LACK OF MODESTY IS ONE OF MY FAILINGS."**

QUOTABLE

Hector Berlioz is considered the ultimate romantic composer. The romantic movement, which rejected the rationalism of the Enlightenment and emphasized emotion over reason, found its musical form in Berlioz compositions that did away with the defined harmonies and established structures of previous generations for an intuitive, emotional approach to music.

But Berlioz was also romantic in the modern sense of the word: Think flowers, valentines, candles, piña coladas, long walks in the rain. Berlioz's life was a succession of overwhelming passions for various women. If he could have stood outside their windows holding a giant boom-box playing Peter Gabriel, he would have.

Instead, he wrote music—powerful, towering music—about the anguish and triumph of love. Certainly, not all of his romances went well, and Berlioz had to learn the sad lesson that living with your beloved is not nearly as romantic as pining hopelessly for her. But even into his old age, Berlioz the lover couldn't be stopped. The heart wants what it wants.

If At First You Don't Succeed, Try Again and Again and Again and Again

Louis Berlioz was a respected provincial physician, and he expected his son, Louis Hector, to follow in his footsteps. The elder Berlioz provided a comprehensive education for Hector, and although this coursework included music lessons, Louis frowned on the passion his son showed for composing. (He did not allow Hector to have a piano, making him one of the few composers never to master the instrument.)

At eighteen, Berlioz moved to Paris to study medicine, and he eventually received his medical degree. Having fulfilled his father's wishes, he began studying music full time. In short order he entered the competition for the Prix de Rome, an annual composition prize that provided a five-year stipend, but he was eliminated in the first round.

His attention might have been distracted by a different sort of passion. In September 1827, he attended a touring production of Shakespeare's *Hamlet* featuring a young Irishwoman named Harriet Smithson in the role of Ophelia. Berlioz was immediately smitten. He did everything in his power to contact Smithson, showing up repeatedly at the stage door and hand-delivering notes to the theater impresario, but no amount of stalking could get her to return his attentions.

Three years later, Berlioz's head was turned by a young woman named Marie Moke, better known as Camille. The two fell deeply in love. But Camille's ambitious middle-class family doubted an unemployed composer could support her, and so Berlioz applied himself yet again to landing the Prix de Rome in order to win her parents' permission to marry.

He failed again in 1828 and 1829 but had high hopes for 1830. Before he could complete the second round of the competition, however, rioting broke out in Paris in what became known as *Les Trois Glorieuses* or the July Revolution. Despite the fevered atmosphere, Berlioz had the sense to stay in his room and finish his assigned cantata. "I dashed off the final pages of my orchestral score to the sound of stray bullets coming over the roofs and pattering on the wall outside my window," he later wrote. Berlioz finished in time to wander the streets, pistol in hand, on the last night of fighting.

Even more satisfying was the news that he had won the Prix de Rome. Flush with success, Berlioz held a concert to present his new work, *Symphonie fantastique*, a.k.a. *Episode in the Life of the Artist*. Still his best-known composition, this work departs from long-established conventions of symphonic form and adopts a radical approach to orchestration and melody. Surprisingly, it was a big hit. He headed for Italy, rejoicing in Camille's parents' permission to marry.

Dressed to Kill

All that joy was shattered six weeks later when a letter arrived from Camille's mother. Mme. Moke informed him that her daughter was to marry a wealthy piano-maker named Camille Pleyel.

To put it lightly, Berlioz lost it. He decided his only recourse was to murder Pleyel, his fiancée, and her mother. He developed an elaborate plan to disguise himself as a ladies' maid so that he could enter his beloved's house unsuspected; he even purchased a dress, wig, and hat as part of the plot. He stole a pair of pistols and armed himself with vials of strychnine and laudanum.

The long journey north took the edge off Berlioz's rage; along the way he realized he'd left his cross-dressing disguise in a carriage. By the time he reached Nice, he had returned to his senses. He consoled himself by writing an orchestral overture. He then engaged the services of a local prostitute, whose favors he enjoyed on the beach near Nice, crying out, he later claimed, "O Splendid nuptial rites, worthy of the grandeur of our untamed loves." If this all seems rather improbable, remember: The guy was a *romantic*.

You Love Me! You Really Love Me!

After spending slightly less than the two years in Italy mandated by the Prix de Rome, Berlioz returned to Paris. He immediately organized another concert consisting of *Symphonie fantastique* and its newly written sequel, *Retour à la vie*, which includes a young man's spoken monologue on the suffering caused by unrequited love. Coincidentally, in the audience for the December 1832 performance was none other than Harriet Smithson. As the narrator read the words, "Oh, if I could but find this Juliet, this Ophelia, for whom my heart cries out!" Smithson burst into tears.

And so, five years after Berlioz had fallen for the young actress, he was shocked to receive a note of congratulations from her. A few days later, they were introduced for the first time. Berlioz immediately proposed marriage and was accepted.

Why did Smithson suddenly accept a marriage proposal from a man she'd previously refused to meet? It's impossible to tell. Her career had taken a dive. Perhaps she was tired of struggling to make it on the stage; perhaps she found Berlioz fascinating. But the most likely explanation truly is that she was overcome by the pure romance of the situation. The couple married in October 1833. The bride spoke no French and the groom spoke no English, but they found other ways to communicate; ten months later they had a son, Louis.

Women Mourn, Men Replace

Berlioz returned to composing, but earning money was always a challenge. To bring in extra income, he took up music criticism and accepted an appointment as deputy librarian to the Paris Conservatoire. Rounding out Berlioz's career was his work as a touring conductor. He conducted with perhaps more flair than skill, but audiences were fascinated by the figure swooping, crouching, and leaping on the podium and wielding the baton.

Alas, life on the road was becoming more pleasant than life at home. Berlioz first saw Harriet as Juliet and Ophelia, and perhaps it was inevitable that the real woman couldn't live up to his idealized image. By 1840, the marriage was on the rocks. Harriet quit taking care of her house, her son, and herself and kept Berlioz up at night with alcohol-fueled tirades.

Berlioz put up with Harriet for a while, but then decided that if he was going to be subjected to jealous accusations of unfaithfulness, he might as well enjoy the real thing. Sometime in the 1840s, he began an affair with an

Points Required	Reward Value
2,500	$5
4,500	$10
8,500	$20
20,000	$50
35,000	$100

Explore the benefits of plum rewards and become a member for free! Visit indigo.ca/plumrewards to learn more.

Chapters   Indigo   COLES   indigo.ca

plum™ rewards

Points Required	Reward Value
2,500	$5
4,500	$10

Indigo

Store# 00280 Indigo Bay & Bloor
55 Bloor Street, West
Toronto,ON M4W 1A5
Phone: (416) 925-3536

YOUR FEEDBACK MATTERS
Tell us about your visit today
for a chance to win a $500 giftcard
Complete our survey at:
www.indigofeedback.com

Store# 00280 Term# 002 Trans# 1092107
Operator: 815ECS   12/19/2017 18:31
GIFT RECEIPT

****
SECRET LIVES OF GREAT COMPOS   BIJF
9781594744020

****
A GIFT FOR YOU
****

Holiday refunds accepted until January
13, 2018. Items brought back with a gift
receipt and in store-bought condition
may be exchanged for a gift card for the
value of the item on the receipt.
Store# 00280 Term# 002 Trans# 1092107
GST Registration # R897152666

0028000210921072

opera singer named Marie Martin (stage name Marie Récio). By 1844 he was living with her in Paris. Marie has gone down in history as a gossipy, overbearing shrew, but it's unclear how much of this is slander from enemies of her husband. (She and Wagner, for one, had a running feud.) In any case, when Harriet died of a stroke in 1854, Berlioz waited only six months to marry Marie.

Ever the Romantic

In 1862, Marie died unexpectedly of a heart attack. She was buried in a vault in Montmartre Cemetery. As the years went by, Berlioz would often walk there. One evening, he encountered a young woman some thirty years his junior. All we know about her is her name, Amélie, and that she and Berlioz fell suddenly, deeply in love. However, after a few months, the relationship ended—we don't know why, although in one version of the story Amélie was married—and Berlioz headed out on tour. A year later, the composer walked through Montmartre Cemetery and found a new grave: that of Amélie. Apparently she had been extremely ill and died while Berlioz was on tour.

In 1867, Berlioz's son, a sailor, died of yellow fever in Havana. The blow seemed to make Berlioz suddenly old. In January 1869, he took to his bed; he died on March 8.

Berlioz's reputation today remains in dispute: Although many see him as an unconventional rebel and genius innovator, others despise what they see as all flash and no substance. Whatever the case, this most romantic romantic gave music-lovers a treasure-trove of symphonic works to debate for years to come.

EVERYONE'S A CRITIC

Many contemporary reviewers found Berlioz's orchestral experiments bizarre and incomprehensible. Here's a sampling of their reactions:

"Berlioz, musically speaking, is a lunatic."

"I can compare Le Carneval Romain by Berlioz to nothing but the caperings and gibberings of a big baboon, over-excited by a dose of alcoholic stimulus."

"In the finale 'Bacchanale of the Brigands' in Berlioz's symphony *Harold in Italy*, the brigands seem to be holding a church sociable or a conference, and the way that the percussion section is let loose adds much to the percussedness of the proceedings."

"Berlioz is, in our opinion, by far the least respectable of the composers of the new school. . . . It needs no gift of prophecy to predict that he will be utterly unknown a hundred years hence to everybody but the encyclopedists and the antiquarians."

WHEN BERLIOZ LEARNED THAT HIS TRUE LOVE PLANNED TO MARRY ANOTHER MAN, HE DISGUISED HIMSELF AS A WOMAN, GRABBED TWO PISTOLS, AND SET OUT TO COMMIT MURDER.

SUFFERING THROUGH BEETHOVEN

Berlioz was a huge fan of Beethoven and reacted with unrestrained emotion to all of his music. On one occasion, someone sitting next to Berlioz at a Beethoven performance was touched to see the young man sobbing controllably. "You seem to be affected, monsieur," the stranger said kindly. "Had you not better retire for a while?"

"Are you under the impression that I am here to enjoy myself?" replied Berlioz.

YOU NEVER FORGET YOUR FIRST LOVE

Before Amélie, before Marie, before Harriet or even Camille, there was Berlioz's first love, Estelle Duboeuf. Estelle was the eighteen-year-old neighbor of Berlioz's grandfather, and Berlioz met her when he was only twelve years old. He was immediately infatuated. Despite exchanging only a few words with her, he never forgot her.

In 1864, when Berlioz was sixty-one and Estelle seventy, he visited Lyon determined to see her again. By then she was the widow of a respected attorney, with four adult children. She received him graciously—certainly she remembered him and knew he had become famous. But the letters that followed appear to reflect Berlioz on the verge of another fatal attraction.

Berlioz begged Estelle to let him take her to Paris; when she visited friends in Switzerland, he pleaded for her address so he could join her there. At first the widow seemed flattered by his attentions, then baffled, then slightly alarmed. Finally, in 1866 matters came to a head. With enormous dignity, Estelle put on the brakes. The frequent visits had to stop. They could still correspond, and the occasional visit was acceptable, but beyond that she drew the line.

In the end, Berlioz's first and last love outlived him. In his will, Berlioz left her a small income, proving that he was a romantic to the end.

FELIX MENDELSSOHN

FEBRUARY 3, 1809–NOVEMBER 4, 1847

ASTROLOGICAL SIGN:
AQUARIUS

NATIONALITY:
GERMAN

MUSICAL STYLE:
ROMANTIC

STANDOUT WORKS:
"WEDDING MARCH" FROM MUSIC FOR *A MIDSUMMER NIGHT'S DREAM* (1842)

WHERE YOU'VE HEARD IT:
AS THE RECESSIONAL IN A BAJILLION WEDDINGS

"EVER SINCE I BEGAN TO COMPOSE, I HAVE REMAINED TRUE TO MY STARTING PRINCIPLE: NOT TO WRITE A PAGE BECAUSE NO MATTER WHAT PUBLIC, OR WHAT PRETTY GIRL WANTED IT TO BE THUS OR THUS; BUT TO WRITE SOLELY AS I MYSELF THOUGHT BEST, AND AS IT GAVE ME PLEASURE."

QUOTABLE

F elix Mendelssohn started composing as a child and published his first piano quartet when he was only thirteen. He went on to publish an amazing collection of symphonies, concertos, and *lieder* (songs) for piano and voice.

Except not all the songs were by Mendelssohn. Tucked in among the young man's works were those of his sister, Fanny. The only way to let her compositions see the light of day was to disguise them as the work of her brother.

And so it goes with the Mendelssohns. You think you're looking at one person, but really there are two. Felix went out into the world and travelled all of Europe while Fanny stayed home and kept house. Felix conducted prominent orchestras while Fanny had to content herself with amateur quartets. Felix became an international superstar while Fanny remained completely unknown. Yet for all their differences, their two lives remained inextricably intertwined— even to death.

What's in a Name?

The Mendelssohns proudly claimed descent from one of the most remarkable German thinkers of the eighteenth century, the esteemed Jewish philosopher Moses Mendelssohn. Moses's son Abraham became a wealthy banker but retained his father's values; education and intellectual achievement were highly prized in his household.

Abraham did not, however, continue his father's religious tradition. All four of Abraham's children were baptized, and Abraham and his wife, Lea, converted to Lutheranism in 1822. They hoped to secure a safer and easier life for their children since prejudice against Jews was widespread, and discrimination—if not outright persecution—was commonplace. To emphasize their new faith, Abraham amended the family's name to "Mendelssohn Bartholdy," "Bartholdy" being the name of the former owners of some family property; he clearly hoped that in time the Jewish *Mendelssohn* would fall into disuse. (His children never fully embraced their new name, although they retained it for their father's sake.)

The first three Mendelssohn children were born in Hamburg (Fanny in 1805, Felix in 1809, and Rebecca in 1811), but the family fled the city in 1811 to escape Napoleon's armies. They settled in Berlin, where the fourth child, Paul, was born.

Two for One

Both Fanny and Felix started piano lessons at age six; four years older than her brother, Fanny held the lead for a long time and was hailed as a prodigy. But when Felix caught up, he amazed audiences with his technical skill and emotional expression. Years of side-by-side training ceased abruptly, however, when Fanny turned fifteen and was informed that she should prepare herself for her true calling as a wife and mother. "Music will perhaps become his [Felix's] profession, while for you it can and should only be an ornament," wrote Abraham.

In 1825, Abraham took Felix to Paris so that he could meet renowned French musicians. Fanny's letters revealed jealousy of her brother's opportunity, jealousy Felix seemed not to notice—or acknowledge. When Felix criticized the quality of Parisian musicians and Fanny replied indignantly, Felix snapped, "Are you in Paris, or am I? So I really ought to know better than you."

In his late teens, Felix concentrated on composing. The summer of 1826 saw the premiere of one of his most enduring works, the overture to Shakespeare's *A Midsummer Night's Dream.* Much less successful was Felix's attempt at opera, *Die Hochzeit des Camacho,* which flopped on the first night. Stung, he never attempted opera again.

He did, however, assemble two volumes of twelve lieder each, published in 1827 and 1830. Three of the songs in each volume were actually written by Fanny—publication under her name was unthinkable.

After four semesters of study at the University of Berlin, Felix was ready to fulfill his destiny as a virtuoso performer and talented composer. He headed for London, where his C Minor Symphony debuted in May 1829 to overwhelming acclaim.

Fanny, meanwhile, fulfilled her destiny by getting married. It had been a long, hard road for Fanny and her fiancé, artist Wilhelm Hensel; the couple had fallen in love back in 1823, but Abraham and Lea opposed the match because Hensel's income was so unsteady. Their relationship received parental sanction only when Hensel was appointed to the Academy of Fine Arts.

Fears that married life would rob her of all opportunity to compose were quickly resolved when, the day after the wedding, Hensel sat Fanny down at the piano with a blank sheet of paper. Of course, domestic duties still took up enormous chunks of her time. In 1830 she had a son, whom she named Sebastian Ludwig Felix after her three favorite composers. She then suffered several miscarriages. However, with Hensel's support, Fanny hosted musical salons, organized a small chorus, and wrote music whenever she could.

Taking on the Paternal(istic) Role

Felix, meanwhile, was in demand at orchestra halls across Europe. One of his few professional blows came in 1833, when the Berlin Singakademie named not Felix but Carl Friedrich Rungenhagen as their new director. Rungenhagen wasn't in the same league as Felix—he wasn't even playing the same game—and rumors persisted that Felix had been rejected because of his Jewish origins. Felix instead concentrated his attentions on the Lower Rhine Music Festival, which he conducted seven times, and the Leipzig Gewandhaus Orchestra, where he was appointed director in 1835.

Abraham died the same year of a sudden stroke. A shocked Felix saw the death as a call to take on adult responsibilities. Determined to get married, he set out to find a bride. He and his wife, nineteen-year-old Cécile Jeanrenaud of Frankfurt, wed in March 1837. Although none of the Mendelssohns warmed to Cécile, the couple had five children, and all reports describe them as devoted to one another.

FELIX MENDELSSOHN BECAME A WORLD-FAMOUS COMPOSER WHILE HIS EQUALLY GIFTED SISTER REMAINED COMPLETELY UNKNOWN.

Another responsibility Felix took on was as dispenser of family wisdom. When discussion arose on the wisdom of Fanny publishing her music, Felix made his disapproval plain. Fanny, he said, was "far too self-respecting a woman" to be a professional composer: "She sees to her house and thinks not of the public, nor of the musical world—nor even of music, except when her primary activity's been carried out."

And yet Fanny's world grew in the 1840s. The Hensel family spent most of 1840 in Italy, where Fanny found herself at the center of admiring fans. On her return to Berlin, she began composing with new energy, and in 1846, she defied her brother and sought publication. Seven collections of lieder quickly made it into print.

Felix wearied of the demanding life of a travelling conductor. He complained of the brutal workload and longed for more time at home with his

children. Just as Fanny's world was expanding, Felix wished his own could contract.

Death Comes in Twos

On May 14, 1847, Fanny began rehearsing her chamber group for the Sunday performance of Felix's *Walpurgis Night*. She sat down at the keyboard, but then her hands seemed to freeze up. This had happened before— it was an unsettling but usually brief handicap. She went to the next room to soak her hands in warm vinegar; listening to the music, she remarked, "How beautiful it sounds." Then she fainted. Fanny died that evening without reawakening, apparently after suffering a stroke.

When the news was broken to Felix, he collapsed in a dead faint. He couldn't bring himself to return to Berlin for the funeral. That summer, friends found him looking "aged and sad." On October 28 Felix suddenly started speaking excitedly in English. Cécile called a doctor, who decided the composer had suffered a stroke. Felix drifted in and out of consciousness, once sitting up suddenly and uttering a piercing shriek. He died on November 4 and was buried next to Fanny in a Berlin cemetery; fewer than six months separated their deaths.

Felix's reputation declined as the nineteenth century wore on, particularly in Germany. Even though he had practiced Christianity his entire life, Germans insisted on thinking of him as Jewish. Wagner lead the way when he wrote that the composer "was not able, even one single time, to call forth in us that deep, that heart-searching effect which we await from art"— because he was a Jew. By the Nazi era, Mendelssohn had been eliminated from German musical history. His statue before the Leipzig orchestra hall was torn down and sold as scrap iron. And yet the end of World War II brought a reappraisal of Mendelssohn in both Europe and America, and today he is placed in the first ranks of musical geniuses.

Fanny, had no reputation to lose. Her few published compositions were forgotten, and it was barely remembered that Felix had had a sister. Interest in her was revived in the 1960s when feminism began to influence classical music studies. Today her music is being reprinted, although critical reaction remains mixed—some see her as a genius equal to her brother, others as an undeveloped talent, and still others as an uncompelling and even banal composer.

MY SISTER, MYSELF

Mendelssohn made multiple tours to England and was eventually introduced to Queen Victoria and Prince Albert. The German prince and highly musical queen got along very well with the composer, and soon Mendelssohn was invited to private musical evenings at Buckingham Palace. One evening, the queen asked Mendelssohn to play while she sang from his first volume of lieder. The queen turned to her favorite song, "Schöner und Schöner" ("More and More Beautiful"), and sang both "prettily and in tune," according to Mendelssohn.

It was only at the end of the song that Mendelssohn felt compelled to admit that the song really was his sister's.

STUMP THE PIANO PLAYER

Mendelssohn possessed a prodigious memory that amazed fellow musicians. In 1844, when asked to play the solo in Beethoven's Fourth Piano Concerto, he arrived at the concert hall to find that no one had the piano score. Despite not having seen the score for at least two years, he played the piece perfectly from memory.

Many years earlier, he performed an even more impressive feat at his monumental revival performance of Bach's *St. Matthew's Passion*. In addition to conducting the event, he planned to play the piano, but when he took his seat the night of the performance, he realized that the score before him was not that of the *Passion* but one that looked similar. Mendelssohn could have delayed the performance to get the right score, or he could have closed the wrong score and played from memory. Instead he kept the score open, seemed to refer to it periodically, and regularly turned the pages—as he conducted and performed. No one knew the whole thing was an act.

THE REINCARNATION OF BACH

Mendelssohn's deep affection for the music of Bach led to the widespread rediscovery of the early master's music. The revival of *the St. Matthew's Passion* inspired its performance across Europe, and before long Mendelssohn's name was inextricably linked with Bach's. This close connection did not fail to elicit comment. Berlioz once remarked, "There is but one God—Bach—and Mendelssohn is his prophet."

BRATWURST EQUALS HAPPINESS

Mendelssohn spent months at a time on tour. Like any traveler, he came to miss the comforts of home. On a trip to England in 1846, he was honored with one formal dinner after another. But the occasion he later remembered with the most pleasure was his discovery of a butcher shop that sold genuine German sausages. He immediately purchased a long string and consumed them on the spot.

FUGUE, INTERRUPTED

On another trip to England, he provided the closing music for the Sunday evening service at St. Paul's Cathedral in London. However, the vergers (the lay staff of the cathedral) were annoyed that the congregation wasn't clearing the sanctuary so they could close up. Mendelssohn sat down at the organ and began playing one of Bach's magnificent fugues. The audience sat breathless while the music built toward a triumphant climax—when suddenly the organ's lush sound faded away into nothing. The vergers had stopped the organ blower responsible for keeping the pipe organ full of air. Mendelssohn was, however, able to complete the Bach fugue two days later. Another church's organist invited him to hold a recital in place of the one so rudely interrupted at St. Paul's.

Women Composers

You will look in vain for a woman's name in the table of contents of this book. That's because every single Western composer on the all-time-best lists came equipped with a Y chromosome.

Blame a long history of excluding women from musical training and performance. Back in the Middle Ages, women were forbidden from singing or playing in public—although in the privacy of abbeys, nuns ran their own orchestras and even composed. The ban on women's public performances was lifted only when the demand for high voices could no longer be met by castrati. (The use of castrati fell out of favor in the late eighteenth century.) Women could then make names for themselves as opera singers, although it was hard to be taken seriously as an artist when everyone assumed you were a prostitute.

If a woman wanted to be any other kind of musician, the barriers were high. Well into the nineteenth century, women were forbidden from attending music academies, so the only place to learn was at home. Even if a woman managed to obtain a solid musical education, she couldn't do much with it without defying convention and raising eyebrows.

It wasn't until the middle of the twentieth century that women broke into mainstream orchestras. With World War II raging, female musicians took the positions of their male counterparts who were serving in the military. To this day, however, even as there are more female members in orchestras worldwide, women conductors struggle to succeed—although recent stars such as Baltimore Symphony Music Director Marin Alsop have proven women can successfully wield a baton.

That leaves composing to catch up with the times. It's not that there haven't been women composers. For example, British composer Elizabeth Maconchy (1907–1994) wrote moving arrangements of popular poems such as Dylan Thomas's "And Death Shall Have No

Dominion." Maconchy was considered the best student in her class at the Royal College of Music, but she was not granted the prestigious Mendelssohn Scholarship because, according to the school's director, "You will only get married and never write another note." No woman's compositions have made it into the standard repertoire, although there are some heartening signs that this may change as more female composers make their marks.

FRÉDÉRIC CHOPIN

MARCH 1, 1810–OCTOBER 17, 1849

ASTROLOGICAL SIGN:
PISCES

NATIONALITY:
POLISH

MUSICAL STYLE:
ROMANTIC

STANDOUT WORKS:
PIANO SONATA NO. 2 IN B-FLAT MINOR, A.K.A. "THE FUNERAL MARCH"

WHERE YOU'VE HEARD IT:
WHENEVER A CHARACTER DIES IN OLD BUGS BUNNY CARTOONS

"I WISH I COULD THROW OFF THE THOUGHTS WHICH POISON MY HAPPINESS. AND YET I TAKE A KIND OF PLEASURE IN INDULGING THEM."

QUOTABLE

A udiences had one complaint about Frédéric Chopin: He was too quiet. His piano playing failed to fill a concert hall, and his restrained compositions got lost in big spaces.

Of course, low volume was all of piece with Chopin's personality. In an era dominated by such over-large composers as Liszt and Berlioz, Chopin stood out for his restraint. He lacked the ego to organize massive, self-promoting tours; he lacked the charisma to inspire fans to hysterical devotion; he lacked the audacity to make himself a celebrity.

But whatever Chopin lacked in arrogance he more than made up for in talent. Few people heard Chopin play, and fewer heard him play to best advantage, but those who did were swept away by his delicate, evocative style. Chopin serves as a counterweight to the romantic tendency toward bigger and bolder music: His compositions are intimate, personal, *quiet*—thus proving that genius doesn't have to be loud to get noticed.

You Can't Go Home Again

Fryderyk was the second child and only son of Nicolas Chopin and his wife, Justyna Krzyżanowska. Nicolas was born in France but moved to Warsaw to escape the French Revolution. Fryderyk was born in the village Żelazowa Wola, where Nicolas was working as a tutor, but the family moved to Warsaw when the baby was seven months old. Nicolas then taught French at the Warsaw Lyceum and ran a boarding house for students.

Fryderyk's elder sister, Ludwika, was his first piano teacher. He showed immediate talent and gave his first public performance at age seven. After a few years of study at the Warsaw Conservatory, Chopin sadly acknowledged that his homeland offered few opportunities for a professional musician. He wasn't eager to travel—the political situation in his homeland was dicey, with a Polish nationalist movement angling for independence from Russia.

Nevertheless, Chopin left Warsaw for Western Europe in early November 1830, carrying with him a handful of native soil in a silver cup. Later that month, Polish army troops rebelled, only to be brutally crushed by the vast Russian army. Chopin feared for his family and blamed himself for not returning to support his homeland. He also faced the fact that return to Poland was no longer an option. He had become a political refugee.

Chopin arrived in Paris in September 1831 with no idea how long he would stay in France. These were heady days: Chopin befriended the composers Mendelssohn, Liszt, and Berlioz as well as the writer Honoré de Balzac, novelist Victor Hugo, and painter Eugène Delacroix. To introduce himself to Paris audiences, he organized a debut concert on February 1832. The hall was only a third full, but critics declared the event unforgettable. One praised the pianist's "elegant, effortless, and graceful" manner—although he complained that Chopin's soft tone made the piano hard to hear.

Another virtuoso would have followed up such a success with more of the same. Not Chopin. Putting together concerts was a headache, and Chopin preferred not to bother. He ended up performing in public fewer than thirty times.

Even when he planned to perform, he was often too sick to go on stage. All through the 1830s, the composer endured bouts of "bronchitis" or "influenza" that left him coughing and weak. Chopin clung to the belief that he had a weak constitution—a more reassuring self-diagnosis than a fatal case of tuberculosis. Without income from concerts, he struggled to make a living from music sales and piano lessons. Sheet music netted composers a pittance, and no one ever got rich giving lessons, so he barely scraped by.

Setting Sail on the Love Boat

One the brighter side, Chopin did find some romance. On a trip to meet his parents at a German spa in 1835, he fell in love with Maria Wodzińska, the daughter of family friends from Warsaw. The next year, he travelled again to Germany and proposed marriage. Maria accepted, but her mother insisted a public announcement be delayed until Maria's father in Poland could give his blessing. Weeks of waiting turned into months. After more than a year, Maria's mother informed him that the relationship was at an end. Chopin took Maria's letters, tied them up with a ribbon, and wrote across the envelope "Moja bieda": "my sorrow."

An entirely different kind of woman eased the blow. In 1837, Liszt introduced Chopin to Amandine Aurore Lucille Dupin, the Baroness Dudevant, better known as George Sand. Already famous for her proto-feminist novels, Sand was a notorious figure who wore men's trousers and smoked cigars. Chopin initially disliked her, writing to a friend, "What a repulsive woman Sand is! But is she really a woman? I am inclined to doubt it."

ACCOMPANIED BY HIS LOVER, BRITISH NOVELIST GEORGE SAND, AND DYING FROM CONSUMPTION, CHOPIN TRAVELED TO FRANCE ON A TINY BOAT FILLED WITH PIGS.

Yet when he met Sand again several months later, dislike turned into desire. Sand responded in kind, and matters were off to a great start—except for one hiccup: Sand's lover, a playwright named Félicien Mallefille. Mallefille took his rejection poorly and haunted the sidewalk in front of Chopin's apartment with a pistol. It behooved the couple to get out of town.

They settled on the island of Majorca, apparently envisioning a Mediterranean paradise. Instead they found conservative Majorcans disapproving of the unmarried couple, particularly the married, trouser-wearing Sand. A villa in the countryside might have been delightful in the spring, but autumn rains made it damp and miserable. Then Chopin started coughing up blood. The landlord realized Chopin's illness was not a cold, or bronchitis, or influenza, but tuberculosis. Chopin was forced to leave the villa immediately.

Sand cast about for a refuge, finally finding an abandoned monastery. Accompanied by Sand's two children and a maid, they endured the primitive conditions of dark, dank cells intended for monks renouncing the sins of the world, not lovers on a holiday. By February, Chopin was so ill he could barely walk; he and Sand returned to France on a tiny boat carrying a cargo of smelly, squealing pigs.

Some People Just Can't Take a Hint

It took months of bed rest in Marseilles for Chopin to recover enough to return to Paris. There would be no more exotic vacations for the couple. Winters were spent in adjoining apartments in Paris, and summers found them at Sand's country estate, Nohant. Chopin did some of his best composing during the long, quiet days.

For several years, Sand babied Chopin and tended to his health, but such devotion eventually wore thin. Rather than break with him in person, she wrote a novel—*Lucrezia Floriani*—in which a character thinly disguised

as herself takes a lover immediately recognizable as Chopin. The relationship ends when the saintly Lucrezia, her nobility of spirit matched only by her luminous beauty, casts off the insanely jealous, parasitic Prince Karol. Chopin's friends were outraged, but the composer merely praised Sand for her superb creative skill.

Hints having failed, Sand sent the grand piano Chopin used in Nohant back to the manufacturer. And that was the end of that.

Sicker than ever, Chopin faced a new crisis as civil unrest broke out in France. An invitation to come to England was irresistible, even if his host-ess, an indefatigable singer named Jane Stirling, got on his nerves. In April 1848, he headed for London. Stirling swept him into a whirl of social engagements, never seeming to notice her idol's exhaustion or the blood he coughed into a handkerchief.

Perhaps illness accounted for his lack of success in London. The unde-terred Miss Stirling hauled him off to Scotland, where stays in damp, ill-heated castles chilled him to the bone. Chopin did his best to dispel the rumors he and Stirling were about to be married; not only was he not attracted to her, his physical condition made marriage out of the question. He told a friend, "I'm nearer to a coffin than a wedding bed."

Gone but Not Forgotten

The England trip ended in the fall of 1848 when Chopin finally extricated himself from Miss Stirling, who had taken to reading him Bible verses for hours on end in an attempt to convert him to Calvinism. He arrived in Paris desperately weak; friends got him an apartment and arranged for his sister, Ludwika, to come to France. Chopin died early in the morning of October 17. His mourning friends organized a performance of Mozart's *Requiem* at the funeral, and when Chopin's coffin was lowered into the earth, the cupful of Polish soil he carried with him from his homeland was tossed into the grave. Today Chopin's entrancing, delicate works are an indelible part of the stan-dard repertoire, and his music has never gone out of favor. Chopin's life is proof positive that you don't need a big personality to make a lasting imprint for the ages.

HOME IS WHERE THE HEART IS

Chopin never returned to Poland after his departure in 1830—at least not during his lifetime. An autopsy was performed on the composer's body, and Chopin's sister, Ludwika, requested that her brother's heart be removed. When the rest of his remains were laid to rest in Paris, Ludwika took the heart with her back to Poland and arranged for it to be interred in a pillar of the Church of the Holy Cross in Warsaw.

LAST WORDS . . . AND WORDS . . . AND WORDS

Chopin's death at such a relatively young age gave rise to a number of romantic stories about his last days. A remarkable number of "last words" were later reported, although it seems unlikely that a man barely able to breathe would have been so chatty. According to one story, he murmured of Sand, "She told me that I would die only in her arms." Another has him saying to friends, "You will play Mozart together in my memory," and a third has him commenting, "It is a rare favor for God to let man know the hour when his death pains begin." A fourth version, written by a priest, has him clutching a crucifix to his chest and exclaiming, "Now I am at the source of Blessedness." Perhaps the most poignant final tale has him pleading, "When this cough suffocates me, I beg you to have my body opened, so I will not be buried alive."

THE CHOPINZEE

One of the greatest interpreters of Chopin was Vladimir de Pachmann, a Ukrainian pianist who lived from 1848 to 1933. De Pachmann frequently arrived late to his own concerts, but whenever he entered he fixed the audience with a piercing gaze. If anyone displeased him, he didn't hesitate to order him or her out of the concert hall; he once objected to an overly elaborate hat and refused to play until its wearer departed.

When de Pachmann played, he maintained a running commentary on both the score and his performance. "Now the melody," he would announce, or "This part is very difficult." When approaching a challenging passage, he would encourage himself with a hearty, "Courage, de Pachmann!" Once it had passed successfully, he congratulated himself with, "Bravo, de Pachmann!"

Although many found de Pachmann's affectations insufferable—Rachmaninoff called him a charlatan—others claimed all the eccentricities were worth it. His eloquent interpretations of Chopin were particularly prized, with Liszt once telling an audience, "Those who have never heard Chopin before are hearing him this evening." So connected did the two become in the public's mind that an American critic dubbed the sometimes clownish, sometimes brilliant de Pachmann "The Chopinzee."

ROBERT SCHUMANN

JUNE 8, 1810–JULY 29, 1856

ASTROLOGICAL SIGN:
GEMINI

NATIONALITY:
GERMAN

MUSICAL STYLE:
ROMANTIC

STANDOUT WORKS:
"TRÄUMEREI" FROM *KINDERSZENEN* ("DREAMING" FROM *SCENES FROM A CHILDHOOD*)

WHERE YOU'VE HEARD IT:
IN A SURPRISING NUMBER OF *LOONY TUNES* CARTOONS, INCLUDING BUGS BUNNY'S "HARE RIBBIN'" (1944)

"TO COMPOSE MUSIC, ALL YOU HAVE TO DO IS REMEMBER A TUNE THAT NOBODY ELSE HAS THOUGHT OF."

QUOTABLE

Robert Schumann's story is a love story. As in all good love stories, there is a strong and ardent boy, a lovely and spirited girl, and a mean and spiteful villain. Love eventually triumphs, and the couple live happily ever after.

Except, of course, that they didn't. Robert Schumann's life—and his marriage to Clara Wieck—was cut short by an illness that left the composer the victim of terrifying delusions of shrieking demons. He would die in an insane asylum so lost to reason that he didn't recognize his beloved.

But even this tragic end has a touching coda. How Clara lived without Robert, the man she had adored since she was eight years old, is a beautiful love story of its own.

Boy Meets Girl

Born in 1810 in Zwickau, Saxony (today eastern Germany), Robert Schumann was the son of a bookseller. He showed early interest in the piano, but his family decided law was a much more sensible occupation. In 1828 Schumann enrolled at the University of Leipzig. Ignoring his coursework, Schumann instead sought out Friedrich Wieck, the man believed by many—most of all himself—to be the best piano teacher in Europe.

It must have been humbling for the young man to realize that Wieck's eight-year-old daughter Clara put his piano skills to shame. Wieck had decided when Clara was five that he would mold her into a musical prodigy, mostly to prove that his teaching skills were so impressive he could make a girl—*a girl!*—into a virtuoso. The two students formed an immediate bond, with Schumann playing the role of an indulgent elder brother who read Clara fairy tales and brought her candy. The hard-working girl had few pleasures in her life, but Schumann was one of them.

Schumann did his best to become a virtuoso himself. He had the talent to pull it off, at least until the third finger of his right hand began to ache and occasionally go numb. To strengthen the finger, Schumann employed a mechanical device intended to bring back flexibility that instead caused permanent injury. Schumann's consolation was composition, in which he gained new confidence. He went to work on his first symphony, which debuted in 1832.

Meanwhile, he enjoyed an affair with a servant named Christel—the result of which was a case of syphilis. A doctor friend lectured Schumann on his morals and gave him some medicine that would have had absolutely no effect on the bacteria. But within a few weeks the initial sores went away, and Schumann rejoiced that he was cured.

Boy Loses Girl—Temporarily

While Wieck took Clara on a several-year tour around Europe, Schumann concentrated on composing. He also founded an influential journal called *Die Neue Zeitschrift für Musik (The New Journal in Music),* in which he promoted composers such as Berlioz, Chopin, and Mendelssohn. He even became briefly engaged to a young woman named Ernestine von Fricken.

Then Clara came back. She was only sixteen to Schumann's twenty-five, but sixteen is a long way from eight. She had been in love with Schumann for years, and in the winter of 1835 he fell in love with her. Their courtship was a whirl of stolen kisses and dances at Christmas parties, all of it innocent and charming—except to Friedrich Wieck. Wieck forbade Clara to ever see Robert again.

For nearly two years Wieck kept Clara and Robert apart, but instead of forgetting each other they grew more committed. Wieck's objections were to some degree reasonable: Schumann was eking out a living composing and writing, and marrying the undomestic Clara was an expensive proposition—the couple would need an army of servants. Wieck's monetary interest in his daughter was less reasonable. Wieck saw his years devoted to coaching Clara as an investment primed to pay off big time. To Wieck, Schumann was trying to rob him of future income.

Wieck went on the offensive. He scheduled his daughter for a lengthy tour; he attacked Schumann as dissolute and immoral; he made impossible demands he knew Schumann couldn't fulfill. Saxon law was behind him: Even though she was eighteen years old, Clara had to get her father's permission to marry. When he refused, she and Schumann had to take him to court. All this dragged on for years. Wieck eventually tried to sabotage Clara's career by telling concert organizers that she was "fallen, depraved, nasty." After all the dramatics, the two finally married on September 12, 1840, the day before Clara's twenty-first birthday. It had been five years since their first kiss.

Brangelina, Meet Clarabert

The marriage that followed has a remarkably modern ring to it. Clara and Robert were two professionals determined to continue their careers. This meant negotiation and compromise because the thin walls of their apartment made it impossible for both to work at the piano at the same time. Money was a continual challenge: Clara could make a lot touring, but tours meant either a long separation or Robert tagging along in Clara's wake.

Pregnancy also made touring harder—and Clara got pregnant *a lot*. She had eight children in fourteen years and at least two miscarriages; seven of the children survived infancy. The couple adored their kids, with Robert taking particular joy in teaching them to play the piano. Some of his best-loved compositions were written for his children.

For the first few years of marriage, the couple lived in Leipzig (where the Mendelssohns were close friends), later moving to Dresden. Then in 1850 the composer was offered the position of music director in Düsseldorf. Schumann relished the opportunity to conduct his own choir and orchestra. Big mistake. Schumann was a lousy conductor. He was miserably nearsighted and could barely see the first violins in front of him, let alone the percussionists at the back of the room. He also lacked the charisma that makes for a good conductor. After a disastrous performance in October 1853, he was fired.

CHASED BY VISIONS OF A CHOIR OF ANGELS THAT TURNED INTO DEMONS, SCHUMANN DOVE INTO THE RHINE WEARING NOTHING BUT HIS BATHROBE AND SLIPPERS.

Angels and Demons

Health problems were also to blame for the Düsseldorf failure. Schumann endured headaches, dizziness, and "nerve attacks" that left him bedridden. The last year in Düsseldorf was particularly bad, with Schumann unable to hear high notes, frequently dropping his baton, and losing his sense of rhythm.

What happened next was utterly terrifying. Schumann heard wonderful music accompanied by the singing of angels. Then the angels turned into demons who tried to drag him to Hell. He warned the pregnant Clara to stay away because he might hurt her.

On the morning of February 27, Schumann slipped out of the house wearing only a dressing gown and slippers. He headed for the river Rhine, scrambled past the toll collector, and threw himself into the water. Fortunately, his odd appearance had attracted attention and he was quickly rescued. Dripping wet and wrapped in a blanket, he was taken home.

Within a week, he was admitted to a private asylum. Sometimes Schumann was quiet and compliant, even composing a little. Other times he screamed at his delusions and fought his keepers. His physical condition deteriorated. By the summer of 1856, he refused to eat. The last time he saw Clara, he could barely talk and couldn't get out of bed. But she believed he had recognized her and tried to embrace her, and no one was cruel enough to tell her that he hadn't recognized anyone for a long time and that his movements were mostly uncontrolled flailings. Schumann died two days later, on July 28, 1856.

What brought down this brilliant man at the relatively young age of forty-six? Today the generally accepted explanation is that he suffered from tertiary syphilis. The infection hid in his body for twenty-four years. Clara wasn't infected because, in its latent phase, syphilis is not transmitted through sexual contact. One dose of penicillin would have cleared it right up.

Clara was left with seven children. She refused charity when friends offered to hold a benefit concert, insisting she could make the money herself. She proceeded to do so with years of successful tours. She continued to play her husband's music and raised her children to love the father the youngest ones didn't even remember. Her long and complex relationship with Johannes Brahms will be treated in his chapter—suffice it to say that even if she eventually fell in love with someone else, she never stopped loving Robert.

Clara lived for forty years after Schumann died. Their marriage had lasted only sixteen years—and for the last two years he was insane—yet Clara was faithful until death.

BATTLE OF THE MUSICAL "SCHU'S"

The similarity between Schumann's name and that of another composer has caused a lot of confusion over the years. Just to clear things up: Franz Schu*bert* was born in Vienna in 1797. He studied under Salieri but struggled to make a name for himself. Like Schu*mann*, he suffered from syphilis; he seems to have been an alcoholic. He died in 1828 and was buried next to his friend Beethoven. Today he is remembered primarily for his *Unfinished Symphony* and the *Trout* Quintet.

The two men had few similarities other than the first syllables of their last names and their professions. Nevertheless, they have been mixed up more than once, with the most famous muddle occurring in 1956 when East Germany issued a set of stamps featuring Schumann's picture superimposed over a score of Schubert's music.

EVEN THE PRUSSIAN ARMY COULDN'T STOP CLARA SCHUMANN

The Dresden Uprising of May 1849 resulted in a democratically minded provisional government kicking out the Saxon royal family and taking control of the city in defiance of Prussian troops. Schumann had been a republican his whole life, but he had four young children and a pregnant wife and thus no intention of manning the barricades. When the radicals arrived to forcibly enlist him, Robert, Clara, and oldest daughter Marie got the heck out of town.

The three younger children were momentarily safe with the housekeeper, but naturally the whole family wanted to be together. So the resolute Clara drove from the safety of their rural retreat back to Dresden. Accompanied by a servant, she set out at three in the morning, left the carriage about a mile from town, and walked past the barricades to the house. She snatched the children from their beds, grabbed a few clothes, and walked back out again, right past the skittish revolutionaries and trigger-happy Prussians. It was a bold and courageous act—one typical of this remarkable woman.

SILENT SCHUMANN

Schumann was famous for his long silences. Berlioz reported in 1843 that he knew his *Requiem* was a success when it caused the taciturn Schumann to actually speak. Wagner, on the other hand, was outraged when, after he had opined on everything from the musical situation in Paris to the politics of Germany, Schumann still said nothing. "An impossible person," he told Liszt. For his part,

Schumann commented that the younger composer had "an enormous gift of the gab . . . one cannot listen to him for long."

TAKE MY WIFE, PLEASE

It's not easy being married to a brilliant pianist. Once, after a spectacular performance by Clara, a gentleman approached the couple to congratulate her. Seeming to feel that something was due her husband, the man turned to Robert and politely inquired, "Please tell us, sir, are you musical?"

FRANZ LISZT

OCTOBER 22, 1811–JULY 21, 1886

ASTROLOGICAL SIGN:
LIBRA

NATIONALITY:
HUNGARIAN

MUSICAL STYLE:
ROMANTIC

STANDOUT WORKS:
HUNGARIAN RHAPSODY NO. 2

WHERE YOU'VE HEARD IT:
IN THE ACADEMY-AWARD-WINNING *TOM AND JERRY* CARTOON
"THE CAT CONCERTO" (1946)

"MY FATHER FEARED THAT WOMEN WOULD TROUBLE MY EXISTENCE AND DOMINATE ME."

QUOTABLE

*I*t's one thing to be a good musician—it's another to be a star.

Nineteenth-century concert-goers got to see some amazing piano virtuosos: the flawless Mendelssohn, the confident Clara Schumann, the sensitive Chopin, not to mention half a dozen others not mentioned in this book.

But Liszt put them all to shame. The difference was not simply technique or talent. Schumann's technique was flawless, and Mendelssohn had talent oozing from every pore. The difference was star power.

Liszt had the inborn ability to wow audiences. The minute he stepped onstage, they forgot everything else. Sure, he played dazzling piano pieces of his own composition, but it didn't matter—he could have played "London Bridge Is Falling Down" and had them fainting in the aisles.

The only problem? Even stars can't live their entire lives onstage. Step out of the spotlight, and things start to get messy.

The Perils of Prodigy

The Liszts were a modest family from the Hungarian village of Raiding. Father Adám was an amateur musician who had been slightly acquainted with Haydn. When he realized his son Franz (*Ferencz* in Hungarian) exhibited early proficiency at the piano, he declared him a prodigy and quit his job. Obviously, a Hungarian village was no place to raise a virtuoso, so the family headed for Vienna. Young Liszt even met Beethoven, who supposedly listened to the boy play and planted a kiss on his forehead, thus passing the torch of musical genius to the next generation. (This tale has many questionable details, not the least of which is that by the time Liszt arrived in Vienna Beethoven was entirely deaf, but Liszt, at least, believed it was true.)

When Liszt was twelve, Adám deemed the boy's training complete, moved the family to Paris, and hawked his son like a performing monkey until dropping dead in 1827. The young Liszt immediately cancelled all of his public performances. Only after the memory of his prodigy days faded did he play in public again.

Lisztomania!

After his self-imposed hibernation, Liszt emerged in the 1830s as a social butterfly and scintillating conversationalist. He was also devastatingly handsome: tall, fair, with alluring blue eyes and a cascade of hair. One of those who fell for him hard was the Countess Marie d'Agoult, an aristocrat with an impressive family tree and unimpressive husband. For a while, Marie was content with a less-than-discreet affair in Paris, but Liszt's other flirtations drove her into torments of jealousy. Marie decided to claim Liszt for herself, and in the summer of 1835 she left her husband, fled to Switzerland, and summoned her lover to her side. Liszt seems to have been as startled by this turn of events as Marie's husband. Only after Liszt arrived in Geneva did Marie mention she was pregnant.

Liszt's daughter Blandine was born in 1835; a second daughter, Cosima, was born in 1837, and a son, Daniel, in 1839. The couple paid them no attention; they were shuttled off to servants, schools, and Liszt's mother.

Oddly, Marie praised her lover as a musical genius but took zero interest in his compositions and found his public performances vulgar. Her riches could have supported them all in luxury, but Liszt refused to be financed by her. Matters came to head after the birth of Daniel, when Liszt resolved to take up the life of a touring virtuoso.

For the next nine years, Liszt dashed from one end of Europe to the other. The resulting "Lisztomania" saw adoring fans rushing him in the streets, stealing his handkerchiefs, and trying to clip locks of his hair. His playing was dramatic, emotional, and flamboyant—he tossed his hair, gazed up at the ceiling, and heaved heavy sighs. Sometimes he asked audiences for themes on which to improvise and then came up with musical interpretations of subjects such as the Milan Cathedral, a railway, and the question, "Is it better to marry or remain a bachelor?" (Answer: Whatever you choose, you'll regret it.)

Marie dourly observed these escapades from Paris and listened to every rumor of his romantic encounters. Most of the rumors happened to be true. He did, for example, have a fling with the courtesan Lola Montez, who forced her way into a men-only dinner in honor of Beethoven and danced a fandango on the table. After years of long-distance squabbling, the ill-fated affair with Marie ended for good in 1844, when she announced she wished never to see him again. Liszt readily complied.

The Princess and the Pianist

The break with Marie couldn't have come at a better time: Liszt had met another woman, the Princess Carolyne zu Sayn-Wittgenstein. The daughter of an immensely wealthy Polish nobleman and the wife of a comparatively

indigent Russian one, Carolyne made up for her lack of physical attractiveness with a brilliant mind and strong dash of eccentricity (like Chopin's lover George Sand, she smoked cigars.)

Life on permanent tour had begun to wear thin. Liszt was nearing forty, and how many times can you play the *William Tell* overture without getting sick of it? He headed for Weimar, where he had been named choirmaster in 1842 but had previously made only flying stops. His new goal was to promote "the music of the future," that is, music that united the disparate arts of poetry and music, so that a symphony could be accompanied by a poem that gave it meaning. This musical ideal was shared by a certain volatile composer named Richard Wagner, who saw Liszt as a kindred spirit (as well as a source of ready cash) and convinced him to premiere several of his long, expensive operas. And so Liszt's lush, emotional compositions became affiliated with Wagner's hyper-dramatism, to the point younger, more traditional composers such as Brahms lashed out against the both of them.

Carolyne settled herself in a villa outside of town. Liszt lived with her, unofficially; his official residence was a hotel in the middle of town. (All his letters were delivered to the hotel and then forwarded.) But Carolyne wasn't content to remain a composer's mistress forever—she wanted to be

FRANZ LISZT WAS SUCH A HEARTTHROB THAT WOMEN CHASED HIM IN THE STREETS, STEALING HIS HANDKERCHIEFS AND TRYING TO CLIP LOCKS OF HIS HAIR.

his wife. Two issues interfered with her plan, however: She was already married, and she was a devout Catholic. After years of struggle to obtain an annulment, Carolyne moved to Rome so she could have direct access to the clerics. She got the annulment in 1860.

After fifteen years in Weimar, Liszt had grown tired of the intellectual struggle of introducing unfamiliar music to unappreciative audiences, so he welcomed the chance to move to Rome for his wedding and a prolonged stay. The church had been filled with flowers and guests invited, but the night before the wedding, Vatican officials came banging on the door. A last-minute hitch had cropped up in the annulment, and the wedding was off.

Piano-Playing Priest

Liszt was left at loose ends in Rome, but he seemed to find the quiet comforting. His sexual shenanigans notwithstanding, he had always been a practicing Catholic, and the ritual of the church gave him comfort, particularly after the death of daughter Blandine in 1862.

What came next shocked everyone: Liszt took what are called minor orders and became a priest in 1865. Although forbidden to say Mass, he was entitled to wear clerical garb and took his new calling very seriously.

The person most startled by Liszt's turn toward religion was his daughter Cosima. Cosima had married one of Liszt's favorite pupils, Hans von Bülow, in 1857, but by 1862 she was madly in love with Liszt's old friend Wagner. We'll save the sordid details for the Wagner chapter—but suffice it to say that when Liszt learned of his daughter's adulterous relationship he flipped his lid. He did all he could to keep the pair apart and delivered long lectures to Cosima on the sanctity of marriage and her duty to her children. (Surely he was aware of his own hypocrisy.) After Cosima married Wagner in 1870, Liszt rebuilt his relationship with his daughter, but he and Wagner remained at loggerheads.

During the 1870s and early 1880s, Liszt divided his life between Rome, Weimar, and Budapest, teaching extensively. In 1881, he fell down a flight of stairs and had health problems thereafter. But in 1886 he traveled to Bayreuth for the annual Wagner festival, managed by Cosima after her husband's death. Cosima housed her father in a nearby inn and paid him little attention, except to demand he attend lengthy performances that exhausted him. He caught pneumonia, and Cosima declared only she would be allowed to nurse him. Devoted students were outraged, particularly when Cosima banned them from Liszt's bedside. Liszt died on July 31, 1886.

The Protestant Cosima hadn't bothered to summon a priest for her Abbé father, so he was denied the Last Rites; she proceeded to ignore his will, which had requested he be buried in a monk's robe without ceremony. Instead he was laid to rest in Bayreuth with great pomp. Back in Rome, Carolyne was outraged, not the least by the choice of burial site: At Bayreuth, Liszt would always be outshone by his son-in-law.

SHOWDOWN AT THE PIANO BENCH

In his twenties, Liszt was so confident he was the best piano player in the world that he took any rival's claims very seriously. Mendelssohn and Chopin had no time for such nonsense, but the Swiss virtuoso Sigismond Thalberg seemed ready for the challenge. Fans and the press got wind of the rivalry and called for a head-to-head match-up. On March 31, 1837, the two came face to face in a piano-playing virtuosos' *High Noon.*

Thalberg's approach was cool and detached—a vivid contrast to the thunderous Liszt. The poet Heinrich Heine reported that "the keys seemed to bleed," and that "everywhere in the room were pale faces, palpitating breasts, and emotional breathing during the pauses." At the end of the night, the two were proclaimed joint winners. Their hostess announced, "Thalberg is the best pianist in the world; Liszt is the only one." History, of course, has been less kind to Thalberg. His name is remembered only for his rivalry with Liszt.

YOU DON'T DISS THE LISZT

Liszt made several lengthy tours of Russia in the 1830s and '40s and became a favorite with the royals—although he found the arrogance of these pampered audiences hard to take. When Liszt played at a St. Petersburg *soirée*, Tsar Nicholas began an animated conversation that drowned out the music. Suddenly Liszt went silent. The puzzled tsar asked the musician, "Why have you stopped playing?" "Music herself should be silent when Nicholas speaks" he replied. After that, Nicholas kept his mouth shut.

CORRESPONDENCE INTERCOURSE?

Taking advantage of Liszt's reputation for romantic escapades, numerous individuals claimed to be his illegitimate offspring, including a pianist named Franz Servais. When asked about the young man, Liszt replied, "I know his mother only by correspondence, and one cannot arrange that sort of thing by correspondence."

RICHARD WAGNER

MAY 22, 1813–FEBRUARY 13, 1883

ASTROLOGICAL SIGN:
GEMINI

NATIONALITY:
GERMAN

MUSICAL STYLE:
ROMANTIC

STANDOUT WORKS:
"RIDE OF THE VALKYRIES" FROM *DIE WALKÜRE*

WHERE YOU'VE HEARD IT:
AS HELICOPTERS SWOOP IN TO ATTACK A QUIET VIETNAMESE
VILLAGE IN *APOCALYPSE NOW* (1979)

"THE [*RING* CYCLE] AS A WHOLE WILL BE . . . THE
GREATEST THING EVER WRITTEN."

QUOTABL

When Richard Wagner composed his *Ring* cycle of operas, he envisioned a ritual performance for the enlightenment of all Germans. After the last note rang out, the specially constructed wooden opera house and all four opera scores were to be burned to bits. With the message of the music received, the world would no longer need the scores.

No one except Wagner himself took any of this very seriously. What's amazing is that anyone ever took Wagner seriously. This was a guy who believed Jews worldwide were trying to destroy him and that opera had magical powers to restore humankind. Yet no matter how wacky his ideas, he always found someone to nod in sympathy and then hand him a wad of cash.

Did Wagner's convictions rub off on his fans? Or did they listen to the music and, amazed by its scope and vision, believe the guy who wrote it couldn't be all that bad?

Young Wagner

Confusion surrounds Richard Wagner's origins. His mother, Johanna Rosine, claimed multiple maiden names to hide a liaison with a German royal prince. The composer's father may have been her first husband, Friedrich Wagner, who died when Richard was a few months old, or her second husband, Ludwig Geyer, whom she married after an all-too-brief widowhood.

Geyer, an actor, involved the entire family in his theatrical endeavors, and young Wagner grew up backstage. Richard burned with ambition and planned on debuting a *Hamlet*-inspired verse-tragedy to bring him instant fame. After writing in secret for two years, he finally unveiled his 4,000-plus-lines to his family, expecting them to be stunned by his remarkable talent. Instead, his sisters giggled at the overwrought melodrama. He was mortified. Determined to prove his worth, Wagner fixed his attention on music. He had learned to play the piano as a child; now he focused on compositional theory and orchestration. Ultimately, his goal was to compose an opera. Opera, to Wagner, represented the highest form of Art. By combining drama, poetry, music, and visual spectacle, opera offered a complete experience, one he believed had the power to lift human beings to a higher plane of existence. Wagner was to become a leading figure in the New German School and the foremost champion of the quest for *Gesamtkunstwerk* or "total work of art."

Run, Wagner, Run

In 1834, with his family's assistance, Wagner was hired as music director of a Magdeburg-based opera company. There he met Christine Wilhelmine ("Minna") Planer, an actress of dubious reputation. Minna saw Wagner as a source of stability and security. This was a dead-wrong reading of Wagner's character, but by the time she figured that out, they were married. Wagner thereafter lost multiple jobs and ran up enormous debts. His most humiliating failure had the couple fleeing Riga by hiding in a ship storeroom with an enormous dog named Robert.

RICHARD WAGNER LOVED TAILOR-MADE SILK DRAWERS, LACE NEGLIGEES, AND VELVET COATS SO MUCH THAT HE DEDICATED A PRIVATE ROOM OF HIS HOUSE TO ALL THINGS FRILLY.

After Wagner spent a miserable few years in Paris, the Dresden theater agreed to produce his opera *Reinzi*. It was his first operatic success, and it even netted him a prestigious job offer as Kapellmeister to the Royal Court of Saxony. For several years Wagner spent his days attending court—and his evenings associating with radical republicans and the occasional anarchist. And so in 1848, when the Dresden Uprising broke out, Wagner headed to the barricades, distributed anti-royalist pamphlets, and did sentry duty in a high tower lined with mattresses to absorb bullet fire. When the uprising collapsed, Wagner faced trial, imprisonment, and even execution. He fled to Weimar, where Franz Liszt arranged—and financed—passage out of Germany for Wagner, Minna, a dog named Peps, and a parrot. Minna was unable to pack Wagner's library, which had been seized by creditors.

Soon thereafter, Minna washed her hands of her husband. This might have come as a relief to Wagner, since it meant he no longer had to hide his affairs. He had a positive gift for attracting aristocratic women willing to fork over cash. He moved to Zurich, where his forced inactivity prompted an outburst of composition. He conceived the *Ring* cycle, based on a mélange of German and Norse myths, and completed its first two operas, *Das Rheingold* in 1854 and *Die Walküre* in 1856.

Mad King Ludwig and Liszt's Crazy Daughter

German authorities granted Wagner a partial amnesty in 1860. The next few years saw the composer bouncing from city to city trying to arrange performances for his operas. *Tannhäuser* opened in Paris in 1861 and was an utter fiasco, and an attempted premiere of *Tristan and Isolde* in Vienna had to be cancelled after more than seventy rehearsals when the complex music and staging were deemed "un-performable." By 1864, the composer was destitute.

Then, as if a fairy godmother had waved a magic wand over him, Wagner's fortunes changed. In this case, the fairy godmother took the unlikely form of the eighteen-year-old Ludwig II of Bavaria, the handsome, flamboyant king who was already rumored to have a thing for stable boys. Ludwig simply adored Wagner's works. One of his first royal acts was to invite Wagner to Munich, settle all of his debts, and grant him a generous salary. It was a miracle.

Wagner had only one request: Could a job be found at court for his good friend Hans von Bülow? Bülow was a talented composer and former protégé of Franz Liszt—but that wasn't what made him Wagner's BFF. Wagner had the hots for Bülow's wife, Liszt's daughter Cosima. Courtesy of Ludwig, the Bülows moved in right around the corner from Wagner. Soon Cosima was pregnant; she gave birth to a daughter, Isolde, in 1865. There was no question which composer had created *this* Isolde.

Munich was shocked. They were also appalled by the amount of money Ludwig spent on Wagner's elaborate productions and the amount of influence the composer had on the government. Ludwig finally had to ask his pet composer to leave town.

Wagner returned to Switzerland with Cosima in tow. The couple had another daughter, Eva, in 1867, and a son, Siegfried, in 1869. Eventually, even the tolerant Bülow reached the end of his rope, and he divorced Cosima in 1870. Since Minna had died in 1866, Wagner and Cosima were free to marry. Cosima devoted the rest of her life to promoting her husband.

For Whom the Ring Tolls

With another quiet period in Switzerland, this time with Cosima to baby him and Ludwig to finance him, Wagner soon finished the *Ring* cycle, completing *Siegfried* in 1871 and *Götterdämmerung* in 1874. These works were intended to be that *Gesamtkunstwerk* he always talked about—a total work art that would bring renewal to the German people.

But an ordinary opera house wouldn't do for the *Ring.* Wagner envisioned a home designed especially for the *Ring,* where the entire cycle could be performed under his control every year. He and Cosima settled on the town of Bayreuth in northern Bavaria, moving there in 1872. Wagner directed every element, from the architecture of the concert hall to the costumes of the characters. He was particularly famous for showing singers how to act their parts, floating around the stage as an elderly, balding Rhine maiden.

The opening performance in August 1876 attracted an audience that included Kaiser Wilhelm and the emperor of Brazil. The show wasn't perfect: A mechanical dragon prompted titters instead of horror, and the ring itself kept getting lost backstage. Most distressingly, when the box office receipts were tallied, the Wagners realized they were a stunning 148,000 marks in the red. Only an infusion of cash from the benevolent Ludwig kept the enterprise from going under.

By now Wagner's health was starting to suffer—he frequently endured chest pains. The family spent winters in Italy to escape the cold German winters. A source of conflict developed between Wagner and Cosima in the form of Carrie Pringle, a talented English soprano. It's not clear if the two progressed to the point of an affair, but Cosima, who had stopped Wagner's flings in the past, was on high alert. When the family moved to Venice for the winter of 1882, Pringle asked if she could visit. The couple had a magnificent fight over her letter; when it ended, Cosima, who rarely played the piano, marched to the keyboard and played a composition by her father, Franz Liszt. Wagner despised his former friend for having opposed their marriage, so Cosima's performance no doubt was meant as a spiteful insult. Whether Cosima had intended it or not, her arrow hit its mark. Wagner suffered a massive heart attack and died.

Wagner's coffin was carried back to Bayreuth for burial. Later stories described Cosima clinging to her husband's body for twenty-four hours, but this is contradicted by her own diaries and other accounts. In a sense, however, she never gave up clinging to his legacy. She devoted every ounce of energy to promoting Wagner and Bayreuth. Today devoted followers wait up to ten years to obtain tickets to Bayreuth, in the ultimate tribute to this brilliant, but infuriating man.

MEET THE WAGNERS

The Bayreuth festival is as famous for its backstage dramas and melodramatic cast of characters as for its onstage tragedies. Cosima ruled the festival with an iron fist until 1906, when she deemed her son Siegfried old enough to take over. In 1915 the apparently bisexual Siegfried tried to stop the rumors about his sexual orientation by marrying an Englishwoman named Winifred Klindworth. She immediately proved his virility by bearing four children in as many years (Wieland, Friedelind, Wolfgang, and Verena). Siegfried died of a heart attack in 1930, not long after Winifred met her hero, a rising star of German politics named Adolf Hitler.

Hitler adored Wagner and frequently dropped in at Bayreuth to frolic in the garden with Winifred's children. So devoted was Hitler to the festival that he provided government support during the war and kept the seats full by shipping in factory workers and soldiers on leave. Friedelind was the only Wagner who had any sense of the implications of Hitler's ravings, and early in the war she fled Germany for England and wrote a series of devastating newspaper articles about the man she used to call "Uncle Wolfie."

After the war, the family was left with a Bayreuth as scarred by its close affiliation with the Nazi Party as by Allied bombs. Winifred was eventually sentenced to probation for her close relationship with Hitler, although she always claimed (with a straight face) that she hadn't known a thing about his politics.

Wieland and Wolfgang resolved to keep the festival going. Wieland died in 1966, and Wolfgang soldiered on. In 2008, the Bavarian culture minister announced that Wolfgang's daughters Eva Wagner-Pasquier and Katharina Wagner would take over the festival. Bayreuth seems poised to take the Wagner legacy well into the twenty-first century with Wagners at the helm.

WAGNER'S "JEWISH QUESTION"

It's widely known Richard Wagner was anti-Semitic; what's not clear is how to put his anti-Semitism into context. It's been claimed that Wagner's beliefs were a product of his time, and there's no question the anti-Jewish sentiment floating around nineteenth-century Europe would shock modern minds. However, Wagner's beliefs trended toward the far end of the spectrum.

It's worth noting that Wagner's antipathy toward Jews didn't appear until he decided two very specific Jews were his enemies: the composers Giacomo Meyerbeer and Felix Mendelssohn. (Wagner ignored the fact that Mendelssohn was a devout Lutheran.) Wagner saw Meyerbeer's and Mendelssohn's coolness toward his operas as a sign of their alien natures; it was a short step to making them representatives of all of his enemies.

Eventually, Wagner's anti-Jewish sentiments became a centerpiece of his elaborate and frankly unhinged personal mythology. Wagner asserted that a master race from the east had been corrupted when they moved west, encountered Jews, and started eating meat. (You might think Wagner therefore advocated vegetarianism, but intellectual consistency was not his forte.) It now behooved the descendants of this master race, the Aryans, to regain their superhuman status by eliminating the influence of the Jews.

If all this sounds familiar, it should. Hitler read all of Wagner's essays as he prepared to write *Mein Kampf.*

POOR RICHARD
Everyone seems to have an opinion when it comes to critiquing Wagner. Here's a small sampling:

I have been told that Wagner's music is better than it sounds.
—American author Mark Twain

One can't judge Wagner's opera *Lohengrin* after a first hearing, and I certainly don't intend hearing it a second time.
—Italian composer Gioacchino Rossini

I love Wagner, but the music I prefer is that of a cat hung up by its tail outside a window and trying to stick to the panes of glass with its claws.
—French poet Charles-Pierre Baudelaire

Parsifal is the kind of opera that starts at six o'clock and after it has been running for three hours you check your watch and it says 6:20.
—American conductor David Randolph

I can't listen to that much Wagner. I start getting the urge to conquer Poland.
—American humorist and filmmaker Woody Allen

IN TOUCH WITH HIS FEMININE SIDE

Richard Wagner liked to present himself as a man's man, a fighter in revolutions, a wooer of women; but the composer also adored silks and satins, particularly *pink* silks and satins. In fact, Richard Wagner habitually wore women's underwear.

It's not clear when this behavior began, but by the time Wagner lived in Zurich, he had developed a passion for tailor-made silk drawers as well as lace negligees and velvet coats. Naturally, he was at some pains to conceal this little quirk. Sometimes he pretended his orders were for Cosima; other times, he arranged for his contraband to be shipped to his barber. Since he couldn't traipse around the house in a petticoat, he needed a special sanctum for their delectation, and so all of his later homes included a private room covered from floor to ceiling in pale silk and ornamented with as many rosettes, ruchings, and tassels as it could hold.

GIUSEPPE VERDI

OCTOBER 9 OR 10, 1813–JANUARY 27, 1901

ASTROLOGICAL SIGN:
LIBRA

NATIONALITY:
ITALIAN

MUSICAL STYLE:
ROMANTIC

STANDOUT WORK:
"SEMPRE LIBERA DEGG'IO" FROM *LA TRAVIATA*

WHERE YOU'VE HEARD IT:
BLARING FROM RICHARD GERE'S LIMOUSINE AT THE END OF *PRETTY WOMAN*

"NOW THAT I AM NOT MANUFACTURING ANY MORE NOTES, I AM PLANTING CABBAGES AND BEANS."

QUOTABLE

Classical music in the mid-nineteenth century is usually depicted as a battle between the Romantics and the traditionalists—the Liszt/Wagner crowd versus Brahms. But there was a third way that came from the other side of the Alps: the way of Giuseppe Verdi.

Verdi took his own path, creating adored operas full of catchy melodies. You left a Verdi premiere humming the tunes, and by the next morning all the street singers and local bands would be belting out the hits. Wagner's epic tragedies and Brahms's intellectual symphonies never had this kind of popular appeal.

How did Verdi do it? By staying true to his roots. Verdi was a country boy who never lost touch with his native Parma; even at the height of his fame, he liked nothing more than to return to his country house to supervise the fall harvest. This is not to say that Verdi wasn't sophisticated or that his music wasn't of the highest quality. He knew his stuff. He just didn't see any point to the music wars. The result? Music everybody's still humming today.

You Can Take a Boy out of Busseto, but You Can't Take Busetto out of the Boy

The Verdi family had worked and farmed in north-central Italy near the small town Busseto for several generations. Giuseppe Verdi, the only son of Carlo Verdi and Luigia Uttini, was born on either October 9 or 10—reports vary— of 1813. As a child, he was completely captivated by music, and when he was six his family was so convinced of his talent that they scrimped and saved to buy him a used spinet. Soon he was the town's organist and a driving force in the Philharmonic Society.

By 1832, it was time for Verdi to widen his horizons, and so the eighteen-year-old set out for Milan to apply to the Conservatory of Music. Verdi was older than the conservatory's maximum age of seventeen, but no one thought this would be a problem since he was so talented. However, after multiple auditions, the examining board gave its considered opinion that the young man "would turn out to be a mediocrity." Verdi was crushed.

Back in Busseto, a tussle broke out over the position of town music director. Verdi's fans lobbied for him to get the job, but local priests put forth their own candidate. The entire town took sides in the ensuing battle, which included brawls in neighborhood taverns. Verdi got sick of the whole thing and wanted to return to Milan, but his supporters were so committed to his cause they kept him prisoner in his own house. The strife was settled only when Verdi won a head-to-head piano competition with his rival.

The position of *maestro di musica* gave Verdi the financial security to marry his sweetheart, Margherita Barezzi. The couple had a daughter a year later and a son the year after that. Verdi had become a local celebrity, but his ambitions had moved beyond Busseto. He resigned in the fall of 1838, and he and Margherita moved to Milan, where he premiered his first opera, *Oberto*, in 1839. It wasn't a triumph, but it wasn't a failure either, and critics predicted that the young man had a bright future.

And the Hits Just Keep on Coming

These years were marked by enormous loss. The Verdis' daughter, Virginia, had died shortly before the family left Busseto; their son, Icilio, died shortly before the premiere of *Oberto*. Then Margherita passed away after a short illness in 1840. From here on, nothing seemed to go right for the composer. Verdi's second opera, *Un giorno di regno*, was a flop that closed after the first night. Verdi told people he would never compose again.

Then the opera impresario Merelli gave him a copy of a new libretto based on the biblical account of the Babylonian king Nebuchadnezzar— "Nabucco" in Italian. Verdi threw the text into a corner and ignored it for five months. One day he picked it up and flipped through it. Years later he wrote, "One day, one line; one day, another; now one note, then a phrase . . . little by little the opera was composed."

Nabucco premiered in May 1842 at the Teatro alla Scala in Milan. The first night was an overwhelming success, with shouts so loud after the first act that Verdi feared he was hearing angry protests instead of grateful applause.

Finally, his career was secure. Verdi called these his "galley years," and he certainly slaved away. Every opera production came with scenes with soloists, quarrels with management, and disputes with censors. Yet Verdi produced masterpiece after masterpiece—*Rigoletto* in 1851, *Il Trovatore* in January 1853, *La Traviata* in March 1853, and *La Forza del Destino* in 1862. Every Italian knew his songs, every Venetian gondolier and Napolese street singer could belt them out, and the nights of his premieres usually ended with local bands performing his latest hit outside his hotel window.

Just a Stone's Throw Away from Home

Verdi began a relationship with a woman he knew from the Milan stage. Giuseppina Strepponi combined a ravishing voice with a dreadful reputation—the unmarried soprano had taken the stage unmistakably pregnant four separate times. (Her children were abandoned at orphanages.)

It was one thing to shack up with a notorious opera singer in Milan; it was another matter in rural Busseto. Verdi had built himself a sizable estate in Busseto, complete with a villa known as Sant'Agata, and every year he returned to the countryside to oversee work on the harvest and livestock. But for all its bucolic charms, Busseto was a conservative small town, and residents took it as an affront when Verdi brought his mistress to their respectable village. On Giuseppina's first stay in Busseto in 1849, Verdi's brother-in-law reproached him for bringing home a prostitute, and strangers threw stones at the windows of their house.

The couple finally married in 1859—why they waited so long, no one knows. Busseto nevertheless remained hostile, and during the long months in the country Signora Verdi had only the servants to talk to.

Viva Italia!

Although little in Busseto changed over the years, the rest of the Italy underwent dramatic transformations. When Verdi began his career, the Italian peninsula was divided into numerous small states, and most of northern Italy was controlled by Austria. Verdi had been identified with the anti-Austrian bloc as far back as the 1842 premiere of *Nabucco*, when the chorus "Va, pensiero," a lament by exiled Hebrew slaves for their homeland, was used by nationalists to protest Austrian rule.

Over the years, the move to kick out the foreign powers and unify the country gained momentum under the leadership of the king of Savoy, Victor Emmanuel II. A moderate who proposed a constitutional monarchy, Victor Emmanuel became closely allied with Verdi: The slogan "Viva VERDI," was reportedly a secret rallying cry of the nationalists (the acronym VERDI standing for "Viva Vittorio Emanuele, Re d'Italia").

After years of struggle, Italy became one nation in 1861. Almost immediately, Verdi was asked to run for the Italian Parliament; he handily won a seat and served one term. For the rest of his life, Verdi was honored as the composer of *Il Risorgimento* ("The Resurgence") that brought Italy's unification.

Once a Composer, Always a Composer

Verdi slowed down as he entered his sixth decade, telling people he had retired. But that didn't stop him from writing *Aida* in 1871, *Otello* in 1887, and *Falstaff* in 1893—when he was seventy-nine years old. Honors poured in. He was appointed to the Italian Senate, made a member of the French Legion of Honor, and named a *Cavaliere* of the Great Cross of Italy. (The king also offered to make him a marchese, but Verdi declined, saying simply, "I am a peasant.")

But all was not awards and honors. Giuseppina's peace had been shattered in the mid-1870s when Verdi began an affair with a soprano named Teresa Stolz. Matters had come to a head around 1877, with Verdi choosing to remain with his wife rather than his mistress. In the 1890s, Giuseppina was frequently ill, and she died in November 1897.

Her octogenarian widower remained spry and lively until 1901, when he suffered a stroke while staying at a hotel in Milan. News of Verdi's illness swept across Italy. The hotel manager closed the establishment to other guests, kept a press office on the ground floor, and posted updates on the sidewalk outside. Police rerouted the traffic outside the hotel to cut down on noise, and the king and queen received telegram updates once an hour. Verdi died at 2:50 in the morning of January 27. By dawn, most of the shops in Milan were closed for mourning.

What he left behind were operas that remain hugely popular to this day—just as enjoyable and hummable as the day they were first performed.

NOBODY INSULTS OUR MAESTRO!

Although most Italians adored everything Verdi wrote, a few were harder to please. After the premiere of *Aida*, one operagoer so disliked the work that he wrote Verdi complaining that he had wasted thirty-two lira on his rail journey, theater tickets, and dinner. The letter-writer, one Prospero Bertani, wanted his money back.

Verdi was more amused than offended. He requested his agent send Signor Bertani twenty-seven lira, thereby paying for the train fare and tickets but not dinner. "He could very well have eaten at home," Verdi wrote. He asked that his agent publish the exchange in all the papers. Fans were so outraged by this attack on the maestro that letters from all over Italy poured in to Signor Bertani, including several death threats.

STOP WITH THE ADULATION ALREADY

On vacation one year, Verdi hosted a friend who was surprised to find the composer's villa crowded with several dozen piano-organs, mechanical pianos used by street musicians. "When I arrived here," said Verdi, "all these organs were playing airs from *Rigoletto, Travatore*, and all my other operas from morning til night. I was so annoyed I hired the whole lot for the season. It has cost me about a thousand francs, but at all events I am left in peace."

WHEN VERDI WAS SHACKING UP WITH A NOTORIOUS OPERA SINGER IN THE COUNTRYSIDE, ANGRY VILLAGERS STONED THEIR HOUSE, CALLING HER A PROSTITUTE.

LA DONNA UNDER WRAPS

When Verdi wrote his new aria "La donna è mobile" for *Rigoletto*, he sensed he had a hit on his hands—but he didn't want the song to reach the public before opening night. So before he handed the score to the tenor, he took the man aside. "Give me your word," he said, "that you will not sing this melody at home, that you will not even whistle it—in a word, that you will allow no one whatever to hear it." Of course, one promise wasn't enough, and before rehearsals Verdi implored everyone at the theater—the orchestra, the singers, even the stage hands—to keep the song a secret. And so at the premiere, "La donna è mobile" was a complete surprise and an immediate success.

EVERYBODY KNOWS YOUR NAME

Verdi's fame in his home country was so great that everyday matters like his mailing address were never an issue. When Verdi once asked a new acquaintance to mail him something, the man asked for Verdi's address. Verdi replied, "Oh, address it simply 'Maestro Verdi, Italy.'"

JOHANNES BRAHMS

MAY 7, 1833–APRIL 3, 1897

ASTROLOGICAL SIGN:
TAURUS

NATIONALITY:
GERMAN

MUSICAL STYLE:
ROMANTIC

STANDOUT WORK:
"WIEGENLIED," ALSO KNOWN AS "CRADLE SONG" OR "BRAHMS'S LULLABY"

WHERE YOU'VE HEARD IT:
TINKLING FROM ANY NUMBER OF CHILDREN'S MOBILES AND MUSIC BOXES

"IF THERE IS ANYONE HERE WHOM I HAVE NOT INSULTED, I BEG HIS PARDON."

QUOTABL

B y the mid-nineteenth century, the Romantic composers Berlioz, Liszt, and Wagner had made such an impression on audiences that everything that had come before was considered hopelessly out of date. If music didn't pour out of you in an emotional torrent and sweep the audience along in its headlong flight, it was nothing.

But hang on a minute, said Johannes Brahms. Music doesn't have to be overwhelmingly emotional and structurally radical. Sonatas, canons, and fugues have value, too. Sounds like a reasonable stance, but remember, we're not dealing with reasonable people. As soon as Brahms set himself up as an alternative to Liszt and Wagner, he exposed himself to withering attacks in what came to be known, believe it or not, as the War of the Romantics. It was a war the curmudgeonly Brahms was all too willing to fight.

The *Bierfiedler* from Hamburg

Johannes Brahms came from a musical family, but the music of his father, Johann Jakob, was a long way from refined court fare. Johann Jakob was a *bierfiedler*—a beer fiddler, an entertainer who played in small bands and local dives. Although he eventually landed a job at the Hamburg Philharmonic, he lost huge chunks of money trying to breed pigeons, and his family lived in the slums. He and wife, Christiane, had four children, with Johannes the middle child and first son. It was clear by age six that the boy had native musical talent, and Johann Jakob rejoiced that his son would follow in his footsteps.

But young Johannes had other ideas. He demanded to learn the piano, and then asked for instruction in composition. Johann Jakob was baffled: Why would you bother with the uncertain world of composing when you could be a *bierfiedler*?

No matter how hard he tried to escape it, Johannes ended up in exactly the kind of dives his father frequented. His father decided the teenager was old enough to earn a living and arranged for him to play piano at waterfront bars; these establishments offered drink, dancing, pretty girls, and little rooms upstairs for more private entertainment. Brahms played waltzes, polkas, and mazurkas until dawn, usually reading a novel as his fingers effortlessly banged out the tunes.

Rule Number One: Stay Awake

Eventually Brahms began teaching piano and left the *bierfiedler* world for good. He also turned his passions to composition. So enthusiastic was he about his works that in 1850, when he learned Robert and Clara Schumann would be in town, Brahms bundled up some of his efforts and sent them to the Schumanns' hotel. A busy Robert Schumann returned the parcel unopened. Brahms was devastated.

Soon, however, other opportunities presented themselves. In 1853, the twenty-year-old Brahms set out on a concert tour with violinist Eduard Reményi. Reményi introduced Brahms to Joseph Joachim, a violin prodigy; they immediately recognized one another as kindred spirits.

Reményi also introduced Brahms to the great Franz Liszt. Liszt asked Brahms to play one of his compositions, but Brahms was paralyzed with nervousness and declined. "Well then," said Liszt, "I shall have to play." He picked up the handwritten score of Brahms's E-flat Minor Scherzo and played it by sight, flawlessly. Liszt then played one of his own works, but this time Brahms's critical faculties kicked in. He thought Liszt's music was over-dramatic, emotional overwrought, and generally over the top.

AS A YOUNG MAN, BRAHMS RELUCTANTLY CONTINUED HIS FATHER'S PROFESSION, PERFORMING BAWDY BARROOM BALLADS IN SQUALID DIVES.

Most of all, however, during his meeting with Liszt, Brahms was *tired*. He and Reményi had been barreling across Germany for weeks, spending their nights at concerts and days bouncing along rough roads. At one point, Liszt looked up to see Brahms had dozed off in his chair. Brahms would never join the ranks of Liszt's protégés.

A New Kind of Messiah

Joachim prodded Brahms to again pursue a meeting with Schumann. Brahms resisted, remembering the unopened package, but his friend waved all his protests aside.

So in the fall of 1853, Brahms knocked on the door of the Schumann house in Düsseldorf. Robert was wearing a dressing gown and slippers and didn't seem particularly welcoming, but he asked Brahms to play. Brahms

started in on his C Minor Piano Sonata, but Schumann stopped him mid-chord and rushed out of the room. Brahms though he would sink through the floor in embarrassment, but Robert returned with Clara. "Here, dear Clara," he said, "you shall hear music such as you have never heard before."

So convinced was Schumann of Brahms's bright future that he dashed off an article for his old journal *Neue Zeitschrift für Musik* that lauded the young man as a genius, a prophet, a messiah of music—one who, moreover, would overthrow the false gods Liszt and Wagner and the entire New German School.

The result was staggering: Brahms leapt from complete obscurity to signal bearer for a musical movement. Of course, Liszt, Wagner & Co. weren't going to take this sort of thing lying down. They declared war on the young composer.

Tragic Triangle

A few months later, back on the road, Brahms heard the shocking news: Robert Schumann had lost his mind. Brahms rushed back to Düsseldorf and promised Clara he would stay until the crisis passed. (Everyone assumed Robert's madness was temporary.) Brahms lived in the Schumann house. To the kids, he was a favorite uncle. To Clara, he was an invaluable friend and support. But to Brahms, Clara was the ideal woman: He had fallen desperately in love with his hero's wife.

How much Clara knew or guessed is unclear. A romance would have been an outrageous betrayal of her husband, since she fully believed Robert would recover. The thirty-four-year-old Clara probably heard the gossip over the attention the good-looking, blue-eyed, twenty-one-year-old Brahms was paying her—but Clara never paid attention to gossip.

Robert's illness ran its tragic course. Brahms accompanied Clara on her last visit to her husband and walked behind the coffin on the way to the cemetery.

What happened next? It is possible Brahms proposed and Clara refused. It is also possible Brahms had ruled out marriage with a woman he had always seen as unattainable. In any case, Clara stayed in Düsseldorf and Brahms tried to reclaim his own life.

The Sound of One Hand Clapping

The next few years proved a stark contrast to the grim watch over Robert Schumann. Brahms's reputation grew as he toured Germany composing, conducting, and flirting with pretty girls. In the summer of 1858 he stayed with friends in rural Göttingen, where a fellow guest was the lovely Agathe von Siebold. Before long, Brahms was accompanying Agathe in duets and taking long walks with her in the woods. They became engaged.

Brahms then headed for Leipzig to perform his D Minor Concerto. The famed Leipzig Gewandhaus orchestra had taken Liszt's side in the War of the Romantics and was already hostile toward Schumann's *Messiah*. At that time, it was customary for the audience to applaud after ever movement of a piece, but when Brahms completed the first movement, he was met with total silence. After the second movement, the same. After the final movement, Brahms sat trembling at the piano. Nothing. Finally a few hands came together in tentative claps, but they were immediately silenced by a spate of hissing. Brahms rose, bowed, and walked off the stage.

The debacle shook Brahms to the core. From his turmoil, he wrote a short letter to Agathe that read in part, "I love you! I must see you again! But I cannot wear fetters!" The implication, to a well-brought-up girl like Agathe, was clear: I will sleep with you, but I won't marry you. She returned his ring and never saw him again.

Soon, however, Brahms's fighting spirit was roused, and he told friends he longed to "write anti-Liszt." Joseph Joachim shared this goal, so in 1860 the two penned a manifesto attacking the New German School as vain and arrogant and exerting an "evil influence" on music. They called for a return to the pure music of Mozart and Beethoven, music uncomplicated by stories and programs and true to classical forms and harmonies.

But the New Germans had been playing this game for a long time. They learned about the manifesto when it had only received a pitiful four signatures, and they hurried to publish it before it was complete. His manifesto the subject of ridicule, Brahms decided to fight back the only way he knew how: By continuing to write his elegant, classical compositions in defiance of the New Germans.

Give Me That Old Time Tradition

In 1862, Brahms learned that the Hamburg Philharmonic was looking for a new conductor, and he assumed he would be their first choice. It came as an ugly surprise, then, when he learned Hamburg had awarded his dream job to someone else. Feeling the sting of rejection, Brahms went to Vienna, where he found audiences appreciative of his traditionalism. He was to live there for the rest of his life. For next three decades, the composer pursued a quiet round of composing and conducting. On his frequent tours around Europe, he performed his own works; back in Vienna, he wrote music and socialized with a select group of friends. In time, he became a fixture at a pub called the Red Hedgehog and a regular at the Wurstelprater, a park crammed with puppet theaters, acrobats, and clowns. Sometimes the increasingly portly composer took a ride on the carousel.

The War of the Romantics had by now ended in a draw. Each side declared itself the winner, with Hans von Bülow announcing that Brahms had become the third "B" alongside Bach and Beethoven. In 1894, the Hamburg Philharmonic finally offered him the music director position. He turned it down, saying their offer had come too late. Although only sixty-one and apparently in good health, he started describing himself as old and worn-out. Bewildered friends described him as aged beyond his years.

Clara Schumann, his longtime love, was failing as well. The two spent a day together in the fall of 1895 and parted laughing, as Brahms stuffed packages of his favorite tobacco into his pockets to smuggle back to Vienna. They never saw one another again: Clara died in May 1896.

Brahms never really got over her loss; he became jaundiced, perhaps the result of liver cancer. On March 7, 1897, he attended a performance of his Fourth Symphony at the Vienna Philharmonic. At the end, the ovation roared on and on as Brahms stood before the audience, tears running down his face. He died less than a month later.

PRETEND I WAS NEVER HERE

When Brahms grew ill, his doctor told him he would have to start a strict diet at once. "But how can I!" exclaimed the composer. "I am invited to dine with Strauss, and we are going to have chicken with paprika!"

"That is out of the question," replied the doctor.

"Very well, then," said Brahms, suddenly thinking of a solution, "please consider that I did not come to consult you until tomorrow."

YOU SING LIKE A GIRL

According to accounts, Brahms was a remarkably handsome young man with blue eyes the color of forget-me-nots, light brown hair, and a square jaw. The only feature that interfered with this divine picture was his voice, which remained as high-pitched as a young boy's. This was an enormous source of embarrassment as he entered his late teens and twenties, and finally Brahms decided to do something about it. He developed a series of "exercises" to lower his register and took to shouting over choir rehearsals. As a result, he ruined what had been a pleasant singing voice and rendered his speaking voice hoarse, barking, and still high. For the rest of his life, at moments of strain his voice would break like that of a thirteen-year-old boy.

SPARE ME THE ADULATION!

Brahms's curmudgeonly side often expressed itself when he had to deal with adoring female fans. When one young woman asked him which of his *lieder* she should buy, he recommended some of his posthumous works. Another lady asked him, "How do you write such divine adagios?" He replied, "Well, you know, my publisher orders them that way."

Brahms clearly found it embarrassing to be praised to his face. Once at a dinner, a friend stood and said, "Don't let us lose this opportunity of drinking to the health of the greatest composer." Brahms leapt to his feet and called out, "Quite right! Here's to Mozart's health!"

PYOTR ILYICH TCHAIKOVSKY

MAY 7, 1840–NOVEMBER 6, 1893

ASTROLOGICAL SIGN:
TAURUS

NATIONALITY:
RUSSIAN

MUSICAL STYLE:
ROMANTIC

STANDOUT WORKS:
"DANCE OF THE SUGAR-PLUM FAIRY" FROM *THE NUTCRACKER*

WHERE YOU'VE HEARD IT:
AS THE DEW-FAIRIES DANCE IN THE 1940 DISNEY ANIMATED MOVIE *FANTASIA*

"HAVING LIVED THIRTY-SEVEN YEARS WITH AN INNATE AVERSION TO MARRIAGE, IT IS VERY DISTRESSING, THROUGH FORCE OF CIRCUMSTANCE, TO BE DRAWN INTO THE POSITION OF BRIDEGROOM WHO, MOREOVER, IS NOT IN THE LEAST ATTRACTED TO HIS BRIDE."

QUOTABL

For a guy who didn't like women, Tchaikovsky sure was dominated by them. And truth be told, it's not that he didn't *like* women—he just didn't want to sleep with them. By modern standards this isn't a big deal, but in nineteenth-century Russia, public exposure as a homosexual could land in you prison.

So Tchaikovsky decided to hide his sexual preferences by getting married. The marriage turned out to be an unmitigated disaster, leaving him with a wife who tried, periodically, to wreck his life. As for the second woman who dominated Tchaikovsky's life—well, their relationship was so strange that they met on only one incredibly awkward occasion.

In the midst of all this sexual turmoil and emotional angst, it's amazing that Tchaikovsky was able to compose at all, let alone create the light and sparkling music that has made him one of the world's most beloved composers.

The Artistry of a Civil Servant

The middle-class Tchaikovsky family had six children, of which Pyotr Ilyich was the second. They lived in a small Imperial Russian town called Votkinsk. Pyotr's interest in music was sparked when his father brought home a barrel-organ called an orchestrion. The fascinated four-year-old tried to pick out its tunes on the piano. His parents tried to limit his playing time, but he would continue to practice on every available surface, once pounding so vigorously on a windowpane that he broke the glass and cut his hand. His parents gave in and arranged for piano lessons.

It didn't occur to anyone to train young Pyotr as a virtuoso, so he attended boarding school in St. Petersburg and later got a job in the Ministry of Justice. Through these years he continued to practice and study and, after three years of civil-service work, convinced his father to support his training at the St. Petersburg Conservatory. As soon as he graduated in 1865 he became professor of harmony at the Moscow Conservatory.

Tchaikovsky wrote his first symphony in 1866, his first opera in 1868, his first overture in 1870, and his first string quartet in 1871. He also accepted a commission to write a ballet—an odd choice since first-rank composers then rarely bothered with ballet music. But Tchaikovsky remembered some amateur family theatrics he had organized several years earlier at his brother's country house, a show with his nieces and nephews based on a Russian folktale. The result was *Swan Lake*, one of the most popular ballets of all time.

Fate or Fatale?

The stigma against homosexuality was so strong in Russian society that Tchaikovsky's love life is impossible to reconstruct. Nevertheless, it's clear from scattered references that he participated in the Moscow gay subculture. To prevent exposure, in 1877 Tchaikovsky decided to find a bride. Out of the blue, he received a letter from Antonina Milyukova, a former Conservatory student nine years his junior. She announced she had been in love with him for years. This alone should have set off alarm bells, since the two had never even met, but instead Tchaikovsky believed that Fate had handed him a bride. Less than two months later, they married.

He regretted it immediately. On the train headed for their honeymoon, the sobbing, hysterical groom explained to his bride that they could not have a sexual relationship. It is unclear whether or not Antonina grasped what he was saying. Tchaikovsky was so embarrassed by his new wife's denseness that he avoided friends; unable to bear her presence in his apartment, he went for long walks every evening in the cold. One night, he decided to throw himself in the icy Moscow River in hopes of catching a deadly cold—not the most efficient suicide plan, but the first that occurred to him. He staggered home half-frozen, but his constitution was strong and he suffered no ill-effects.

Finally, Tchaikovsky had his brother send a fake telegram summoning him to St. Petersburg; he fled his wife and never returned. Within a few weeks he was holed up in Paris, and his brothers began paying Antonina to keep her mouth shut. It took months for him to compose again.

Out of Sight, Out of Mind, and in the Money

As Tchaikovsky's marriage fell apart, he developed a far more rewarding relationship with another complete stranger. Yet again a letter arrived out of the blue, this time from a wealthy widow named Nadezhda von Meck. She wanted to commission some chamber pieces. A correspondence sprang up, and soon the two were writing each other lengthy letters about music, art, books, love, and life. Von Meck offered Tchaikovsky a stipend that would allow him to quit his work at the Moscow Conservatory. There was only one caveat: They could never meet.

Von Meck's insistence on a letter-only relationship defies understanding, but Tchaikovsky kept his end of the bargain. They ended up going to ridiculous lengths to keep apart. They told each other their travel itineraries so they wouldn't bump into one another in Paris or Florence; when Tchaikovsky stayed at von Meck's country estate, she provided him a daily schedule so that they wouldn't accidentally cross paths. As fate would have it, one day Tchaikovsky started his walk early while von Meck was running late. The two encountered one another on a country road. Neither spoke, but Tchaikovsky raised his hat in greeting and went on his way. It was all profoundly weird, but in von Meck, Tchaikovsky found a truly sympathetic friend and supporter.

Antonina he could mostly ignore. Sometimes she asked for a divorce, but Tchaikovsky always dissuaded her by sending her more money; he feared what might come out in court. Once she appeared at Tchaikovsky's apartment, threw her arms around his neck, and announced that she now knew how to arouse his passions. One hundred rubles later, she was on her way.

The relationship with von Meck ultimately ended as strangely as it had begun. She had suffered several financial losses, and in 1890 she wrote that both her financial support and letters must cease. Tchaikovsky was devastated. The decline in his income was regrettable, but more distressing was the loss of her unwavering friendship.

Love and Death?

As the years went on, Tchaikovsky's fame grew. On tours of European capitals, he was delighted to be met at rail stations by adoring fans. In 1888 he even visited America. He returned to ballet in 1892 and wrote his best-known work, *The Nutcracker.*

All this success and acclaim makes what happened next all the more mysterious. On November 6, Tchaikovsky died. Accolades and memorials poured in, the state paid for an enormous funeral, and the Imperial Chapel Choir sang at the service. The tsar himself remarked, "We have many dukes and barons, but only one Tchaikovsky."

The cause of death was given as cholera, which the composer allegedly contracted by drinking a glass of un-boiled water. But there are problems with this story. Reports of how and where Tchaikovsky drank the fatal glass contradict one another, as do depictions of the course of his illness. Rumors circulated for years that the death was in fact a suicide.

In 1979 a new story surfaced. The widow of Nikolay Jakobi, a powerful

government official who had attended school with Tchaikovsky, claimed that the composer had been involved in a homosexual relationship with the nephew of a duke. The duke wrote a letter of accusation and gave it to Jakobi to hand over to the Tsar. Jakobi supposedly called Tchaikovsky to a meeting at his house with other alumni, and they debated what to do next. They decided Tchaikovsky must kill himself—the only way for Jakobi to withhold the letter with honor.

We'll never know if this story is true. Many prefer to believe his death a tragic accident rather than a suicide brought on by societal prejudices. Ultimately, however, the end was the same: A brilliant man died too young at age fifty-three, leaving behind a legacy of delightful music enjoyed around the world.

> FORCED INTO MARRIAGE BY SOCIETAL CONVENTIONS, TCHAIKOVSKY HAD A HARD TIME CONVINCING HIS WIFE THAT HE WAS JUST NOT THAT INTO HER—OR ANY WOMAN.

MY, HOW TIMES HAVE CHANGED

Rumors of Tchaikovsky's homosexuality and suicide circulated for years. When composer Vladimir Dukelsky discussed the matter with ballet impresario Sergey Diaghilev, Diaghilev commented, "Poor Pyotr Ilyich Tchaikovsky was always on the verge of suicide, so afraid was he that people might discover he was a pederast. Today, if you're a composer and *not* a pederast you had better put a bullet through your head."

TAKING A CRACK AT THE *NUTCRACKER*

Tchaikovsky's *Nutcracker* ballet was generally praised when it was released, but it certainly wasn't a hit. In fact, the reviews were generally dismissive; one critic wrote: "For dancers, there is rather little in it, for art absolutely nothing, and for the artistic fate of our ballet, one more step downward."

For years it was rarely performed, but in the 1930s ballet companies rediscovered the score and performed it outside of Russia. In 1940, the ballet premiered in the United States in a production by the Ballets Russes de Monte Carlo. But it took off when it caught the attention of the great choreographer George Balanchine, who created a full-length version for the New York City Ballet in 1954. Ballet companies around the United States immediately tried to imitate his huge success, and by the 1960s *The Nutcracker* was a Christmastime ritual in most major cities. Today, more people have seen *The Nutcracker* than any other ballet, and the show often accounts for more than fifty percent of a ballet company's annual revenue.

CANNON FODDER

Tchaikovsky's *1812 Overture* (written in commemoration of the Russian defeat of Napoleon, *not*—as is sometimes assumed—the American-English War of 1812) is one of the loudest pieces of music in the classical repertoire. In addition to the usual complement of flutes, oboes, trumpets, and trombones, it is scored for cannons. Thus it is usually performed outdoors, where the pyrotechnics can be extraordinary.

They can also be a disaster. At a 1978 performance of the Royal Liverpool Philharmonic Orchestra, orchestra members were surprised to find two cannons aimed over the heads of the brass section, right at the audience, rather than facing away from the crowd. The conductor expressed concern, but the munitions experts assured him that they did this all the time and never had any trouble.

When the first cannon blast went off, a sheet of flame shot out of the cannon's mouth with an incredible roar. The orchestra was half-deafened and struggled to continue, despite clouds of smoke obscuring the conductor's podium. When the second blast hit, one of the first violinists leapt out of her chair and ran screaming off the stage. A tuba player was knocked off his seat and huddled on the floor for the rest of the performance. Somehow, the piece staggered to the end. The stunned audience was covered in soot, once-white dresses and shirts were filthy gray. Backstage, a horn player had to be physically restrained from slugging one of the pyrotechnicians.

The poor violinist who had fled the stage seems to have suffered a sort of an *1812 Overture*-induced post-traumatic stress syndrome; she received a special dispensation from management so that she did not have to participate in performances of the piece ever again.

ANTONÍN LEOPOLD DVOŘÁK

SEPTEMBER 8, 1841–MAY 1, 1904

ASTROLOGICAL SIGN:
VIRGO

NATIONALITY:
CZECH

MUSICAL STYLE:
ROMANTIC

STANDOUT WORKS:
LARGO FROM SYMPHONY NO. 9 FROM *THE NEW WORLD*

WHERE YOU'VE HEARD IT:
IN THE 1994 MOVIE *CLEAR AND PRESENT DANGER*

"ALTHOUGH I HAVE MOVED WELL ENOUGH INTO THE GREAT WORLD OF MUSIC, I AM STILL WHAT I WAS—A SIMPLE CZECH JOBBING COMPOSER."

QUOTABLE

*T*hrough a combination of history, geography, and bad luck, the nations of Eastern Europe have had more than their fair share of invasions, repressions, rebellions, and revolutions. In the midst of all that chaos, it has been difficult for composers to create a national musical idiom, develop schools, cultivate musicians, and promote the work of native sons and daughters. Even though Chopin adored his native Poland and Liszt his native Hungary, they had little opportunity to contribute to Polish or Hungarian music.

Dvořák was different. Although technically a citizen of the Austrian Empire, he considered himself Czech through and through. He created music of the Czech people, for the Czech people—operas in their native tongue, sacred music of their native faith, symphonies drawn from their native songs.

And yet he ended up in Manhattan writing an American classic. History's funny that way.

Of Meat and Organs

When Antonín Dvořák was born in 1841, German-speaking Austria controlled Bohemia, so Dvořák's hometown was known by two names: Nelahozeves to its Czech residents and Mühlhausen to the German-speaking rulers. Dvořák's father, Frantisek, owned a small inn and butcher shop, following in the footsteps of his father and his father's father. Antonín was the eldest of the family's nine children and was expected to become a butcher in turn—but his first love was always music. When he turned sixteen years old, he begged his father to let him give up butchering. The practical Frantisek insisted that his son train for a career and sent him to the Organ School in Prague.

As a student, Dvořák couldn't afford a piano of his own—he could barely afford food—so he befriended wealthier students and convinced them to let him practice at their homes. These arrangements never lasted long because Dvořák would show up and play day and night. Renting apartments in buildings with pianos didn't work, either, since the budding composer was likely to spring out of bed in the middle of the night and pound away with no thought for others' sleep.

After graduation and several years of scraping together gigs, Dvořák landed a job as a violinist at the Provisional Theater, so named not because it was temporary but because it was the theater of the Bohemian province.

The nearby National Theater put on plays and operas*in German, but the Provisional Theater cultivated native Czech works. There wasn't much of a repertoire for them to choose from, however. The country had so far produced only one outstanding composer, Bedfiich Smetana, who basically invented Czech classical music with his opera *The Bartered Bride*.

Dvořák aspired to follow in Smetana's footsteps. Dead broke, he had no money for a libretto, so the texts he worked from were dismal. And his music, frankly, wasn't much better: He rehashed Wagner, mostly. His first attempt at opera, *Alfred*, never got off the ground. The second, *King and Charcoal Burner*, premiered in 1874 at the Provisional Theater and then was thankfully forgotten. Although his compositions improved over the years, his librettos remained weak. It seemed clear that Dvorák waš not going to further the cause of native Czech music with opera.

Turning away from opera, Dvořák achieved his first real success with music inspired by a Czech poem called Heirs of the White Mountain. His reputation as a topnotch composer was cemented soon afterward with a second work, the Nocturne for String Orchestra.

That Old Time Religion

Now flush with confidence and cash, Dvořák married Anna Čermákova, a former piano student of his. Dvořák, like Mozart and Haydn before him, had originally been in love with his wife's sister, but Josefina Čermákova threw him over to marry a count. Fortunately for Dvořák, his marriage was much happier than Haydn's.

But it was a family soon beset by tragedy. First a baby died in infancy, then a year and half later the couple's eleven-month-old daughter died in a poisoning accident. Three weeks later their three-year-old son, Otaker, died of chicken pox. The devoutly Catholic Dvořák poured all of anguish into a new composition set to a famous thirteenth-century meditation poem on the sorrows of the Virgin Mary. His *Stabat Mater* of 1877 became not only the first great sacred work in Czech but also an achingly beautiful masterpiece.

The success of Stabat Mater seemed to open the floodgates. The same year, Dvořák began a correspondence with Brahms, who recommended him to his publisher, Fritz Simrock. Simrock published Dvořák's *Moravian Dances* to such acclaim that he quickly commissioned something similar; the resulting *Slavonic Dances* were an immediate hit.

In time, Dvořák and his wife had six more children, and their home buzzed with activity as students came and went, servants bustled about, and the children were everywhere underfoot. It was a simple household. Some of Dvořák's happiest days were spent at his modest country house in Vysoká, where he tended a garden, raised doves, and hung out with villagers in the local inn.

If I Can Make It There . . .

In 1891 the composer received a staggering offer: fifteen thousand dollars to come to New York to direct the National Conservatory of Music, a new institution founded by a music-loving millionaire's wife. Dvořák hesitated a long time before accepting, but in September 1892 he set out for the long sea voyage to the United States.

The Dvořáks settled in a comfortable house on East 17th Street opposite Stuyvesant Square. Mornings the composer took long walks to Central Park or down to the harbor. He then taught composition three days a week to small classes that included several African-American students. Afternoons were for composing, and evenings he usually stayed at home playing cards. Dvořák rarely made his way to concerts and only went to the Metropolitan Opera twice. It wasn't that he disliked the New York music scene, he just preferred quiet nights at home. The family considered returning home for the summer, but then they received an invitation to visit Spillville, Iowa. With all six children in tow, the Dvořáks headed for the small Czech-speaking village, where they found themselves completely at home.

AS THE ELDEST OF NINE CHILDREN, DVOŘÁK WAS EXPECTED TO BECOME A BUTCHER DESPITE HIS MUSICAL TALENTS.

Dvořák's impressions of the United States glowed with enthusiasm. He praised the lack of social distinctions and wrote in amazement that both a millionaire and his servant addressed each other as "Sir." He delighted in the music of "native" America, particularly African-American spirituals and Native American songs, although it seems unlikely that he heard genuine versions of either. In fact, Dvořák seems to have confused Native American and black Southern music and claimed not only that he found the two types of music practically identical, but also that it bore a remarkable similarity to

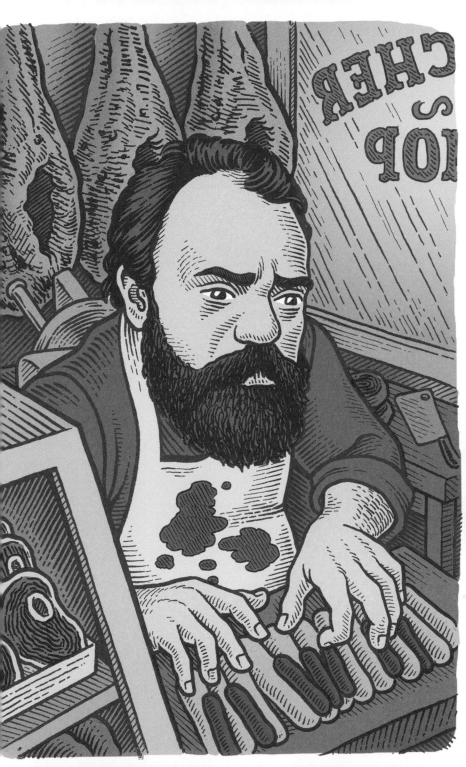

the music of Scotland. Frankly, Dvořák's view of America was generally naïve and simplistic: He knew nothing about the segregated South, the harsh West, or the overcrowded, disease-infested tenements of New York City—but he saw the best of nineteenth-century America and gloried in its strengths.

This romantic vision resulted in his most famous composition: Symphony no. 9, *The New World*. Dvořák claimed he drew upon American folk songs for inspiration, but he didn't quote them directly. Although some critics have noted greater similarities with Bohemian dances than American melodies, Dvořák's intention was to reflect the vast, striving young country, and audiences from Boston to San Francisco have loved the work since its premiere.

No Place Like Home

Dvořák returned to Prague in 1895 after two and a half years in America. He was now financially and professionally secure, and he enjoyed playing the Grand Old Man of Czech music. He kept on writing Czech operas, none of which got off the ground. Dvořák simply did not seem to have the skill to pick a good libretto. ("Any new libretto will do!" he once wrote a friend, which shows how little he felt it mattered.)

During the premiere of his latest opera *Armida* in 1904, Dvořák suddenly took ill. The composer had never been sick in his life, but now he was tormented by recurrent abdominal pain. He died of a stroke on May 1. Tens of thousands of people lined the route of his funeral procession in Prague. The long-oppressed Czech people recognized Dvořák not only a great composer but as *their* great composer.

The great irony is that, beyond his homeland, he is best-known for a symphony about America.

CAN I INTEREST YOU IN A DVOŘÁK TIE CLIP?

When Dvořák made a name for himself in England, he was surprised to find his face reproduced on cigarette cards. Similarly, during his time in America, he entered the public consciousness through a succession of collars, ties, and walking sticks—none of which he actually endorsed or profited a dime.

PENCIL PUSHER

In 1901, Dvořák was honored by the Austrian government with an appointment to the Second House of Parliament, a body that was roughly equivalent to the English House of Lords, but with even less authority. He made only one appearance at the House for his swearing-in, although he was delighted to find he had been given his own desk, complete with an inkwell, pens, paper, and several sharpened Hardtmuth no. 2 pencils—an excellent brand, with a lead both soft and firm. Dvořák pocketed the pencils, later showing them to his wife and saying, "Look at these, they're just the thing for writing music!"

SPIRITUAL RIPOFF?

Dvořák wrote the slow and haunting second movement of his Symphony no. 9 as a deliberate evocation of African-American spirituals. He did such a good job that many people believed the melody was not his own. Numerous sources claim the melody is based on a hymn or even a Scottish folk tune, but they're all wrong: Adaptations of the melody as a stand-alone song all came after the symphony. The best-known of these was composed by a student of Dvořák's named William Arms Fisher; Fisher adapted the melody into a hymn and called it "Goin' Home." Today this wholly invented "spiritual" is played by military bands, wailing bagpipes, and a cappella choirs across the United States as a moving tribute to loss and sorrow.

MARK MY WORDS

Dvořák's appreciation of African-American music raised eyebrows in segregated, racist America, but in time his remarks came to be seen as remarkably prescient. In an article in the *New York Herald* on May 21, 1893, Dvořák wrote:

> I am now satisfied that the future music of this country must
> be founded upon what are called the negro melodies. . . . All
> of the great musicians have borrowed from the songs of the
> common people. . . . In the negro melodies of America I discover

all that is needed for a great and noble school of music. They are pathetic, tender, passionate, melancholy, solemn, religious, bold, merry, gay, or what you will. It is music that suits itself to any mood or any purpose. There is nothing in the whole range of composition that cannot be supplied with themes from this source.

Most American musicians pooh-poohed this statement, insisting American classical music would be based on European models. In fact, composers from Gershwin's day to today have drawn inspiration from African-American music, just as this quintessentially Czech composer predicted.

EDWARD WILLIAM ELGAR

JUNE 2, 1857–FEBRUARY 23, 1934

ASTROLOGICAL SIGN:
GEMINI

NATIONALITY:
ENGLISH

MUSICAL STYLE:
ROMANTIC

STANDOUT WORKS:
POMP AND CIRCUMSTANCE MARCH NO. 1

WHERE YOU'VE HEARD IT:
AT EVERY SINGLE GRADUATION CEREMONY YOU'VE EVER ATTENDED

"THERE IS MUSIC IN THE AIR, MUSIC ALL AROUND US, THE WORLD IS FULL OF IT AND YOU SIMPLY TAKE AS MUCH AS YOU REQUIRE."

QUOTABLE

England had the hardest time producing musical geniuses. Although Germany and Italy were bursting with them and France and Russia held their own, England could make only a half-hearted claim to the German-born Handel.

Enter Edward Elgar, England's claim to composing fame. Of course, being an English composer had cons as well as pros. Elgar had to endure a multitude of English prejudices, including entrenched hostility toward Catholics and deep-seated class biases. But Elgar struggled through, married a woman above his station, hobnobbed with kings and queens, and achieved worldwide recognition. It's the classic story of a self-made man—one that's decidedly un-English.

Just Because You Hang Out at an Asylum Doesn't Mean You're Insane

Elgar's father, William Elgar, was a proficient musician and music-dealer who conducted local choirs and played the organ. William's shop was a superior type, selling sheet music and instruments and offering piano tuning services. He and his wife, Anne, had seven children, of whom Edward was the fourth. Surrounded by music, Edward became an expert violinist. He also taught himself music theory by studying the scores of Bach and Beethoven.

Leaving school at age fourteen, Elgar went to work as an office boy. He quit after a year and made money by teaching violin and piano—a grueling regimen that required that he walk miles between students' houses. He saved up every penny to travel to London once a week for lessons in violin and composition.

Another source of income was the Worcester and County Lunatic Asylum. The director of the institution believed music had recuperative powers, and he formed a band to play regularly for patients; Elgar became the bandleader. In this odd and inauspicious setting, Elgar rejoiced in having musicians to play his compositions.

Elgar's compositions soon outpaced the capabilities of the lunatic asylum band, but music publishers, conductors, and concert organizers showed little enthusiasm for his work. Elgar felt pushed aside because of his Catholic, working-class origins. Broke and depressed, he worried that his music would never succeed.

The Elgar Enigma

In 1886, he took on a new student named Alice Roberts. Alice was an intim-
idating figure: eight years older than Elgar, a published poet, and the daughter of a major-general. The couple were engaged in 1888 to widespread disapproval. It all came down to class: Alice was a station above Elgar, a fact
that bothered the Elgars as much as the Robertses. Further, no matter how
much Alice believed in his talents, Elgar was still a thirty-one-year-old
unpublished composer who subsisted on teaching and a conducting gig at
an insane asylum: On paper, not much of a match. But Alice had her own
money, so whatever Alice wanted, Alice got. They married on May 8, 1889.
A daughter, Carice, was born the next year.

It was Elgar's invariable habit to improvise on the piano in the evening,
and so after one day's round of violin lessons, he was noodling away at the
keyboard when he happened upon a particularly pleasing melody. "Whom
does that remind you of?" he asked his wife, and Alice replied, "Billy Baker
[a good friend of the couple] going out of a room." And so were born Elgar's
Enigma Variations.

The piece consists of fourteen "variations," each named after a friend
of the composer. Elgar said he had "written what I think they would have
written—if they were asses enough to compose." Some variations represent
characteristics of the individuals: Enigma no. 10, "Dorabella," includes a
staccato woodwind section intended to imitate his friend's laugh. Others rec-
ollect events: no. 11, "G.R.S.," recalls a walk with friend George Robertson
Sinclair and his bulldog Dan along the River Wye; Dan fell in the river and
had to be fished out. The "enigma" of the *Variations* is that the theme—
identified on the score as the first six measures of the music—is never actually heard again and is apparently based on a well-known tune, although
Elgar never revealed which one.

How About a Little Pomp for These Circumstances?

After all the years of frustration, with the *Enigma Variations* Elgar had a genuine success. He followed up this victory with another, an oratorio called *The
Dream of Gerontius*, which survived a disastrous premiere to go on to general acclaim. (The only trouble with *Gerontius* was the words, which were
deemed "too Catholic" for the Church of England; the libretto had to be
revised before it could be performed at Anglican churches.)

Then in 1901, Elgar began his best-known composition, *Pomp and*

Circumstance March no. 1. Shortly after he finished the march, Queen Victoria died and the coronation of King Edward VII was announced. It occurred to Elgar that, if combined with appropriate lyrics, the tune would make a great commemorative piece. The result was the "Coronation Ode" with lyrics by the poet A. C. Benson. The finale of the ode was also released as a separate song titled "Land of Hope and Glory," an immediate hit that became an unofficial national anthem.

Suddenly Elgar—and Alice—had all the success they desired. An Elgar Festival was held at Covent Garden in 1904, with the new king and queen attending. The couple moved into a large house outside of Hereford, and Alice luxuriated in her regained social status.

Not Much Hope, but a Lot of Glory

The Elgars' security came to an end in 1914 with the outbreak of war. The family committed themselves to the war effort: Elgar signed up as a special constable at the Hampstead police station, Alice taught French to departing soldiers, and Carice volunteered with the Red Cross. "Land of Hope and Glory" became more popular than ever, and Elgar considered adding a new verse that would serve as a call to battle. As the war went on and the number of casualties grew, his opinion shifted and he came to hate how "Land of Hope and Glory" was used as jingoistic propaganda.

At the end of the war, Elgar faced what seemed to be a new world. The hardest blow came with Alice's death on April 7, 1920. The composer fell into a deep depression, regaining his peace of mind only in 1923, when he leased a cottage in his beloved West Midlands. Professionally, his success grew: Honors piled up, including a baronetcy; ultimately, he was introduced as "Sir Edward Elgar Bt OM GCVO," which really meant something in England. Elgar bristled when people forgot to recognize his status, but the honors didn't mean as much without Alice around to enjoy them.

Elgar suffered from debilitating pain for several years, finally diagnosed after exploratory surgery as inoperable cancer. When he became bedridden, a radio link was set up between his London apartment and the new Abbey Road studios so he could listen to recording sessions of some of his works. He once asked, with typical Elgarian humor, "Who could have written such beautiful music?" Elgar died on February 23, 1934.

Elgar's music remained out of favor through the middle of the twentieth century, striking observers as nostalgic at best. In the 1970s, however, his reputation began to rebound, particularly in England. Today his music is some of the most popular in his homeland, where he is considered a national treasure. His image even appeared on the back of the £20 note from 1999 to 2007.

ALICE, WE HARDLY KNEW YOU

Alice Elgar had been an aspiring author and poet before her marriage. Her poetry, frankly, has not aged well. *Isabel Trevithoe* of 1879 is an extended meditation on a heroine who aspires to good works. Sample lines:

> Then Isabel,
> Fresh fired to speech, would pour forth such a strain
> Of burning words regarding women's work,
> Their duties high, how they were bound to use
> Their mighty influence to clear the world
> Of wrong and endless sin . . .

THAT'S ONE BUSY RABBIT

In 1905, Carice Elgar brought home a white angora rabbit, immediately naming him Peter in honor of Beatrix Potter's literary creation. After a family trip to Italy, he was promptly renamed "Pietro d'Alba." Elgar fussed over the rabbit's health, buying a book on the care of rabbits and making sure he had a hot-water bottle for his hutch every night in the winter. Peter soon became Elgar's alter ego, offering dour criticisms of new works and penning doleful poetry on the failure of the carrot crop. Pietro d'Alba even received credit on Elgar's scores for his arrangement of folk songs.

Alas, the life of a rabbit is not long, and in 1910 Peter/Pietro went to the great carrot patch in the sky. Elgar wrote to one of his friends, saying, "Why should I tell you this! Because I want to write to somebody (— ? everybody) and say how really grieved I am." He concluded that it was "terrible to think how many human beings could be spared out of our little life's circle so much easier than my confidant & adviser Pietro d'Alba."

WHAT HAPPENS WHEN A COMPOSER HAS A LITTLE TOO MUCH TIME ON HIS HANDS

Elgar had a profound sense of the ridiculous. When a friend moved to a British village named Potters Bar, Elgar speculated over "Who was Potter & why did he possess a Bar?" He suggested Potter had been a soap maker, but dismissed the idea since "he must necessarily have made more than one bar." Potter might have been a composer, although of very limited scope to have only written one measure (or bar) of music. "Produce the bar," Elgar said, "and we can judge its musical value."

Elgar concluded, "I conceive Potter as a philosopher: high & serene musing on & clarifying problems far beyond human knowledge; I see him brought face to face with some impenetrable riddle before which the mighty intellect—even that of Potter—quailed, paled & failed. Surely this was Potter's Bar."

THERE GOES THE NEIGHBORHOOD

Once he became a successful composer, Elgar had the time and income to devote to intellectual pursuits. He set up a chemistry lab in his basement, later moving it to a shed outside when Alice complained of the nasty smells pervading the house. One of his favorite tricks was to make a concoction of phosphorus that would spontaneously combust, to his endless delight. But on one occasion he made too much. Wanting to get back to work and unwilling to dispose of the chemicals properly, he put the volatile paste into a pot and stuck it in the rain barrel beside the house.

Sometime later, a tremendous blast shook the house, the barrel was blown to pieces, and water poured out all over the yard. Elgar calmly lit his pipe and strolled outside amidst soggy, splintered boards, twists of metal hoops, and demolished flower beds. A neighbor peeped through the gate at the wreckage and asked, "Did you hear that noise? It sounded like an explosion!" "Yes," said Elgar, "What was it?"

The neighbor shook his head and walked away.

ELGAR'S SUCCESS AS A COMPOSER ALLOWED HIM TO BECOME AN AMATEUR SCIENTIST WHO PUTTERED ABOUT WITH EXPLOSIVE CHEMICALS.

GIACOMO PUCCINI

DECEMBER 22, 1858–NOVEMBER 29, 1924

ASTROLOGICAL SIGN:
CAPRICORN

NATIONALITY:
ITALIAN

MUSICAL STYLE:
LATE ROMANTIC OR REALIST

STANDOUT WORK:
MADAMA BUTTERFLY

WHERE YOU'VE HEARD IT:
THROUGHOUT THE 1987 EROTIC THRILLER *FATAL ATTRACTION*

"FOR ME, THE COUNTRY IS A NECESSITY, SOME-THING URGENT, AS WHEN YOU ARE DESPERATE TO GO TO THE BATHROOM, AND THERE ARE PEOPLE THERE AND YOU CANNOT GO."

QUOTABL

Giacomo Puccini lived a life of drama and extravagance, full of tragedy, comedy, and excess. Forbidden love? Check. Near-death experience? Check. Triumph over adversity? Check.

Not coincidentally, his operas overflow with overlarge personalities, including jealous opera singers, unfeeling military officers, evil princesses, and perfidious policemen. The wicked Princess Turandot and the saintly, suicidal slave Madame Butterfly are Puccini's fictional creations—but they had real counterparts in the life of their creator.

It just goes to prove the old adage: Write what you know.

The Bad Boy of Lucca

The Puccinis of Lucca were a local musical dynasty. When Michele and Albina Puccini's first son was born in 1858, they named him Giacomo Antonio Domenico Michele Secondo Maria in honor of his musical forebears. After the death of Michele Puccini, all of the family's hopes focused on five-year-old Giacomo, who didn't particularly rise to the challenge. He entered the Istituto Musicale in Lucca but was deplored by his teachers as lazy and disrespectful. He even stole pipes from the church organ and sold them for scrap metal to buy cigarettes. As church organist, he could hide his crime by reworking the hymns to avoid the missing pipes.

Puccini nevertheless seemed prepared to follow his father's footsteps as a local musician. Then in 1876 he walked eighteen miles to Pisa to see *Aida*. "I felt a musical window had opened for me," he wrote. His passion forever more would be opera. After a lot of scrimping and saving, he headed to the Milan Conservatory in 1880. Like Verdi, he was over the school's age limit, but unlike Verdi, he was deemed skilled enough to enter. Despite all concessions and sacrifices made on his behalf, Puccini remained a lousy student, redeemed only by his prodigious talent.

In 1882, Puccini learned about a competition for a one-act opera and decided to enter. He didn't win so much as an honorable mention, but patrons thought the work had merit and paid for its production in 1884. In the audience of that performance was Giulio Ricordi, the grand old man of Italian music publishing. He liked the opera so much he commissioned a new work.

My Heart's on Fire, Elvira

Puccini should have jumped on this opportunity, but he was called home by the news that his mother was dying. The funeral took place, Puccini consoled his sisters, the estate was settled, and still he lingered in Lucca. Friends in Milan were baffled by his reluctance to return, but they had no idea that he had fallen in love with a local married woman: Elvira Bonturi Gemignani, the stylish and sophisticated wife of a former schoolmate.

Naturally, gossiping tongues wagged. Puccini's sisters begged him not to bring shame on the family. Instead, he got Elvira pregnant. The scandal broke in the autumn of 1886 when the two ran off together. Conservative Lucca was aghast. Puccini's respectable sisters—particularly Iginia, a nun—could hardly bear up against the disgrace. Elvira's outraged husband issued so many threats the lovebirds had to keep their location secret.

After years of turmoil, the birth of an illegitimate son, and endless wrangles with his and Elvira's families, Puccini's new work, *Edgar*, appeared in 1889. It was a disappointment and has never gained a following. But Ricordi did not give up on Puccini. He commissioned another opera, and Puccini went to work on *Manon Lescaut*. In search of quiet, Puccini turned to Torre del Lago, an isolated seaside village. He loved the quiet, the desolation, and the great hunting. Elvira *hated* it. Stylish, sophisticated Elvira in a primitive fishing village? Horrors.

Manon Lescaut premiered in 1893. Finally, Puccini had an outright success. He followed it with *La bohème* in 1896 and *Tosca* in 1900. Royalties rolled in, and Puccini could live it up. He dressed in impeccable suits, hats, and shoes; he built multiple houses, each more comfortable than the last. He developed a passion for cars and adored auto shows.

A World-Class Soap Opera

One might have thought wealth and success would have satisfied Elvira—but nothing satisfied Elvira. The years of scandal and hardship had transformed her into a middle-aged shrew consumed by jealousy. She had cause. In 1900 Puccini fell for a young woman named Corinna. (Accounts don't reveal her last name, or her age.)

Elvira tried everything from temper tantrums to hunger strikes, but nothing could stop Puccini from seeing Corinna. One day, when Puccini told her he was going hunting, she headed for a nearby village where she suspected the two had a love nest. In fact, Puccini had just left, and Corinna was in a carriage on her way out of town. Elvira ran shrieking to the carriage and started poking Corinna with her umbrella. The coachman whipped the horses to get away from the crazy lady, and Elvira was unceremoniously dumped into a ditch. This didn't improve her mood. She made it home before Puccini, and the minute he walked in the door from his "hunting" trip she descended upon him with fists and fingernails. The next day he said the bloody scratches all over his face were from falling into a bramble bush; no one believed him.

A few years later, Puccini, Elvira, their son, Tonio, and their chauffeur drove home on a foggy night. The car missed a curve, ran down a gully, and flipped over. Elvira and Tonio were bruised and shaken but otherwise unhurt; the driver's leg was broken. Puccini couldn't even be found. Finally he was discovered underneath the overturned car, his right leg crushed. The composer spent months in bed and would use a walking stick for the rest of his life.

To complicate matters, Elvira's husband, Gemignani, died the day after the crash. Puccini's sisters begged him to marry Elvira, but he wavered. Corinna threatened to sue for false promises. Puccini eventually caved, bought off Corinna, and married his lover of nearly eighteen years. "Iginia will be glad," Puccini wrote.

A World-Class Tragedy

Somehow Puccini continued work on his next opera, *Madama Butterfly*. The day after his wedding, Puccini left Torre del Lago for rehearsals in Milan (so much for the honeymoon). Puccini's hopes were high, but the opening night turned into a howling fiasco. Ricordi believed anti-Puccini factions had staged the protests, but Puccini recognized that the opera had serious flaws. He worked on revisions, and a new version of *Butterfly* premiered four months later. It's been a hit ever since.

A marriage certificate had not improved Elvira's state of mind. She read all the mail, listened behind doors, and followed Puccini when he left the house. On tour she went through his clothes to find incriminating evidence, once making a scene in New York when she found a note from a dinner-party acquaintance tucked behind his hat band. Then she decided Puccini was sleeping with a servant girl named Doria. Puccini and Doria denied it, but Elvira didn't believe them. She followed Doria around Torre del Lago, calling her a slut and showed up at Doria's house to shout abuse at her. Matters of honor were a serious matter in rural Italy, and Doria's brothers threatened Puccini for defiling an innocent girl. The despairing Doria went to a pharmacy, bought a jar of corrosive disinfectant, and swallowed it; she died after five days of horrendous pain.

A horrified Puccini considered suicide, yet Elvira, unrepentant, spread the rumor that Doria had died after a botched abortion. When an autopsy revealed that Doria had died a virgin, her family brought charges against Elvira. After a widely publicized trial, Elvira was sentenced to five months in prison and a hefty fine. Puccini's lawyers convinced Doria's family to withdraw the suit with a large settlement, and the court nullified the conviction.

AS A TEENAGER, PUCCINI STOLE PIPES FROM HIS CHURCH'S ORGAN AND SOLD THEM AS SCRAP METAL TO BUY CIGARETTES.

The couple separated for a while, but then Puccini returned to Elvira. Why they stuck together after so much unhappiness is a mystery. Perhaps the habit was too hard to break.

Puccini did not let World War I affect him much, unlike his friend, the conductor Arturo Toscanini, who once led a military band so close to the fighting that the performers' instruments were damaged by falling shrapnel. (Toscanini, who had premiered several of Puccini's operas, was so angry at Puccini's indifference to the bloodshed that they didn't speak for years.)

Puccini decided his next opera would be based on a play called *Turandot*. Before he could finish the score, however, he was rushed to Brussels for emergency medical treatment. For years he had endured a painful sore throat; after repeatedly dismissing it as laryngitis or a cold, doctors diagnosed throat cancer. His only hope was surgery and experimental radiation treatment. These failed to have any effect, and Puccini died on November 29, 1924.

The score of *Turnadot* sat unfinished. In April 1926, Toscanini premiered the opera at La Scala in Milan. At the point in the third act where Puccini's score ended, the conductor stopped the orchestra, put down his baton, and turned to the audience. "Here the opera ends," he said, "because at this point the Maestro died." Only the next night was a com-

plete opera presented, with a finale written by Franco Alfano based on Puccini's sketches. *Turnadot* is not the most popular of Puccini's operas: *Madama Butterfly*, *La Bohème*, and *Tosca* rank as nos. 1, 2, and 8 on the list of most-performed operas in North America, with *Turandot* coming in at no. 12. But with the haunting aria *Nessum Dorma*, Puccini created an immortal piece of music, known and loved around the world long after his death.

ON THE REBOUND

The celebrated end of the opera *Tosca* has its title character jump to her death from a high tower. Usually, sopranos leap through a window at the back of the stage onto mattresses below. However, according to opera legend, at one performance at the Lyric Opera of Chicago, English soprano Eva Turner got the shock of her life when instead of landing on a mattress she hit a trampoline. Tosca bounced into view two or three more times, much to the audience's amusement. It's not clear if the mattress-to-trampoline switch had been a thoughtful effort to improve safety or a practical joke intended to punish a too-demanding performer.

WHO, ME?

Shortly before World War I, Puccini attended the Wagner Festival in Bayreuth with his mistress-of-the-moment, Josephine von Stängel. Word leaked around the event that the famous Puccini was in attendance, but the composer, attempting to keep his name out of the papers and Elvira off his back, had registered under a false name. When someone actually pointed him out to Cosima Wagner, she went up to him and asked to be introduced. In a moment of desperation, he decided to keep up the masquerade. "No," he said, "I'm not Giacomo Puccini," and walked off.

WHEN YOU CARE ENOUGH TO SEND THE VERY BEST

During the years of Puccini and Toscanini's feud, they had very little contact—except for one Christmastime incident. That year Puccini forgot to remove the conductor's name from the list of friends to whom he sent the traditional Italian holiday gift, a pannetone cake. When Puccini realized his error, he sent Toscanini a telegram reading "PANNETONE SENT BY MISTAKE PUCCINI." Toscanini replied, "PANNETONE EATEN BY MISTAKE TOSCANINI."

Opera Libretti

A libretto (plural: *libretti)* is the written text of an opera; a librettist is the person who writes the text. A good libretto contains not only singable lines but also a strong dramatic structure. Although many operas are based on sources such as plays or novels, the librettist often has great difficulty adapting the original source work. Writing a three-act opera containing arias, duets, and choruses that keeps audience engaged is no small feat.

Despite all their hard work, librettists rarely get the credit they deserve. People go to see Verdi's *Aida* and Mozarts *Così fan tutte*, not Antonio Ghislanzoni's *Aida* or Lorenzo Da Ponte's *Così*. Furthermore, many composers give their librettists no end of grief. Puccini, for example, was the bane of his writers, hounding them mercilessly for drafts and demanding endless rewrites.

Wagner ignored the problem altogether by writing his own libretti. This eliminated several problems, including the need to pay anyone else, but also had its drawbacks. Critics from Wagner's day forward have lambasted his verse as pretentious and dull, and, with a running time of five hours, *Götterdämmerung* could certainly have used an editor.

So the next time you're at an opera, take a moment to pay your respects to the unsung librettist. Hard work went into those words—toil that has meant the difference between an opera's success or failure.

GUSTAV MAHLER

JULY 7, 1860–MAY 18, 1911

ASTROLOGICAL SIGN:
CANCER

NATIONALITY:
AUSTRIAN

MUSICAL STYLE:
ROMANTIC

STANDOUT WORKS:
KINDERTOTENLIEDER

WHERE YOU'VE HEARD IT:
IN THE 2006 DYSTOPIAN POLITICAL THRILLER *CHILDREN OF MEN*

"THE IMPORTANT THING IS NEVER TO LET ONE-SELF BE GUIDED BY THE OPINION OF ONE'S CONTEMPORARIES; TO CONTINUE STEADFASTLY ON ONE'S WAY WITHOUT LETTING ONESELF BE EITHER DEFEATED BY FAILURE OR DIVERTED BY APPLAUSE."

QUOTABLE

Gustav Mahler considered music the most important thing in the world. Great music could melt hearts, transform lives, and redeem souls. Great symphonies could encompass every possible emotion and experience. Great performances could improve the lives of audiences.

The only problem for Mahler was the price of all this greatness. He worked harder than almost any other composer, no matter how much it annoyed his orchestras, exhausted his audiences, damaged his relationships, and hurt his own health. The question for Mahler was always whether he'd wear himself out before he wore out the tolerance of everyone around him.

Somebody Yell "Fire!"

The Mahler family lived in Iglau, Austria, a German-speaking enclave in Bohemia, where father Bernard ran a brewery and bakery. Young Gustav, born in 1860, found all types of music fascinating. At three, he was so entranced by a military band that he escaped his house and followed the soldiers for some distance until someone noticed the tiny boy and escorted him home. He started piano lessons, and his Jewish parents even convinced the local priest to let him to sing with the Catholic children's choir.

Mahler started composing as a teenager, but after graduating from the Vienna Conservatory and Vienna University, he realized composition wouldn't pay the bills. He decided to conduct. His first gig? Leading a small band at a second-rate spa named Bad Hall, where his duties included setting up music stands and stacking chairs. Bad Hall was followed by work in Laibach, then Olmütz, Kassel, Prague, and Leipzig. In 1889, Mahler took the post of chief conductor in Budapest, where on the opening night of *Lohengrin* the prompter's box caught fire. Mahler continued conducting as flames lit up the stage and smoke filled the rafters. When the fire department arrived, he halted the orchestra long enough for them to extinguish the blaze, then started up again where he had let off.

Orchestra members were likely to be amused the first time they met Mahler. Thin and wiry, he wore horned-rimmed glasses that slipped off his nose the moment he started waving his arms. His movements were energetic to the point of frantic; a critic said he looked like a cat having convulsions. Any inclination to laugh ended, however, as soon as work began. He dressed down performers for the most minor mistakes; when he fixed musicians with his withering stare, they became so paralyzed they couldn't lift their instruments. Orchestras hated him, but they played their best for him.

The triumph of Mahler's conducting career came in 1897, when the thirty-seven-year-old was appointed director of the Vienna Opera. This Imperial appointment, however, came with strings attached: No Jews allowed. Mahler had never been particularly observant, and so in advance of the appointment he blithely converted to Catholicism, treating his new faith with as much indifference as his old.

Single-Minded Symphony-Writing

Brilliant as an opera conductor, Mahler never wrote an opera. Nor did he write sonatas, concerti, oratorios, overtures, tone poems, or any of the other forms of classical music. Mahler focused all of his energies on song cycles and, primarily, symphonies.

And what symphonies! Mahler's works are huge in every way. First, they're long: the shortest lasts an hour and the longest nearly two. (Beethoven's never went longer than seventy minutes.) Second, they require an enormous number of musicians: Mahler's 8th is nicknamed "The Symphony of the Thousand" because it takes that many people to pull it off. Finally, they are musically huge, with sweeping themes and overwhelming emotions. Critics attacked the works as overwrought, torturous, and ponderous, and audiences left the concert hall exhausted and baffled. Mahler believed "symphonies should contain everything," and he poured every bit of his energy into these vast works.

All About Alma

Not long after Mahler arrived in Vienna, he met a young woman named Alma Schindler at a party. Dazzling, charming, and tempestuous, the twenty-two-year-old Alma was twenty years younger than the conductor and already had a reputation for attracting brilliant men. Previous flirts included composer Alexander von Zemlinsky, Arnold Schoenberg's brother-in-law, and Gustav Klimt, the Austrian painter. The couple married on March 9, 1902.

It wasn't an easy relationship—neither the grouchy, workaholic Mahler nor the moody, emotional Alma was easy to live with. Further, Mahler demanded that his career come first, to the point that Alma had to give up her musical aspirations. Alma had written a handful of songs, but Mahler insisted there could be only one composer in the family.

For a while, it worked. The couple had two daughters, Maria in 1902 (Alma was pregnant when they got married) and Anna in 1904. But before long Alma got fed up; serving as a handmaiden to genius isn't nearly as romantic as it sounds. Then came a horrible blow: Maria caught scarlet fever and diphtheria and died. She was four years old. Soon after, doctors diagnosed Mahler with heart disease.

He resigned from the Vienna Opera the next year. All his losses contributed to his decision, but the tipping point was an offer from the Metropolitan Opera to conduct in New York City. Mahler's 1909 season with the Met was followed by a 1910 season with both the Met and the New York Philharmonic.

SO GREAT WAS MAHLER'S CONCENTRATION WHILE CONDUCTING THAT NOTHING—NOT EVEN A FIRE THAT THREATENED TO BURN DOWN THE CONCERT HALL—COULD DISTRACT HIM.

Baby, Come Back

Back in Austria for the summer of 1910, Mahler holed up in a mountain retreat to compose while Alma headed for a luxurious spa. She soon met a fellow guest, the aspiring architect Walter Gropius. Gropius was twenty-seven years old and a long way from the work that would make him famous, but Alma had a nose for talent. They started a passionate affair.

Alma returned to her husband, but Gropius "accidentally" sent a letter intended for Alma to Mahler, and the cat was out of the bag. Rather than apologize, Alma lashed out at her husband, accusing him of repressing her talents and ignoring her needs. (Since Alma routinely locked her door at night, Mahler might well have also complained about his needs. On the other hand, Alma complained Mahler was lousy in bed and often impotent.) Mahler plunged into despair. He wrote her pleading notes, wept all night outside her door, and filled their house with roses. He even unearthed her songs and insisted she have them published. Alma gave in, or at least pretended to. She sailed for New York with her husband in October, although he had no idea that she and Gropius had had a secret meeting the day before their departure.

That February, a sore throat that had been bothering Mahler off and on flared up, and his temperature soared to 104 degrees. Doctors discovered he

was suffering from bacterial endocarditis, an infection of the heart valves. Before the advent of antibiotics, no treatment was available. Nevertheless, he and Alma returned to Europe to try an experimental serum in Paris. The treatment failed, and doctors recommended Alma hurry if she wanted to get her husband back to Austria. Mahler died on May 18, 1911, in Vienna.

Critical appreciation for Mahler's music has only grown in the years since his death. It is not music that is easy to love—no one leaves a Mahler concert humming the tunes—but his legacy extended far into the twentieth century, influencing a new generation of composers who, like him, grapple with the vast sweep of universal themes.

ALL ABOUT ALMA

After Mahler's death, Alma didn't immediately resume contact with Gropius. Instead she had a turbulent affair with the artist Oskar Kokoschka, who painted a famous work of her called "Bride of the Wind." After World War I began and Kokoschka enlisted, she returned to Gropius, and they married in 1915. Gropius also served in the army, and during his lengthy absences she began an affair with novelist Franz Werfel.

Gropius and Alma eventually divorced, and some time later she married Werfel. In 1938, the couple fled Germany to escape Nazi persecution. Two quiet years in France ended with the Nazi invasion, and they had to flee again, this time crossing the Pyrenees on foot and making for Portugal, where they arranged voyage to New York. Alma died of a heart attack in 1964. She was a fascinating figure with an amazing talent for attracting brilliant men. One can only wonder what career she may have had in her own right, if she had been born in a different time.

SILENCE!

Attending the opera had always been a delightful way to spend an evening in Vienna—until Gustav Mahler came to town. He insisted on absolute silence—the merest cough or rustled program could result in a ferocious glare. He ordered the auditorium lights dimmed and relentlessly barred entry to latecomers. Programs featured the most obscure and demanding works.

Audiences accepted Mahler's dictums, but that didn't mean they had to like them. Emperor Franz Joseph was among those baffled by the new regime. "Is music such serious business?" he once asked. "I always thought it was meant to make people happy."

MUST WE INVITE GUSTAV?

The tales of Mahler's eccentricities spread far and wide. He was notoriously absentminded, known to stir his tea with a lit cigarette or sit for hours in an empty train car, unaware that the engine had been uncoupled and hauled away. His social skills appalled friends. Invite Mahler to a dinner party and you had to be prepared not only for his special diet (whole-wheat bread and apples) but also his mercurial behavior. Either he ate in a glowering silence, ignoring all those around him, or he ranted endlessly on some topic. Not surprisingly, he didn't get invited out very often.

WHEN GUSTAV MET SIGMUND

After Alma revealed her affair with Gropius, the desperate composer cast about for help, eventually contacting the father of psychoanalysis himself, Dr. Sigmund Freud.

Mahler met with Freud on August 26, 1910. Over the course of a four-hour stroll around Vienna, the esteemed doctor pondered at length the fact that Mahler's mother, Marie, shared the name with Alma, who had been baptized Maria Alma. When Mahler caught the train back to Austria, Freud reported with some satisfaction, "I achieved much with him." Mahler seems to have been less impressed. He wired Alma, "Interview interesting. Mountains made out of molehills."

HOW ABOUT CALLING IT "SYMPHONY NO. TEN MINUS ONE"?

Alma wrote extensively of her life with Mahler, and her accounts were initially so trusted that they formed the foundation of Mahler scholarship. Later biographers, however, uncovered numerous discrepancies between Alma's accounts and the truth, and current Mahler research is plagued by what's come to be known as the "Alma problem."

Take, for example, Alma's contention that Mahler suffered from a paralyzing "fear of the ninth," a superstition that symphony composers die after they write their ninth symphony (see Beethoven). Mahler supposedly feared writing his own ninth symphony so much that he did not number his ninth symphonic work, but gave it the name *Das Lied von der Erde.* Mahler then went ahead with a symphony that he gave the number 9, and then, sure enough, he died.

Recent biographers question this account, noting that if Mahler had such a terror of a ninth symphony he could have simply called the composition after *Das Lied von der Erde* the tenth symphony. Nevertheless, many Mahler fans believe the legend. Schoenberg, for example, said of Mahler and his Ninth: "It seems that the ninth is a limit. . . . It seems as if something might be imparted to us in the Tenth which we ought not yet to know, for which we are not ready. Those who have written a Ninth stood too close to the hereafter."

REDEMPTION LIMITED TO ONE PER CUSTOMER

The glowering, moody Gustav Mahler and the bon vivant Richard Strauss were two of the most unlikely friends in music history, yet they promoted each other's works and appreciated each other's talents. That doesn't mean the course of friendship always ran smooth. Mahler frequently imagined slights and insults from Strauss, and Strauss found Mahler's brooding exasperating. And a fundamental difference marked their attitudes toward music. After the premiere of Strauss's opera *Feuersnot*, Strauss spent their celebratory dinner calculating his royalties. Mahler was horrified, later writing Alma that it was "better, by far, to eat the bread of poverty and follow one's star than sell one's soul like that."

After Mahler's death, Strauss told a friend he had never really understood Mahler's music, particularly Mahler's insistence that he found redemption in composition. "I don't know what I am supposed to be redeemed from," Strauss complained.

CLAUDE DEBUSSY

AUGUST 22, 1862–MARCH 25, 1918

ASTROLOGICAL SIGN:
LEO

NATIONALITY:
FRENCH

MUSICAL STYLE:
IMPRESSIONIST

STANDOUT WORKS:
CLARE DE LUNE

WHERE YOU'VE HEARD IT:
AT THE END OF THE 2001 VERSION OF *OCEAN'S ELEVEN*, WHEN THE GANG OF CROOKS WATCHES THE DANCING FOUNTAINS OF THE BELLAGIO

"AN ARTIST IS IN THE MAIN A DETESTABLE INTERIOR KIND OF MAN, AND PERHAPS ALSO A DEPLORABLE HUSBAND."

QUOTABLE

Sometimes the different arts of an era—music, literature, architecture, painting—align in powerful ways. The cheerful charm of Renaissance English music breathes the same spirit as Shakespeare's comedies. The purity and strength of neoclassical architecture finds musical expression in Mozart's symphonies. The fractured surfaces of Picasso's cubist period visually reflect the shrieking sounds of Stravinsky's modern period.

There's a reason why Claude Monet's seascapes and Claude Debussy's *La Mer* have the same shimmering, luminous quality: They were impressionist works created with the same intentions.

That's not to say that Debussy *liked* the term. He probably would have preferred being called a symbolist, or a modernist, or some other –ist, but composers don't always get to pick these things. But maybe it's better that way: Debussy's own choices—on matters such as women and money—didn't turn out so well.

Give the People What They Want Already

The Debussys lived on the fringe of respectable middle-class French society, trying and failing to succeed with numerous jobs and businesses, including a china shop. Their make-and-scrape finances meant the family moved four times before young Achille-Claude (nicknamed Chilo) was five years old. An aunt arranged for seven-year-old Chilo to have piano lessons after he tried to pick out chords on her piano.

Politics disrupted family life in 1871 when the socialist Commune seized control of Paris. Father Manuel Debussy joined the pro-Commune National Guard and was promoted to captain. In an ill-organized attack on a government-held fort, most of his soldiers ran away, and he surrendered. When the Commune collapsed two weeks later, Manuel Debussy was in a tight spot: Many of his comrades faced a firing squad. Apparently the government decided the ineffectual revolutionary deserved only four years in prison (he ended up serving a year).

The Debussys' luck finally turned when a friend of a friend brought the talented child Claude to Madame Mauté de Fleurville, an aristocratic personage who claimed to be the widow of the Marquis de Sivry and a former pupil of Chopin. In fact the "Marquis" had been a hat-maker, and Madame Mauté had never even met Chopin. Whatever her deficiencies in truth-telling,

Madame Mauté was an excellent teacher who groomed Debussy for the Paris Conservatoire.

Debussy's parents hoped he could become a piano virtuoso, but in school competitions he never won more than fourth place. In composition class he learned the rules of harmony and could crank out traditional pieces, but you could tell his heart wasn't in it. The compositions he cared about horrified his instructors. His professor of harmony once muttered over an exercise, "Of course, it's all utterly unorthodox, but still, very *ingenious*." Summer jobs included a stint working for Tchaikovsky's patron Nadezhda von Meck. Von Meck tried to interest Tchaikovsky in Debussy's compositions, but the older composer found their radical harmonics baffling.

Debussy entered the Prix de Rome competition twice, but lost because his innovations irritated the faculty. On his third try in 1884, he won with a deliberately conservative composition. Friends were disappointed that Debussy hadn't shocked the world, but Debussy's parents were delighted by their son's success.

Impressionist Impression Impresses

After two years in Rome, Debussy returned to France and took up with an intelligent, unconventional blonde named Gaby Dupont. The two lived in a succession of miserable attic apartments in Montmartre and became friends with the crowd of poets, painters, and musicians living the bohemian life straight out of a Toulouse-Lautrec painting. Debussy became particularly close to the writers of the Symbolist movement, a literary style that emphasized morbid romanticism and erotic imagery.

Although most of his life was spent among the down-and-out, Debussy was drawn to the comforts of the upper classes, and in the early 1890s he met Mademoiselle Thérèse Roger, a young woman of good family. Debussy was smitten, he proposed, and the two became engaged in the spring of 1894. The only two hindrances were Debussy's debts and his live-in girlfriend, Gaby. These barriers proved to be too much for the middle-class Rogers, who were shocked to learn about the composer's insolvency and immorality. Why Gaby continued to live with Debussy after his brief commitment to another woman—why, in fact, she stayed through his multiple affairs—is anyone's guess, although on at least one occasion Gaby found a letter from another woman in Debussy's pocket and tried to shoot either her-

self or her lover. The whole affair got written up in the papers.

Debussy finally got to hear one of his orchestral works formally performed in December, 1894. The innovative *Prélude à l'après-midi d'un faune* ("Prelude to the Afternoon of a Faun"), based on a poem by Mallarmé, feels free-form and improvisational, hiding its structural complexity under a shimmering surface of unconventional harmonies. The premiere audience was delighted by the work, but critics seemed bewildered. Only after several years would the real impact of the piece be appreciated by a new generation of composers.

Gaby eventually went on her way, and Debussy started a new affair with a model named Lilly Texier. Friends found Texier pretty but dull, no match for Debussy's intellectualism, but they married in late 1899. Lilly was by Debussy's side at the premiere of his opera *Pelléas et Mélisande* in April 1902. Debussy had based the opera on a play by symbolist Maurice Maeterlinck and lobbied for years to have it accepted by the Opéra Comique.

ONE OF DEBUSSY'S LOVERS THREATENED TO SHOOT HIM WHEN SHE FOUND A LETTER FROM ANOTHER WOMAN IN HIS POCKET.

From the very first night, audiences declared the performance a groundbreaking artistic event. Debussy had rejected two hundred years of operatic tradition: *Pelléas* has no arias, choruses, or recitatives. It doesn't even have melodies. The music flows and pulses, with the singing floating along with the orchestra rather than dominating it. The harmonies were definitely not those taught at the Conservatoire.

Seeking a way to describe Debussy's music, critics compared it to impressionism, the ground-breaking art movement of the previous generation. The haunting lines and faintly dissonant chords of *Pelléas* can be heard as the musical equivalent of Monet's out-of-focus water lilies. The similarity was to some degree deliberate: In the 1890s, Debussy's friend Eric Satie had suggested, "Why not make use of the representational methods of Claude Monet, Cézanne, Toulouse-Lautrec, and so on?"

Lifestyles of the Broke and Famous

After *Pelléas,* Debussy found himself caught up in sudden, startling fame. A popular artist painted his portrait, he moved out of Montmartre, and he was named to the Légion d'Honneur. Then he fell in love again. Emma Bardac had all the brains and sophistication Lilly lacked, but, inconveniently, she was married.

Debussy tried to break things off with Lilly by telling her he needed to spend more time "alone," a claim that doesn't even have the excuse of originality. Lilly did not take this well—she attempted suicide by shooting herself in the chest, but survived. The story got into all the papers, and Debussy and the now-pregnant Emma had to flee to England to escape the spotlight. Their daughter, Claude-Emma, known among the family as Chou-Chou, was born in October, 1905, by which time both of her parents were divorced, although they didn't bother to marry each other until 1908.

Debussy's life was now far removed from the risqué Bohemianism of his youth. He lived in an enormous house in a swanky neighborhood, employed an army of servants, and hired a car. He thought it his due, but the debts kept adding up.

When World War I broke out, Debussy plunged into deep depression, but in time an unusual sort of patriotic fervor gripped him. He deplored the German influence on culture as well as the pervasive horror of war, so he wrote piano *Études* intended to represent all that was good about French music and the peaceful life.

Debussy's health had become increasingly precarious. He was diagnosed with colorectal cancer and a portion of his colon was removed in 1916 in one of the first colostomy operations. But the cancer returned, and in the last years of the war he steadily declined. In 1918, the last German offensive brought long-range guns within the reach of his house, but Debussy was too ill to be moved to the basement for safety. He died on March 25, 1918.

The war ended that November, and Debussy seemed forgotten. His elegant modernism was pushed aside in favor of aggressive atonalism; like Monet's water lilies, Debussy's music seemed an echo of an earlier age. Only in the latter half of the twentieth century was Debussy rediscovered. Today, with the perspective of a century, we can recognize the radical innovations he pursued and appreciate their haunting loveliness. Debussy is proof that you can reject the tradition of Bach, Beethoven, and Brahms and still write beautiful music.

FUELING THE FIRES OF CREATIVITY

Fuel shortages plagued France during World War I, and you had to be either very rich or very clever to get enough coal to heat your home. The perpetually broke Debussy came up with a strategy: He promised to write his coal merchant an original composition in exchange for valuable fuel. The merchant delivered the goods and went home with Debussy's last composition, *Le soirs illuminés par l'ardeur du Le Balcon* ("Evenings Lighted by Burning Coals"—a line from Baudelaire's poem *Le Balcon).*

NIJINSKY'S HIGH-JINKS

Around 1911, Debussy met the ballet impresario Serge Diaghilev, who convinced him to let his Ballets Russes create a dance based on *Prélude à l'après-midi d'un faune.* The famous Vaslav Nijinsky choreographed the work and played the lead role, and it was performed in May, 1912— to appalled audiences.

The story of the ballet is of a sleeping faun (half man, half goat) who is awakened by several passing nymphs; he becomes inflamed by desire, but all the nymphs run away. Today you can find *Hannah Montana* episodes that are less explicit, but the 1912 audience found the odd hip-jutting walk of the faun and his repeated gesturing toward his pelvic region downright obscene. The premiere was booed, but when word got out of the shocking content, the ballet became a runaway hit with sold-out performances.

GET OUT! OUT!

Pelléas et Mélisande was considered so radical by the music establishment that a professor at the Paris Conservatoire announced that anyone who dared to bring the "filthy" score into his class or imitate Debussy's "errors of harmony" would be expelled. He meant it: Not long after, a student was found with a copy of the score and summarily dismissed.

RICHARD STRAUSS

JUNE 11, 1864–SEPTEMBER 8, 1949

ASTROLOGICAL SIGN:
GEMINI

NATIONALITY:
GERMAN

MUSICAL STYLE:
LATE ROMANTIC/EARLY MODERN

STANDOUT WORKS:
ALSO SPRACH ZARATHUSTRA

WHERE YOU'VE HEARD IT:
IN THE DRAMATIC OPENING SEQUENCE OF THE 1968 FILM *2001: A SPACE ODYSSEY*

"THERE HAS NEVER BEEN A GREAT ARTIST YET, WHO THOUSANDS OF PEOPLE DIDN'T THINK HE WAS MAD."

QUOTABL

T he first thing everyone said about Richard Strauss was that his wife was crazy. Sure, he wrote exciting, even shocking music; sure, his tone poems and operas amazed crowds from Munich to Manhattan; sure, he thrilled audiences as a conductor. But what really interested the gossips was his wife, Pauline.

Pauline blew through turn-of-the-century Germany like a tornado. She criticized her husband's music to his face, horrified hostesses by refusing to sit on chairs she declared dirty, and offended just about every important figure in European music. But her husband loved her, and some of his most entrancing works honor this amazing, maddening woman.

The Composer as Doormat

Franz Strauss was an accomplished musician who served as the principal horn player at the Court Opera in Munich, where, to his endless annoyance, he played in many Wagner premieres. Strauss considered modern music an abomination and raised his son Richard, born in 1864, to deplore anything remotely Wagnerian. Franz drilled his heir in classical harmonies and forms and arranged for his friends to give piano, violin, and composition lessons to the boy. By the time Richard was eighteen, his D Minor Symphony had been performed by the Court Orchestra. Over time, exposure to a wide range of music chipped away at Franz's conservatism, and by the mid-1880s Strauss appalled his father by praising the emotional expressiveness of Wagner and Liszt and deploring the traditionalism of Brahms.

In 1893, Strauss conducted a new opera, *Hänsel und Gretel* by Engelbert Humperdinck. The part of Hänsel was sung by a tempestuous soprano named Pauline de Ahna. So impressed was Strauss by her performance that he requested she play a major role in his first opera, *Guntram,* although her temper tantrums at rehearsals became legendary. Apparently he found this entrancing, and they married in September 1894. (The marriage proved far more lasting than *Guntram*, which came off as a pale imitation of Wagner.)

The notorious Pauline reminded his friends of a raging tornado. She shocked people with her screaming rages and outrageous statements; she often announced that, as the daughter of a general, she had married beneath her. She complained that Strauss's music was boring compared to her favorite obscure French composers. In the early years of their marriage, she continued her singing career with her famous husband as her accompanist.

When he got carried away with virtuosic endings, she kept on hand a large chiffon handkerchief to flourish about and finally throw on the floor, in order to keep the attention where it belonged—on her. Her obsession with cleanliness reached OCD levels. Strauss couldn't enter his own house without making use of three separate doormats, and guests had to wipe off their shoes with damp cloths. Despite all this, Strauss absolutely adored his wife; he said she pepped him and kept him on his toes.

The couple had a son, named Franz after his grandfather, in April, 1897. Strauss celebrated their home life in a unique way with his tone poem *Symphonia Domestica*. The work depicts a day in the life of the Strausses, complete with play-time with the baby, a love scene between husband and wife, and a "lively row" that ends with everyone making up. One gets the idea that "lively rows" were a day-to-day experience chez Strauss.

Unfaithfully Yours

After several years' hiatus, Strauss turned his attention again to opera in 1905. His choice of a libretto was the scandalous Oscar Wilde play *Salome*. The work was technically daring, but what shocked audiences most was the seductive "Dance of the Seven Veils" and the provocative ending in which the half-mad Salome kisses the lips of the severed head of John the Baptist. Reaction was mixed. Some proclaimed the piece revolutionary, but Cosima Wagner declared it "madness." The opera was bowdlerized in London and banned outright in New York, Chicago, and Vienna. Nevertheless, Strauss's next opera, *Elektra*, premiered in January, 1909, followed by *Der Rosenkavalier* in 1910 and *Ariadne auf Naxos* in 1912.

Whereas many German composers responded with patriotic fervor to World War I, Strauss tried to pretend politics didn't exist. His new operas included *Intermezzo* of 1924, for which he wrote the libretto as well. The work was based on a real incident from 1902. That year, Strauss was in England for a conducting gig, and Pauline, back in Germany, had no qualms about opening his personal mail. She found a note signed "Mieze Mücke" recollecting a recent meeting at a bar and requesting free opera tickets. Pauline deduced a full-blown affair from these few lines, contacted an attorney to begin divorce proceedings, and withdrew half the money from their bank account. The bewildered Strauss received a curt message from his wife announcing the end of their marriage.

It turned out the whole thing was a mistake—Mücke had been trying to get in touch with someone named Stransky—but Strauss had difficulty convincing Pauline since she returned all his imploring letters unopened. Most people would have been happy to put such an unpleasant episode behind them, but Strauss found it funny and wrote an entire opera about a conductor and his wife who nearly divorce over a comedy of errors. Strauss had kept the subject of the opera a secret from his wife; at the premiere when someone spoke to her about this "marvelous present to you from your husband," she snapped, "I don't give a damn."

The Perils of Pauline

As the Nazi Party gained power in the 1930s, Strauss tried to keep his distance from politics, but politics in Germany were inescapable, and Strauss came to lend his support to some questionable if not downright deplorable people and causes. He socialized with Nazi leaders, went to a 1934 dinner with Hitler, signed a denunciation of writer Thomas Mann, and served as president of Reich Music Chamber from 1933 to 1935. In 1933, Arturo Toscanini withdrew from conducting at Bayreuth to protest Germany's policies, and Winifred Wagner asked Strauss to step in. He was genuinely surprised at the storm of criticism that followed. (Toscanini said, "To Strauss the composer I take off my hat; to Strauss the man I put it back on again.")

However, Strauss did not share Nazism's most hateful attitudes. For example, Strauss had worked for some time with the author Stefan Zweig on the libretto for a new opera *Die schweigsame Frau,* but when it came time for its premiere in 1935 in Dresden, permission to perform it was nearly denied because Zweig was a Jew. Zweig saw the writing on the wall; he told Strauss he would write no more libretti under his own name. If Strauss wanted, Zweig would assist another librettist named Joseph Gregor, but anonymously. Strauss wrote a furious letter to Zweig complaining, "Do you believe that I am ever, in any of my actions, guided by the thought that I am 'German'? Do you believe that Mozart composed as an 'Aryan'? I know only two types of people: those with and those without talent." Not surprisingly, the Gestapo intercepted the letter; Strauss was forced to resign from the Reich Music Chamber for his lack of Aryan loyalty, and Zweig left the country.

As the war broke out, Strauss and Pauline retreated to Garmisch, their Bavarian country house. They were both by now in their mid-seventies and dependent on the help of their faithful servants, particularly their chauffeur, Martin. Strauss had to pull every string he could to keep Martin from being sent to the front. Even more difficult—and more serious—was the effort to protect his son Franz's wife, Alice, a Jew. The couple were repeatedly harassed by Gestapo and were once arrested and interrogated for several days before being released. Late in the war, a warrant was issued for Alice, but a friend in the district office made sure the paperwork got stuck in the bottom of his in-box.

Of course, Pauline created additional anxiety. She just couldn't keep her mouth shut. Early in the war at a gala reception in Vienna, Pauline got in a conversation with Baldur von Schirach, head of the Hitler Youth, regional leader of the Nazi Party, and governor of the city. She decided she liked him, and so she announced, "When the war is lost and over, then Herr Schirach, I'll save a little place for you at Garmisch, when you're on the run. But as for that other trash . . ." She shook her head. Strauss stood paralyzed, beads of sweat popping out on his forehead. "Many thanks for your friendly warning,"

> CONCERNED ORCHESTRA MEMBERS INTERRUPTED A RAUCOUS ARGUMENT BETWEEN STRAUSS AND A CRANKY SOPRANO— ONLY TO FIND THAT THEY HAD JUST BECOME ENGAGED.

Schirach replied. "But I don't believe that I'll need your help." He walked away, and they suffered no repercussions. Strauss must have been glad to have Pauline relatively contained at Garmisch.

On the morning of April 20, 1945, American tanks appeared in the meadow beside the Strauss house. Soon a jeep showed up and an army major announced Garmisch was being commandeered. Strauss went to front door and declared, "I am Richard Strauss, the composer of *Rosenkavalier* and *Salome*." Fortunately the army major was a music lover; he put an official "Off Limits" sign on the house.

Lasting Legacy
After the war, Strauss was widely condemned for his Nazi involvement. He could have protested more than he did and could have chosen not to allow his name to be associated so closely with the party. However, his personal letters and documents fail to show any support for Nazi policies, and he dis-

agreed with party authorities. Certainly Strauss was no Winifred Wagner. The worst most people say about Strauss today is that he was naïve to think that he could keep out of politics.

But Strauss had to rebuild both his reputation and his bank balance after the war. He toured Europe again, happy to find that audiences didn't hold his nationality against him. In the fall of 1949, he fell ill; his heart was failing and he suffered repeated infections. He died September 8. At the funeral, after the concluding trio from *Der Rosenkavalier* was sung, Pauline slipped from her chair and sobbed, "Richard! Richard!" They had been married fifty-five years. Pauline never recovered from her loss—she died less than a year later, on May 13, 1950.

Although Strauss's music continues to be criticized for its unevenness—it seems he cranked out some pieces just for the money—it is celebrated for its emotional depth and inventiveness. A master of orchestration, he created tone poems, symphonies, and operas that are both musically significant and exciting to hear.

CLEANLINESS IS NEXT TO PAULINENESS

Pauline was obsessed by dust. She regularly inspected all of the surfaces of her house as well as the surfaces of any house she happened to visit. When she stayed with friends, she horrified her hosts by running her fingers over the furniture, opening drawers, and looking under beds to check for errant dirt. Any hostess who failed the inspection could count on having her servants summoned and scolded.

On one occasion, Pauline didn't bother to wait for a hostess. She arrived at the house of celebrated soprano Lotte Lehman to find Lehman out for the day. Pauline marched in, summoned all of the servants, and ordered them to clean out and rearrange all of the closets to her exacting specifications. Lehman claimed that when she came home, she laughed until she cried.

WHY BUY THE COW?

Pauline's rages were legendary. Once, when she delivered a scathing lecture to her husband as they rode in a horse-drawn carriage, the driver turned around and shouted at Strauss, "Are you going to stand for that?

Throw the cow out!"

Both Pauline and her husband burst out laughing, and Pauline herself circulated the story.

I HATE YOU—NO, WAIT, I LOVE YOU!

In the years before their marriage, Strauss conducted Pauline in numerous opera productions, and rehearsals were always accompanied by dramatic scenes. During one particularly heated quarrel over tempo, Pauline threw her score at Strauss's head and stormed off to her dressing room. He followed, and the entire orchestra tiptoed behind him so they could listen behind the door to the screaming, shrieking, and occasional thuds as objects flew around the room.

Then, suddenly, there was silence. The orchestra members looked at each other in horror: Had the soloist murdered the conductor, or the other way around?

Finally a delegation of players decided to intervene. They knocked on the door, which was opened by an impassive Strauss. The musicians announced that, in respect for their conductor and in protest of Pauline's outrageous behavior, they would refuse to participate in any further production in which Fraulein de Ahna had a role.

"That distresses me," said Strauss, "as I have just become engaged to Fraulein de Ahna."

STRAUSS VS. STRAUSS

If you thought Schubert/Schumann confusion was bad, or the proliferation of Bachs frustrating to keep straight, try the Strauss/Strauss muddle. Richard Strauss spent his entire career being confused with the Strausses of Vienna, of which, just to complicate things, there were four.

Johann Strauss the Elder lived from 1827 to 1870 and popularized the waltz form in Austria. He had three sons, Johann II (1825–1899), Josef (1827–1870), and Eduard (1835–1916), all of whom took up composing. Johann II was the most famous of the bunch and is remembered best for *The Blue Danube* waltz. Coincidentally, the piece also shows up in *2001: A Space Odyssey* in an extended space docking sequence.

SKATTING WITH STRAUSS

Strauss was obsessed with skat, the national card game of Germany. He played for hours every evening, telling friends it was the only time he didn't think about music. His fondness for the game became well-known in musical circles, and it became a tradition for Strauss to introduce himself to new orchestras by announcing, "I need some players for skat. Who will join me?" Naturally, he got quite good at the game and often fleeced his friends. To keep everyone happy at Bayreuth, Cosima Wagner made a secret deal with singers and musicians: She reimbursed them for their losses.

SERGEY RACHMANINOFF

APRIL 1, 1873–MARCH 28, 1943

ASTROLOGICAL SIGN:
ARIES

NATIONALITY:
RUSSIAN /LATER AN AMERICAN CITIZEN

MUSICAL STYLE:
LATE ROMANTIC

STANDOUT WORKS:
PIANO CONCERTO NO. 2

WHERE YOU'VE HEARD IT:
THE MELODY IN THE 1976 POP HIT "ALL BY MYSELF" BY ERIC CARMEN

QUOTABLE

"I'VE PLAYED [MY CORELLI VARIATIONS] ABOUT
FIFTEEN TIMES . . . GUIDED BY THE COUGHING OF
THE AUDIENCE. WHENEVER COUGHING WOULD
INCREASE, I WOULD SKIP THE NEXT VARIATION.
WHENEVER THERE WAS NO COUGHING, I WOULD PLAY THEM IN
PROPER ORDER. IN ONE CONCERT, I DON'T REMEMBER WHERE,
SOME SMALL TOWN, THE COUGHING WAS SO VIOLENT THAT I
PLAYED ONLY TEN VARIATIONS (OUT OF TWENTY)."

Most people have to content themselves with one talent, but not Sergey Rachmaninoff. He excelled in not one, not two, but three areas.

Rachmaninoff could easily have devoted his life to composing—he produced ravishing melodies with complex harmonies. Or he could have played piano—his virtuoso performances stunned audiences. Or he could have conducted—he brought out the best in orchestras.

The only problem? He couldn't do all three at once. And so Rachmaninoff's life was a constant balancing act, one complicated by world events that eventually drove him and his entire family into exile.

The Education of Sergey

The Rachmaninoffs of Semyonovo, in northwestern Russia, had a distinguished family tree, going back to the fifteenth century and traced from the grand dukes of Moscow. In more recent years, the Rachmaninoffs were known as high-ranking soldiers and respectable land owners. All that ended, however, with Sergey's father, Vasily, who frittered away all five family estates and then abandoned his wife, Lubov, and their six children.

The original plan had been for Sergey and his brothers to attend a prestigious military school, but Vasily's improvidence eliminated that option. When Sergey was nine, he was able to follow his musical inclinations and enroll at the Moscow Conservatory. Sergey was talented, but he wasn't particularly interested in endless practice sessions, and he spent more time at the skating rink than the piano. His mother had no idea her son was failing all his classes until a teacher mentioned it; Rachmaninoff had been doctoring his report card.

Lubov consulted one of her nephews, Sergey's older cousin Alexander Siloti, himself a teacher at the St. Petersburg Conservatory. Siloti suggested Sergey be put under the care of the best piano teacher in Russia, Nikolai Zverev.

Zverev taught at the Moscow Conservatory and also housed a handful of poor but talented students. He imposed rigid discipline on his charges. They practiced for three hours a day, sometimes starting as early as six in the morning; if a sleepy student faltered over the keys, Zverev, clothed only his nightshirt, would leap out of his bed in the next room and run in cursing. As well as providing formal lessons, he took his pupils to the opera, ballet, and theater, introduced them to his own wide circle of musical friends, and drilled them in etiquette. As the boys became teenagers, he introduced them to elegant restaurants, night clubs, and, rumor has it, brothels.

You're Getting Verrrrrry Sleepy

Under Zverev's instruction, Rachmaninoff grew from a lazy good-for-nothing into a serious student of music. When he learned that his favorite Conservatory teacher would be leaving for his last year of studies, Rachmaninoff decided to take his final exams a year early. This was an enormous task, requiring he compose several vocal pieces, a symphony, and an opera. His final student performances were a triumph, however, and he was awarded the Conservatory Great Gold Medal, granted only two previous times. On top of that, a music publisher offered to publish his work, and the Imperial Opera put on his student opera *Aleko.*

The next triumph should have been the premiere of Rachmaninoff's First Symphony. The event took place on March 27, 1897, in St. Petersburg, with Alexander Glazunov conducting. Rachmaninoff worried all through rehearsals: The apathetic Glazunov didn't seem to understand the music. During the performance, Rachmaninoff sat on the fire escape outside the concert hall with his fingers stuffed in his ears so he couldn't hear his music being butchered. (Rumor had it Glazunov was drunk.) The audience was unimpressed and the critics harsh. Russian composer César Cui claimed that the only audience that would like it would be the inhabitants of Hell.

Rachmaninoff was devastated. Until this point, everything had been so easy; now he couldn't even compose. More failures were to follow. When offered the chance to conduct an opera, he completely botched the rehearsal—not surprisingly, since he had never conducted before.

Friends decided to cheer him up by introducing him to the great Leo Tolstoy. The writer was informed that his guest had lost his confidence in himself, so Tolstoy gave him a lecture. "Do you imagine that everything in life goes smoothly?" he asked. "All of us have difficult moments; but that is life." After this far-from-encouraging speech, he invited Rachmaninoff to play. The composer launched into a piece called *Fate,* based on the opening theme of Beethoven's Fifth Symphony. Big mistake: No one had told Rachmaninoff that Tolstoy despised Beethoven. As soon as the music ended, he delivered another lecture on the evils of "modern" music.

Rachmaninoff did not compose for a full three years. He moped, he drooped, he drank way too much vodka. His family finally convinced him to see the doctor Nikolai Dahl. As well as being an accomplished cellist, Dahl was a psychologist trained in the use of hypnotherapy. Rachmaninoff visited Dahl every day to listen to the doctor repeat in a soothing voice, "You will begin to write your concerto. . . . You will work with great facility. . . . The concerto will be of an excellent quality . . ."

It worked. Within a matter of months, Rachmaninoff had begun work on his most famous and most celebrated composition, his Piano Concerto no. 2.

The Red Menace

After the successful premiere of the concerto in October 1901, Rachmaninoff became engaged to his first cousin Natalia Satina. Substantial barriers stood in the way of their marriage. The Russian Orthodox Church issued marriage licenses, and since the lax churchgoer Rachmaninoff never went to Confession, it seemed unlikely he could find a priest willing to marry him. Further, the marriage of cousins required the permission of the tsar. Fortunately, one of Sergey and Natalia's aunts was good friends with a prominent priest who pulled all the necessary strings. The couple married on April 29, 1902. Their first daughter, Irina, was born just over a year after the wedding, in May 1903; another daughter, Tatiana, was born in June 1907.

> A DRUNKEN CONDUCTER SO BUTCHERED RACHMANINOFF'S FIRST SYMPHONY THAT HE FLED TO THE FIRE ESCAPE AND JAMMED HIS FINGERS IN HIS EARS.

In 1904, Rachmaninoff took the post of conductor at the Bolshoi Theater. However, his time there was interrupted by the outbreak of civic violence in 1905. After years of misrule under the autocratic tsarist government, Russians rebelled. The unrest spread to the Bolshoi orchestra, and Rachmaninoff found it impossible to control disruptive members. He resigned.

No matter—if he couldn't conduct, he could compose or concertize. He traveled widely as a touring pianist, including a 1909 trip to the United States. Touring ended in 1914 with the outbreak of World War I, and then the Russian Revolution brought violence and chaos to the entire country. Rachmaninoff represented everything the Bolsheviks despised: a landowner

of aristocratic lineage playing Western-inspired music that catered to the bourgeoisie. Rachmaninoff was no die-hard conservative—he mostly ignored politics—but now his family was in danger.

Just in time, he received an invitation to tour in Scandinavia in 1917. He took the opportunity to flee. The family could tell no one their intentions and certainly couldn't pack as if they were leaving for good. Rachmaninoff carried only a small suitcase crammed with manuscript scores. After a train ride through Finland, they crossed the border to Sweden in an open sleigh, in the middle of a raging snowstorm. They were safe.

In the Land of the Free

For about a year, the family stayed in Sweden and Denmark. Then American musicians invited Rachmaninoff to cross the Atlantic. He could be assured, they said, of an active touring schedule or even a permanent job as a conductor. Once again, Rachmaninoff faced the choice between composing, conducting, and playing. This time, his choice was economic rather than artistic: Life as a touring piano virtuoso had the greatest financial rewards. So he hit the road. All through the 1920s and '30s, Rachmaninoff lived out of a suitcase.

He and Natalia lived in New York and later Los Angeles, but the couple never really integrated into American society. They socialized with fellow Russian émigrés, hired Russian servants, and followed Russian customs. For years, Rachmaninoff hoped the Soviet Union would collapse so they could return home. The realization that his exile would be permanent sunk in slowly. Many biographers believe Rachmaninoff's homesickness contributed to his long creative drought; he didn't compose for fifteen years. Finally, in 1934 he wrote *Rhapsody on the Theme of Paganini*. He followed this work with Symphony no. 3 in 1935–36 and the *Symphonic Dances* in 1940.

Rachmaninoff followed the course of World War II closely, particularly the German invasion of Russia. He donated the proceeds of his 1939–40 winter tour to the Red Army, not in support of the Communist government but in an effort to help the common soldier.

He fell ill in 1942, and doctors told Natalia he was suffering from late-stage melanoma. She refused to let her husband know his diagnosis, and he went ahead with his 1943 tour. His last performance was held February 17, 1943, at the University of Tennessee in Knoxville; he and

Natalia had become American citizens only sixteen days earlier. So sick that he finally had to cancel other appearances, he returned to Los Angeles. Rachmaninoff died on March 28, 1943, four days before his seventieth birthday.

Today Rachmaninoff's struggle over balancing life as a composer, conductor, and pianist is hardly remembered. His performances as conductor and pianist exist only in rare black-and-white films and the occasional recording. But the music he composed lives on, retaining the particular stamp of Rachmaninoff, the composer.

REDISCOVERING THE FIRST

Remember the First Symphony, the one with the disastrous premiere in 1897? Rachmaninoff locked the score away in a drawer. When he left for America, it stayed behind in Russia, and for years, everyone assumed it had been lost.

Then, in 1944, individual orchestra parts were found in Leningrad (formerly St. Petersburg). The complete score was reconstructed, and in October 1945 the Moscow Conservatory played it. Today it is recognized as an early masterpiece and is a part of the standard orchestral repertoire. The fault wasn't in the music but in Glazunov's conducting.

BRINGING DOWN THE U.S.S.R., ONE NOTE AT A TIME

One of the most famous interpreters of Rachmaninoff's music was Van Cliburn, an American pianist born in 1934. In 1958, after attending Julliard and performing at Carnegie Hall, he entered the first International Tchaikovsky Competition, a piano contest held in Moscow and designed to demonstrate Soviet cultural superiority.

At the finale, Cliburn played Tchaikovsky's Piano Concerto no. 1 and Rachmaninoff's Piano Concerto no. 3, and earned a standing ovation lasting an amazing eight minutes. This left the judges perplexed: How could they demonstrate Soviet superiority when this tall, gangly Texan had clearly blown the other contestants out of the water? Finally they appealed directly to Soviet Premier Nikita Khrushchev. "Is he the best?" Khrushchev asked. "Then give him the prize!"

Cliburn returned home a national hero, earning the only New York City ticker-tape parade ever held for a classical musician. He even made the cover of *Time*, accompanied by the headline, "The Texan Who Conquered Russia."

YOU GOTTA BELIEVE

After Rachmaninoff moved to Los Angeles, he met a number of his neighbors, many of whom were film stars. One night he met Charlie Chaplin, and the two got into an extended discussion of religion. Chaplin announced he was an unbeliever.

Rachmaninoff, who himself rarely darkened the door of a church, replied uncomprehendingly, "But how can you have art without religion?"

"I don't think we're talking about the same thing," said Chaplin. "Art is a feeling more than a belief."

"So is religion," replied the composer.

ARNOLD SCHOENBERG

SEPTEMBER 13, 1874–JULY 13, 1951

ASTROLOGICAL SIGN:
VIRGO

NATIONALITY:
AUSTRIAN/LATER AN AMERICAN CITIZEN

MUSICAL STYLE:
MODERN

STANDOUT WORKS:
FIVE ORCHESTRAL PIECES

WHERE YOU'VE HEARD IT:
HARDLY ANYWHERE OUTSIDE THE CONCERT HALL

"MY MUSIC IS NOT REALLY MODERN, JUST BADLY PLAYED."

QUOTABLE

Arnold Schoenberg attracted some of the most outraged criticism in the history of music. Sure, you can find critics calling Beethoven abhorrent and Mozart insipid, but the heights of vituperation reached by Schoenberg-haters can't be matched.

Critics strained to come up with metaphors for his music. It was like "the disordered fancies of delirium," "a pandemonium of cross-eyed devils," "feeding time at the zoo," "self-torture of a flagellant," "a cat walking down the keyboard," and "a lecture on the fourth dimension delivered in Chinese." The effect on listeners was compared to "sharp daggers of white heat . . . [paring] away tiny slices of his victim's flesh."

What on earth did Schoenberg do to prompt such hatred? He merely tried to create a new foundation for Western music. How impertinent!

Chords and Discord

The Schönbergs were Jewish shopkeepers of modest means, setting up their shoe store in the Jewish district of Austria in the late 1800s. Father Samuel ran the business while his piano teacher wife, Pauline, began musical instruction for their son Arnold. The boy picked up the skill so quickly he soon knew more than she did, and he largely taught himself. He learned about different compositional forms from a mail-order encyclopedia, which meant he couldn't write a sonata until the "S" volume arrived.

Samuel died when Arnold was fifteen, and the teen was forced to quit school and go to work. He worked as a bank clerk—and hated it. He continued to play, and in 1893 he met an aspiring composer named Alexander von Zemlinsky, who gave him his only formal lessons in harmony and counterpoint. Then the bank he had been working for went bankrupt. A delighted Schönberg got a conducting gig at a metal-workers' choir in a small town twelve miles from Vienna, although he often had to walk the whole distance because he couldn't afford train fare.

His own compositions received little attention. In 1899, he composed a string sextet called *Verklärte Nacht* ("Transfigured Night") and submitted it to a Viennese music society, but they deplored its Wagnerian emotionalism. "It sounds as if someone had smeared the score of *Tristan* while it was still wet!" complained one judge. They rejected the piece because it contained a chord no one could find in the composition textbooks.

Schönberg struggled on. He further disappointed his family in 1897 when he converted from Judaism to Protestantism. His friendship with Zemlinsky grew closer when he married Zemlinksy's sister Mathilde in 1901. The couple had a daughter the same year and a son in 1908.

I'll Make My Own Rules

Schönberg, meanwhile, had befriended a number of artists and grown interested in expressing himself in painting as well as music. Realizing he couldn't become a self-taught expert in everything, he signed up for art lessons with a young painter named Richard Gerstl. Gerstl pioneered an expressive, psychologically insightful style, and under his tutelage Schönberg became an adept if not brilliant artist.

Mathilde also cultivated an interest in painting—and soon she and Gerstl were having an affair. In 1908, they ran off together. The devastated composer poured his heart into his music, writing a song cycle that used discordant harmonies to express the discord of his own mind. After a few months, Mathilde returned, but not long afterward Gerstl killed himself. The entire family was shaken by the affair, and when Schönberg's String Quartet no. 2 flopped, it's not surprising that the composer fell into a deep depression.

When World War I broke out, Schönberg was twice called for military duty and twice discharged for medical reasons. The war, oddly enough, fit into Schönberg's developing musical philosophy. He had come to believe that classical music—specifically German classical music—had been infected with Frenchified ideas to the point that it was a victim of "inbreeding and incest." Chords and harmonies had become "effeminate," "philistine," "hermaphroditic," and, worst of all, "kitsch." (How a perfectly innocent diminished seventh can be "hermaphroditic" is a mystery to all but the most devoted Schoenbergians.) The only solution was to cast out the decadent harmonies and embrace discordance, atonality, and anti-harmony. The war was Germany's opportunity to defeat the sissified French and their harmonious music once and for all—"Now we will throw these mediocre kitschmongers into slavery, and teach them to venerate the German spirit and worship the German god," he thundered.

Yet he found composing increasingly difficult. He envisioned large-scale works but was unable to bring them to completion. Schönberg had cast off all the old rules that governed music for centuries, only to realize those rules had served a purpose. So Schönberg decided the solution was a new set of rules. In 1923, he invented the "twelve-tone technique," also known as the

"dodecaphonic method." The details are complicated, but it boils down to two basic points: First, twelve-tone music employs a twelve-tone scale instead of the traditional seven-note scale used in Western music from Bach's *Toccata and Fugue* to the "Happy Birthday" song. Second, for each composition, all twelve notes of the scale are combined in a tone row (not a melody per se, but rather a précis of notes and their relationships) that becomes the foundation of the composition. The rules get complicated fast and involve concepts like linear set presentation, isomorphic partitioning, and hexachordal inverstional combinatoriality. In any case, Schönberg had created a new compositional model that gave structure to his most ambitious works. He was thrilled.

The listening audience? Not so much. Chords produced with the twelve-tone method come off as hideously atonal, and audiences had a hard time recognizing (or caring about) the underlying structure. One insightful critic of Schönberg observed that many of his works "are—*on paper*—triumphs of twelve-tonal logic and precisely calculated mathematical organization. Mathematics, however, are not music, and to non-dodecaphonists the effect of such works on the ear is one of unintelligible ugliness."

CRITICS LIKENED SCHOENBERG'S MUSIC TO "A LECTURE ON THE FOURTH DIMENSION GIVEN IN CHINESE," AND "A PANDEMONIUM OF CROSS-EYED DEVILS."

Losing My Religion

Schönberg had gradually lost his faith in Protestantism, although he remained nominally a Lutheran. That didn't stop German and Austrian officials from attacking him as a Jew. As early as 1921, he was kicked out of an Alpine holiday village because Jews weren't welcome. He could have stayed had he provided proof of his Christian baptism, but he wouldn't demean himself to do so. It was an ominous sign of things to come.

Mathilde died after a short illness in 1923. He missed her good humor, but that didn't stop him from falling in love and marrying Gertrud Kolisch, a beautiful woman half his age, in less than a year. They eventually had three children. Schoenberg achieved his greatest career success thus far when he was appointed professor of composition at the Berlin Academy of Art.

In 1933, the president of the Academy announced that Adolf Hitler had resolved to "break the Jewish stranglehold on Western music." Schönberg stormed out, shouting, "This sort of thing you don't need to say to me twice!" Two months later he and his family had moved to Paris. His sense of Jewish solidarity deepening, he formally rejoined the faith of his ancestors.

With Jewish refugees flooding into Paris, Schönberg realized he would have few opportunities in France. He accepted an offer to teach at the Malkin Conservatory in Boston and set out for the United States in October, 1933, dropping the umlaut from his name and becoming "Schoenberg" instead of "Schönberg." He was sixty years old.

California Is the Place You Ought to Be

The Malkin Conservatory proved a disappointment, but in 1935 Schoenberg got an offer to lecture at the University of Southern California. He and his family moved to Hollywood, where his children grew up as genuine American kids. He took up tennis and became a passionate fan of Bruins football when he went on to teach at UCLA. Students adored the crusty German, who tried to bring out the best in his pupils whether they embraced his twelve-tone method or not.

His time at UCLA was cut short by the university's mandatory retirement policy, although it had been extended from age sixty-five to seventy just for him. Since his pension was based on the number of years he had worked, he received only $38 a month. Lacking enough money to support a wife and three young children, he took on private pupils, an increasingly difficult task since his health was failing. In August 1946, he suffered a heart attack and remained in poor health for several years. Schoenberg died July 13, 1951.

Today, he is perhaps the most famous composer that no one ever hears. Although he may have been the most influential composer of the twentieth century, his music is rarely played. But his dedication and daring—not to mention his indomitable spirit in the face of overwhelmingly caustic criticism—mark him as an artist who was willing to take risks and upset the musical order of all who had come before him.

WHEN YOUR NUMBER'S UP, YOUR NUMBER'S UP

Schoenberg suffered from a debilitating case of triskaidekaphobia—the fear of the number 13. So terrified was he of the number that he refused to number the thirteenth bar of music (he preferred 12a) and claimed it was always on the thirteenth page of a new composition that things went wrong. His unfinished opera *Moses und Aron* was originally named *Moses und Aaron*, but he changed the spelling when he realized the letters added up to—you guessed it—13.

Schoenberg faced his 76th (7 + 6 = 13) year with anxiety, particularly Friday, July 13. He had been depressed for several weeks by his poor health, and on that day he decided to stay in bed. That night he awoke and asked the time; it was 11:45. Schoenberg seemed relieved that the day would soon pass, but then he slipped back into sleep—and died. It was thirteen minutes to midnight.

IT'S A DIRTY JOB . . .

When Schönberg was called into the military during World War I, he did his best to remain inconspicuous. Nevertheless, one day an army officer asked if he was "that controversial composer." Schoenberg replied, "Somebody had to be, and nobody else wanted to, so I took on the job myself."

THEY HATE ME, THEY REALLY HATE ME

Schoenberg's attempt at the visual arts fared no better with the critics than his music. At an exhibit in 1910, an observer declared, "Schoenberg's music and Schoenberg's pictures—they'll knock your ears and eyes out at the same time."

DR. SEUSS, MEET HERR SCHOENBERG

After only a short stint at UCLA, Schoenberg's fashion sense transformed from staid-German-professor-look to a more American style—although it's not clear that he really understood quite how to fit in on campus. One student described him as appearing in class wearing "a peach-colored shirt, a green tie with white polka-dots, a knit belt of the most vivid purple with a large and ostentatious gold buckle, and an unbelievably loud gray suit with lots of black and brown stripes."

CHARLES IVES

OCTOBER 20, 1874–MAY 19, 1954

ASTROLOGICAL SIGN:
LIBRA

NATIONALITY:
AMERICAN

MUSICAL STYLE:
MODERN

STANDOUT WORKS:
THE UNANSWERED QUESTION

WHERE YOU'VE HEARD IT:
AS THE THEME OF THE 1998 GERMAN FILM *RUN, LOLA, RUN*

"THE WORD 'BEAUTY' IS AS EASY TO USE AS THE WORD 'DEGENERATE.' BOTH COME IN HANDY WHEN ONE DOES OR DOES NOT AGREE WITH YOU."

QUOTABL

*I*t's easy to forget what a young country the United States really is—until you realize how long it took the country to produce its own art. Classical music didn't exist in America in the days of Bach and Haydn. It wasn't until after the Civil War that opera houses and orchestras really took off, and for years the majority of the performers—and all of the music—was European.

Yet when the first major American composer appeared, he stood out as distinctly American. Rather than embracing the European tradition, Charles Ives rejected classicism as "sissy" and deplored European musicians as "pansies." Rather than follow the old model of education in a French or German conservatory, he went to Yale; rather than build a career as a conductor, he sold life insurance.

Charles Ives is an American's American: a baseball-playing, cigar-smoking, self-promoting, self-made man. His music evokes such American pastimes as gospel singing at tent revivals and brass bands at Fourth of July parades. It's also profoundly weird and like nothing that had ever come before.

But maybe that's American, too.

Dissonance Has Feelings, Too

The Ives family had deep roots in Danbury, Connecticut, with forebears running local businesses, participating in local government, and generally serving as pillars of the community. The young George Ives, however, was considered something of an oddball: He ran off at seventeen to lead a military band in the Civil War. When he returned to Danbury, he conducted brass bands, played at local churches, and organized amateur productions of popular operas. He was well liked, but everyone wondered when he would quit this music nonsense and get a real job.

George married Mollie Parmalee, and the couple had two sons, Charles Edward and Joseph Moss. It didn't take long for George to realize young Charlie shared his love of music. George, himself an eager experimenter, never discouraged his son's creativity; if Charlie played a chord unimaginable to a traditionalist, George applauded his innovation. Before long, Charlie was writing his own pieces, and George was playing them with one of his bands. By age fourteen, Charlie had taken an organist post at a local church. All through his teens, Charlie maintained a furious pace, running to school, dashing to baseball games, flying home to practice piano, then heading over to the church for choir rehearsal. By tradition, the Ives boys went to Yale, and so after a stint at a prep school to improve his academic record, Charlie enrolled in 1894.

Back home, Father George made the momentous decision to give up music because he couldn't support two boys at Yale on his irregular income. He took a job at the Danbury Savings Bank and told his son to avoid his mistake: Music should be a hobby, not a career. It's not clear what the younger Ives made of this. He enrolled in music courses at Yale, although he was surprised to find that the school's strict traditionalists didn't approve of experimentation. When Charlie showed Professor Horatio Parker one of his songs, Parker zeroed in on a dissonant chord that, against all the rules handed down by Bach on high, was not followed by a second chord resolving it into harmony. "There's no excuse for that," Parker snapped. Charlie complained in a letter home, and his father had enough spirit to reply, "Tell Parker that every dissonance doesn't have to resolve, if it doesn't happen to feel like it." It was to be one of the last communications Ives would have with his father. Soon afterward, devastating news came from Danbury: George Ives was dead, felled by a stroke at age forty-nine.

FEW WOULD HAVE GUESSED THAT THE MAN WHO WAS A PLACID INSURANCE AGENT AT IVES & MYNICK BY DAY WAS A COMPOSER OF ATONAL MUSIC BY NIGHT.

Dissonance Loves Harmony

Ives felt his father's loss deeply, but he forged on, taking on a college schedule that was even more punishing than the one he had kept in high school. Friends gave him the nickname "Dasher." Athletics remained important: His coach said he could have been a champion sprinter if he hadn't spent so much time practicing piano. He was tapped for Yale's exclusive fraternities and social clubs and, despite his shyness, was a favorite at parties for his ability to plop down at a piano and play popular songs. His friends had no idea that he took music seriously.

When Ives graduated, he took his father's advice and went into insurance. He and a friend opened their own agency, Ives & Myrick, with offices

near Wall Street. Ives's marketing savvy ensured its success, and the company became the most successful agency in the country. Ives found himself a very wealthy man. Yet every day, he went home and wrote music.

In 1905, Ives fell in love with a young woman named, improbably enough, Harmony. Harmony Twichell was the daughter of a New England minister; her brothers had known Ives at Yale. Devoutly religious, Harmony trained as a nurse and worked with the urban poor. She and Ives had been acquainted for years—she had been his date to Yale's junior prom—but it wasn't until they met again in 1905 that they fell for one another. They married in June, 1908.

Harmony became pregnant almost immediately, but then she suffered a miscarriage so severe that she had to have an emergency hysterectomy. The couple was devastated; they had looked forward to having a large family. In the summer of 1915, the Iveses hosted a poor urban family at a cottage on their property in rural Connecticut. One daughter, Edith, was a sickly fourteen-month-old. The child remained ill at the end of the summer, so Harmony offered to let little Edie stay so she could nurse her back to health. The inevitable happened: Harmony and Charles fell in love with the blonde-haired toddler. They decided to adopt her—not an easy proposition, since both of Edie's parents were alive and well. But Ives had the money to smooth over any conflict. Edie's family continued to pester him for cash for years.

Following the Beat of a Different Drum

Through the years, few people heard the music Ives was working on. With nothing to follow except his own inclinations, he developed a unique approach to every aspect of composing. His harmonies would have given Haydn a heart attack, and his rhythms would have shocked Brahms into a seizure. Ives saw no reason why the entire orchestra should play in one key, or even keep the same beat. In Ives's work, one section might play in march time while another plays a waltz; a few of his pieces even require multiple conductors.

Ives's favorite trick was to incorporate well-known songs and melodies into his compositions—an early version of hip-hop sampling. He quoted from hymns ("Nearer, My God, to Thee," "In the Sweet By-and-By"), marches (lots of John Philip Sousa), and popular tunes ("Turkey in the Straw," "London Bridge Is Falling Down"), sometimes with one melody running into or over another. He also possessed what can only be called a musical sense of humor. He loved creating musical effects that mimicked the real world. In "Country March Band," his homage to amateur brass bands, one confused trumpet player keeps going for two bars after the rest of the band stops. The "Fourth of July" movement from Ives's *Holiday Symphony* ends with a burst of fireworks that catch the town hall on fire, and the song "A Runaway Horse on Main Street" depicts exactly that. Ives sometimes showed his work to professional musicians, but the response was bewilderment at best.

Direct Mail Man

The beginning of World War I found Ives becoming politically active: He supported efforts to pass a constitutional amendment that would have transformed the United States into a direct democracy, with a majority of voters required to authorize the country's participation in any conflict. (It didn't get very far.) Then he decided this war required his personal involvement, so the forty-four year old signed up for six months' service as an ambulance driver.

Within weeks of leaving for France, the astonishing amount of exertion Ives had crammed into every moment of his life suddenly caught up with him. He had a massive heart attack. His close encounter with death transformed Ives. He felt he was facing a death sentence and had limited time to accomplish the two goals most important to him: ensuring the financial security of his family (a natural priority for an insurance salesman) and getting his music heard.

The first goal was easy. He had already made a fortune, and all through the 1920s he expanded it. But the second goal proved not so simple. For one thing, Ives refused to court the approval of the U.S. music establishment of classical societies and orchestras, which he characterized as a bunch of lily-livered wusses. Ives was convinced music needed to become more American, more manly, and music societies, often headed by society women and effeminate men, were not the sort of audience Ives strove to impress. Taking his macho posturing a step further, he condemned the lilting, harmonious music of Mendelssohn, Debussy, and Ravel as sissy. "Can't they take dissonance like a man?" he demanded.

Ives's solution? Take his music directly to the people. He printed up his scores at his own expense and mailed them out to a list of modern composers, adventurous conductors, and sympathetic reviewers. And it worked. In time, Ives interested a handful of modern music aficionados, and slowly, painfully, his pieces were heard. The response was usually negative—although a few discerning listeners praised Ives for his uniquely American style.

Ultimately, he took recognition no better than he had taken rejection: When he was awarded the Pulitzer Prize for his Third Symphony in 1947 (thirty-seven years after it had been composed), he replied, "Prizes are for boys—I'm grown up!"

Ives essentially quit composing in 1926, and in January 1930 he stepped down from Ives & Myrick. He suffered multiple heart attacks and had to spend weeks at a time in bed. In the spring of 1954, he underwent surgery for a double hernia; he seemed to be recovering well but then suffered a stroke. He died on May 19.

Ives had pointed the way toward many trends in modern and even post-modern music. Polyrhythm, polyharmony, polytonality, atonality, tone clusters, dissonant counterpoint—all of these are represented in Ives's works. We call Ives a modernist, but really he fits into no category except his own, remaining a quintessentially American individualist to the end.

AND HERE'S THE PITCH

As a young man, Ives was both delighted and terrified when his father's band played one of his first compositions, "Holiday Quickstep." Ives found himself simply too nervous to take his usual place with the snare drum, so he stayed at home. As the band marched down Main Street past his house, he couldn't even look—he was observed facing the other way and hurling a baseball against a barn door.

In general, Ives disliked displaying his musical prowess in his hometown. His response to the question "What do you play?" was "Shortstop."

MUSIC APPRECIATION

The military band led by Ives's father became known as the best in the army, a fact that did not escape the attention of the commander-in-chief. When President Lincoln visited General Grant to review the Army of the Potomac during the siege of Petersburg, the president observed, "That's a good band." The laconic Grant replied, "You couldn't prove it by me. I only know two tunes. One is 'Yankee Doodle,' and the other isn't."

IVES VS. IVES

Perhaps you have been wondering through this entire chapter—wait, isn't Ives the guy who sang "It's a Holly, Jolly Christmas"? Welcome to yet another case of musical identity overlap.

Burl Ives (1909–1995) was an Academy-Award-winning actor and acclaimed folk singer. He performed on Broadway and in movies; Tennessee Williams wrote the part of Big Daddy in *Cat on a Hot Tin Roof* specifically for him. He is, however, better known for playing Sam the Snowman in the animated TV favorite *Rudolf the Red-Nosed Reindeer*. Charles Ives, in contrast, kept to the worlds of insurance and composition.

MEASURING UP TO MARK

Harmony Twichell's father, Joe, was a close friend of Mark Twain who traveled with him around Europe and once suggested that the author turn his old stories of life on the Mississippi into a novel. When Harmony and Ives became engaged, Harmony naturally introduced her fiancé to their old family friend. "Well," said Twain, when they walked in the door, "the fore seems all right; turn him around and let's see about the aft."

MAURICE RAVEL

MARCH 7, 1875–DECEMBER 28, 1937

ASTROLOGICAL SIGN:
PISCES

NATIONALITY:
FRENCH

MUSICAL STYLE:
IMPRESSIONIST

STANDOUT WORKS:
BOLÉRO

WHERE YOU'VE HEARD IT:
ENDLESSLY PLAYED IN THE DUDLEY MOORE/BO DEREK HIT MOVIE *10*

"WE ARE NOT MADE FOR MARRIAGE, WE ARTISTS.
WE ARE SELDOM NORMAL, AND OUR LIFE STILL
LESS SO."

QUOTABLE

*O*ne of the vagaries of copyright law is that musicians can continue to earn money long after they're dead. Elvis Presley, for example, made $52 million in 2007, more than most living performers. (Justin Timberlake raked in a paltry $44 million in comparison.)

So, which departed French musician is still bringing in the dough decades after his death? The late, lamented Maurice Ravel, whose *Boléro* earns more than $2.2 million every year. From the composer's death in 1937 to 2001, his estate made approximately $63 million for *Boléro* alone.

No one, the composer included, could have predicted that the oddly structured orchestral piece would be so popular. Ravel himself said of the work, "There isn't any music in it." *Boléro* turned out to be Ravel's last great composition—and may even contain clues to his ultimate fate.

Keeping His Eyes on the Prix

Maurice Ravel was the son of Swiss inventor Joseph Ravel, who never succeeded in popularizing any of his inventions. His early loop-the-loop rollercoaster "The Whirlwind of Death" never quite caught on because of the number of fatalities associated with it. The family moved to Paris when Maurice was a child. He picked up music early, and at age fourteen, he entered the Paris Conservatoire. He had little interest, however, in formal exercises such as fugues and canons, and for several frustrating years he tried and failed to win the Prix de Rome competition. On one occasion he was kicked out in the first round for "terrible errors in writing." One senses he wasn't trying very hard. During the same period he composed the haunting *Pavane pour une infante défunte* ("Pavane for a Dead Princess"; a *pavane* was a type of sixteenth-century dance) It remains one of his most beloved works.

On Ravel's fifth Prix de Rome attempt, he was thirty years old and celebrated by the French press. Nevertheless, judges eliminated him in the first round—again. The French art world erupted in a rage, deploring the stuffy traditionalism of the Conservatoire. Newspapers picked up the story, declared it "l'affair Ravel," and lobbied for the resignation of the Conservatoire's director. When the dust settled, the Conservatoire had a new director, and Ravel was the darling of the art set.

How Do I Look?

Ravel ate up the attention. He was a small man—just over five feet tall—but he dressed to kill in snappy suits and exotic ties. He cultivated the dandyish attitude of the aesthete and socialized with a group of artists and intellectuals known as "Les Apaches." ("Apache" was Paris slang for *street thug*, which Ravel's circle most certainly weren't; the name stuck after a street vendor shouted "Hey, watch out, you Apaches!" when the group brushed into him in the street.)

Several of the Apaches were homosexual, and some recent biographers have asserted Ravel, too, was gay. Certainly he never married, but all the evidence one way or another is anecdotal or circumstantial. Ravel was circumspect about his sexuality, but his habit of putting on tights, a tutu, and falsies and dancing around on tiptoes to entertain his Apache friends must have given rise to talk.

Ravel also became associated with one of the most openly gay artists of the day, the ballet impresario Sergey Diaghilev, who was engaged in a torrid affair with choreographer Vaslav Nijinsky. Ravel created *Daphnis et Chloé* for Diaghilev, deliberately including swooping sections of music to accommodate Nijinsky's soaring leaps.

TO AMUSE HIS FRIENDS, RAVEL DANCED AROUND IN TIGHTS, A TUTU, AND FALSIES.

In Memoriam

When World War I broke out, the nearly forty-year-old Ravel tried to enlist in the most dangerous branch of the service, the air corps. But instead, he became a military truck driver. His base didn't even have a piano, and he refused transfer to more amenable quarters. Although never at the front line, he saw his share of horrors, including the bloody aftermath of the Battle of Verdun.

Ravel deeply mourned the young soldiers he saw sent to the slaughter. ("If the war lasts any longer, it will be necessary to distribute baby dolls and rattles to the Army of the Republic," he noted to a friend.) Before the war he had begun a piano piece called *Le Tombeau de Couperin*. (A *tombeau* is an

old-fashioned term for memorial music, and François Couperin was a French Baroque composer.) Ravel intended to evoke a seventeenth-century mood of delicacy. He dedicated each of the six sections to a friend killed in the war. When asked why the piece seems paradoxically light-hearted rather than sad, Ravel replied, "The dead are sad enough."

Duel Personalities

By the end of the war, Ravel had achieved considerable fame. In January, 1920, he was awarded the Legion of Honor, but he shocked everyone by refusing to accept it. He felt that most Legion of Honor recipients had schemed to win the honor, and he didn't want to be associated with any of them.

Ravel went to work on another ballet, a commission from Diaghilev titled *La Valse*. In the interim, Nijinsky broke Diaghilev's heart by getting married, and Diaghilev not only cut off all contact with the dancer but also expected his friends to do the same. When Ravel remained friendly with the dancer, Diaghilev saw it as a betrayal, and so rejected *La Valse*.

Ravel moved on to other projects, including the opera *l'Enfant et les Sortilèges*, a surrealist piece that includes dancing armchairs, singing teacups, and flying squirrels. The dances in *l'Enfant* were to be performed by members of Ballets Russes, which meant again dealing with Diaghilev, whether he liked it or not. When Ravel encountered the impresario in a hotel lobby, Diaghilev held out his hand, but Ravel abruptly challenged him to a duel.

As entertaining as it might have been to see the petite Frenchman and suave Russian meet at dawn with pistols, friends convinced them to let the matter drop—but not until Diaghilev threatened to wreck *l'Enfant* by pulling his dancers from the opera. Diaghilev died in 1929, unreconciled with his old friend to the end.

Roughing It with Ravel

In 1927, Ravel was invited to tour the United States. Prohibition was going strong, and Ravel feared he would be deprived of his beloved French wines. Organizers assured him that all forms of liquor would be available, Prohibition or not, and they arranged for a full case of his favorite cigarettes to be imported. The dandy Frenchman awed American audiences as much with his appearance as with his piano playing. He once refused to go onstage because he had misplaced his monogrammed handkerchief. He socialized with George Gershwin, Bela Bartók, Mary Pickford, and Douglas Fairbanks. When Gershwin took him to Harlem to hear jazz, he was bewildered by the cigarettes on the table labeled "grass."

Back in France, Ravel lived in the quiet Paris suburb Montfort-l'Amaury in a house he dubbed *Le Belvédère*. The house overflowed with bibelots and curios picked up at street fairs and secondhand shops. Ravel adored buying crude, dirty canvasses and telling guests that they were original Renoirs or Italian Old Masters. Friends would ooh and aah, only to have him burst out laughing and announce, "They're all fakes!" Montfort's quiet residents looked on the exotic Ravel with a mixture of fascination and horror; after a party welcoming him back from America, a rumor flew around the village that guests had stripped naked and indulged in an orgy. When Ravel was told the story by a friend he remarked, "Isn't it a disgrace?"

Am I Repeating Myself?

In 1928, Ravel penned his most famous composition, *Boléro*. The work's popularity today has robbed us of the ability to hear just how strange it was to contemporary audiences. For about fifteen minutes, *Boléro* consists of a single melodic line, repeated nine times. The only variation is in the orchestration, as different instruments take over the melody or join in the insistent rhythm.

The work earned Ravel a fortune—but not everyone was bowled over by *Boléro*. At one early performance, Ravel's brother claimed he saw an old woman gripping the back of her chair and shrieking, "*Au fou! Au fou!*"— "The madman! The madman!" There was perhaps more to her reaction than even she knew. In the early 1930s Ravel began experiencing odd memory lapses. One day at the beach, he suddenly forgot how to swim. He went blank on names and could only cast about for ways to communicate his meaning. He would say, "You know, the lady who takes care of the house, who has a nasty personality," to mean his housekeeper, Madame Révelot. Friends assumed the problems stemmed from an accident in 1932 when Ravel's taxi had been struck by another car. Prominent neurologists examined him but could offer little aid. Finally, in 1937, a doctor proposed experimental surgery to "reinflate" one of the lobes of his brain with fluid. Ravel woke briefly after the operation and asked for his brother, but then sank into unconsciousness and died nine days later.

Today it's theorized that Ravel suffered from a condition called "frontotemporal dementia," in which certain parts of the brain atrophy while other parts actually grow. The form that Ravel may have had actually causes bursts of creativity in its early stages, although this creativity often includes a high degree of structure and repetition. Contemporary neurologists suggest that *Boléro*'s repetitive form was an early sign of Ravel's illness.

BECAUSE I SAID SO

In 1929, Ravel received one of his most unusual commissions: to write a piano concerto for one hand. The commission came from Paul Wittgenstein, an Austrian pianist who lost his right arm while serving in World War I. Determined to continue his piano career, Wittgenstein reached out to all the great composers of his day and asked them to write music specifically for the left hand. Benjamin Britten, Paul Hindemith, and Richard Strauss all responded, but the most well-known of the resulting works was Ravel's Piano Concerto for the Left Hand Alone.

Wittgenstein initially disliked the jazz-influenced concerto, and at the premiere he casually mentioned that he had made a few modifications to the piece. Ravel didn't hide his disapproval, and Wittgenstein replied in anger, "I'm an old pianist and it doesn't sound right." Ravel snapped back, "I'm an old orchestrator and it sounds right!" Wittgenstein later sent the composer a letter saying, "Interpreters must not be slaves!" Ravel's response? "Interpreters *are* slaves!"

In time, Wittgenstein came to agree with Ravel and began playing the concerto as it had been written. Few pianists have had the courage to attempt the challenging piece. One pianist named Alfred Cortot insisted on playing it with both hands, to Ravel's endless annoyance.

PICKING UP THE PACE

Ravel found it particularly frustrating when orchestra conductors changed the tempos of his compositions. He had a running feud with Toscanani, who insisted on gradually increasing the tempo of *Boléro* rather than keeping it steady. Similarly, he hated it when pianists slowed down the pace of *Pavane pour une infante défunte.* At one rehearsal, the pianist elongated all the phrases and generally slowed the piece to a plodding pace. Ravel rushed to the piano and shouted, "Listen, I wrote 'Pavane for a Dead Princess,' not 'Dead Pavane for a Princess!'"

IGOR STRAVINSKY

JUNE 17, 1882–APRIL 6, 1971

ASTROLOGICAL SIGN:
GEMINI

NATIONALITY:
RUSSIAN/LATER AN AMERICAN CITIZEN

MUSICAL STYLE:
MODERNIST

STANDOUT WORK:
THE RITE OF SPRING

WHERE YOU'VE HEARD IT:
AS THE LUMBERING DINOSAURS FIGHT IT OUT IN THE 1940 DISNEY
ANIMATED CLASSIC *FANTASIA*

"MY MUSIC IS BEST UNDERSTOOD BY CHILDREN AND ANIMALS."

QUOTABI

L ots of musical performances go badly. Some audiences clap politely, but you can sense their lack of interest. Some sit in silence. And some actually hiss their disapproval.

Igor Stravinsky's *Rite of Spring* prompted none of these reactions. Silence would have been welcome—hissing preferred. Instead, the audience, shouted, screamed, booed, and stomped. They pounded on the backs of chairs and slugged other patrons. Elderly Parisian women whacked tuxedoed men with their umbrellas. What on earth could have prompted such a scene? Only the most shocking music of the modern era.

Ballet Is Not for Sissies

The bass-baritone Fyodor Stravinsky achieved significant acclaim in late 1800s Russia for his magnificent singing voice and powerful stage presence. Igor, his next-to-youngest son, grew up attending first-class performances and meeting the stars of the St. Petersburg music scene. He had shown early interest in music, but Fyodor insisted he attend university. While half-heartedly studying law, Stravinsky sought out Russian composer Nikolai Rimsky-Korsakov and began intensive one-on-one composition lessons.

In 1905, Stravinsky proposed to his cousin Katerina (Katya) Nossenko. Like the Rachmaninoffs, the couple had to overcome the taboos regarding marriage between first cousins; they finally found a village priest they could lie to, and were married in January, 1906. The couple had four children: Fyodor in 1907, Lyudmila in 1908, Soulima in 1910, and Miléne in 1913. Stravinsky befriended Serge Diaghilev, who had just begun his efforts to revitalize dance. Diaghilev invited Stravinsky to write music for the Ballets Russes, and he accepted despite the objections of his old friends and teachers. Rimsky-Korsakov had died in 1908, but his circle looked down on ballet as suitable for only the dirty old men who took binoculars to performances. But Stravinsky persisted, and in 1910, he went to Paris for the premiere of *The Firebird*. Soon afterward, he decided to move his family to the West, settling in a suburb of Montreux.

What a Riot!

After the success of *The Firebird*, Stravinsky created a second ballet, *Petrushka*, in 1911. Then he began to play with a story idea about a girl who danced to her death. The result would change Western music.

Conductor Pierre Monteux reported he wanted to run out of the room the first time Stravinsky played *The Rite of Spring* on piano for him. Diaghilev, however, was fascinated by the artistic possibilities the piece might present for his lover and protégé, Vaslav Nijinsky. Nijinsky's choreography for the work turned every principle of classical ballet on its head: The dancers walked with their feet turned in and their knees jutting out; they jumped flat-footed and landed with bone-jarring thumps. Rehearsals staggered along as the dancers tried to understand their steps and the orchestra tried to understand the score. At one rehearsal, after a particularly discordant shriek from the horn section, the entire orchestra broke into nervous, hysterical laughter.

The mood was tense in the theater on the night of May 29, 1913; word had gotten out this new ballet was "difficult." But nothing could have prepared the audience for the harsh, throbbing chords that assailed their ears. People started hissing, then booing, then shouting, screaming, and fighting. Stravinsky fled backstage to find Nijinsky standing on a chair shouting the beat to the dancers; Stravinsky clung to Nijinsky's coattails so he wouldn't topple over onto the stage. Diaghilev flicked the lights, and the theater manager went onstage between the first and second movements to urge calm—to no effect. The police had to be called.

It was a genuine musical riot.

The next night was better—you could actually hear some of the music—and the third night better still. But Stravinsky was no longer in the audience. He had been admitted to a hospital for severe abdominal pains, the result, he believed, of eating a bad oyster. In fact he had come close to death; he was later diagnosed with typhoid.

Love Me, Love My Lover

After the *Rite*, Stravinsky retreated for a time to recover from his illness. His wife also needed long-term care: Katya had been diagnosed with tuberculosis and required lengthy, expensive treatment. Then World War I began, further isolating the Stravinskys from their family in Russia. When news of the Russian Revolution arrived, Stravinsky greeted it with enthusiasm, but his hopes were crushed by the brutal Bolshevik takeover of the country. The aftermath of so much violence prompted Stravinsky to draw back from aggressive modernism. He adopted a neoclassical style characterized by emotional restraint.

The Stravinskys moved to southern France after the war, but Igor spent most of his time in Paris. He fell in love with a Russian émigré named Vera Sudeykin. Charming, witty, and sophisticated, Vera had all the social graces the withdrawn Katya lacked; she was also married, but that proved as little an inconvenience for her as it was for Stravinsky. All through the 1920s and early 1930s, Stravinsky spent half of each year with Katya, the children, and his widowed mother in the country, and the other half with Vera in Paris or on tour. Stravinsky insisted his wife and his lover accept one another without question. When he traveled alone, he even made Katya deliver Vera's allowance in person. Vera handled it all with aplomb, but the increasingly ill Katya retreated into spirituality and prayer, and the children's worship of their glamorous father was tinged with resentment.

Daughter Milène had contracted tuberculosis, and mother and daughter spent months together at sanatoriums. As the Nazi presence loomed over Europe, the two grew increasingly frail. Milène died on November 30, 1938, and Katya followed her to the grave four months later. The final blow was the death of Stravinsky's mother the following June.

Rite of Passage

Overwhelmed by loss and concerned by the political situation, Stravinsky was relieved to receive an invitation to give a series of lectures at Harvard. He and Vera took off for Boston. On March 9, 1940, a year after Katya's death, he and Vera wed in Bedford, Massachusetts. The couple told the judge Vera had divorced her first husband in 1920. This was a lie. They apparently preferred bigamy to the risk of American disapproval of "living in sin."

The Stravinskys settled in Hollywood, where they socialized with Edward G. Robinson, Marlene Dietrich, and Cecil B. De Mille. Studios requested film scores, but Stravinsky refused to cede control of his music to movie makers. He was still smarting over Disney's *Fantasia,* in which the animators had dictated that his music be chopped up and reorganized.

The war ended, but Stravinsky stayed in the United States; he and Vera became American citizens in 1946. In 1948 he befriended a young conductor named Robert Craft, who eventually became his secretary, contributor, general servant, and adopted son. Craft had studied the twelve-tone work of Schoenberg and introduced Stravinsky to the finer details of the approach. Soon Stravinsky was writing dodecaphonic music himself. This return to modernism coincided with his increased interest in spirituality, and he wrote the works *Canticum Sacrum* and *A Sermon, a Narrative, and a Prayer*.

For years, composers in the Soviet Union urged Stravinsky to return to his homeland. The affair got twisted up in Cold War politics, with Soviet officials eager to honor the composer. After numerous delays and near-cancellations, Stravinsky, Vera, and Craft arrived in Moscow in September, 1962. The couple was overwhelmed by the enthusiastic reception, and Stravinsky made a number of positive statements about the Soviet Union. He was bitterly criticized for this in the West—particularly when, ten days after his departure, President Kennedy revealed the existence of ballistic-missile launching pads in Cuba.

THE PRIMITIVE BEAT OF STRAVINSKY'S *RITE OF SPRING* WAS SO SHOCKING TO ITS FIRST AUDIENCE THAT THEIR CONFUSION DEVOLVED INTO A VIOLENT RIOT.

Strife After Death

As Stravinsky's eighth decade wore on, he was troubled by ill health. Craft assumed a greater and greater role, taking over Stravinsky's communications and even handling financial matters. Stravinsky's children viewed his involvement with suspicion, and before long the family had fractured into two camps, with the children convinced Craft and Vera were scheming to disinherit them and Craft and Vera sure that the children were gold diggers interested only in their father's wealth.

In search of the best possible medical care, Vera and Craft moved Stravinsky to New York City. He died there on April 6, 1971, at age eighty-eight. Vera decided to bury her husband in Venice, claiming it was his favorite city. The financial dispute kicked into high gear before the dirt had settled over the grave. The family tore into a series of drawn-out lawsuits that continued even after Vera's death in 1982.

SEND IN THE ELEPHANTS AND THE DANCING GIRLS!

In 1946 Stravinsky received an unusual commission: a ballet for elephants. The idea originated with choreographer George Balanchine, who had been approached by the Ringling Brothers and Barnum and Bailey Circus. Stravinsky whipped out a brisk, cheerful piece that premiered at Madison Square Garden in 1942 starring, according to the program, "Fifty Elephants and Fifty Beautiful Girls in an Original Choreographic Tour de Force."

The show closed in two months. But while it lasted, Stravinsky was the only elephant-ballet composer in the world.

MAKING A NAME FOR HIMSELF, AMERICAN STYLE

After arriving in the United States, Stravinsky and Vera had to go through an extensive interview as part of the citizenship process. An immigration official asked the composer for his name and he replied, carefully enunciating, "Stra-vin-sky." "Oh," said the official. "Do you want to change it? Most of them do."

HEY! TORO!

Travel in turn-of-the-century Russia was always an adventure. On one occasion, when Stravinsky was trying to leave the countryside, he missed his connection and realized that the next passenger train wouldn't arrive until the next day. A goods-train was, however, taking the same route, so he bribed the conductor to let him get aboard.

He was escorted to a cattle car where the only other occupant was an enormous bull tied by a "single, not-very-reassuring rope," according to Stravinsky. He barricaded himself as best he could in the corner with his suitcase and hoped for the best. "I must have looked an odd sight in Smolensk as I stepped from that *corrida* carrying my expensive (or, at least, not tramp-like) bag and brushing my clothes and hat, but I must also have looked relieved."

GEORGE GERSHWIN

SEPTEMBER 26, 1898–JULY 11, 1937

ASTROLOGICAL SIGN:
LIBRA

NATIONALITY:
AMERICAN

MUSICAL STYLE:
MODERNIST

STANDOUT WORKS:
RHAPSODY IN BLUE

WHERE YOU'VE HEARD IT:
IN ALL THOSE UNITED AIRLINES COMMERCIALS

"RUMORS ABOUT HIGHBROW MUSIC RIDICULOUS. AM OUT TO WRITE HITS."

QUOTABLE

George Gershwin couldn't keep anyone satisfied. Sure, he wrote sparkling, witty show tunes as well as moving, dramatic orchestral works. But the classical music critics complained that he was too lowbrow and popular, and movie and theater producers fretted he was too highbrow and sophisticated.

Gershwin shrugged and went on creating both serious and not-so-serious music—and a good thing, too. Today, when the distinctions seem less important, his compositions are crowd-pleasers wherever they're performed.

And the Hits Just Keep on Coming

Moishe Gershowitz and Rosa Brushkin were part of the flood of immigrants fleeing Russian pogroms who landed on New York's Lower East Side. The two apparently knew each other back in St. Petersburg, and the couple, now known as Morris Gershvin and Rose Bruskin, married on July 21, 1895. They had four children: Israel in 1896, Jacob in 1898, Arthur in 1900, and Frances in 1906. Not recognizing anyone yet? That's because Israel and Jacob became Ira and George the minute they walked out of the house.

George had an early and passionate interest in music. He later remembered standing outside a penny arcade barefoot and in overalls, listening to the tinkling sounds of a player piano. In 1910, when the family had a secondhand upright piano hoisted through their second-story window so Ira could take music lessons, George plopped down on the bench and started playing a popular hit. His parents were amazed—and Ira was relieved to be off the hook.

After a course of music lessons, fifteen-year-old George changed his surname to Gershwin and quit school. He became a "song plugger" for a music publishing firm, an unusual job that required him to learn all the latest popular tunes and then play them at bars, music halls, and cafes. It was grueling and low-paying work, but one thing lead to another, and soon Gershwin was picking up odd jobs as a rehearsal pianist for Broadway shows. He started writing songs—forgettable, many of them, but a few were significant. "Swanee," for example, was recorded by Al Jolson and became a big hit. Ira started helping his brother with lyrics, and before long the two were cranking out tunes.

Who Cares What the Critics Say?

George Gershwin wasn't satisfied writing show tunes. He took lessons in composition and theory through the 1910s and early '20s, even as his stock on Broadway soared. Then one day in 1924, George was playing pool with a buddy and Ira was reading the newspaper, when Ira asked his brother if he knew he was supposed to be writing a jazz concerto for the Paul Whiteman orchestra. Whiteman was a classically trained conductor who wanted to prove that jazz could be a viable idiom for serious music. He and Gershwin had talked about the concerto idea, but Gershwin didn't realize that Whiteman had set a date.

With only five weeks left, Gershwin set to work on *Rhapsody in Blue*. He envisioned the piece as "musical kaleidoscope" of America, and when it premiered on February 12, 1924, it was an immediate hit. Classical critics, however, were less impressed—they claimed Gershwin had only strung together a series of songs. They also attacked him for using a professional orchestrator; unlike Broadway songwriters, *real* composers considered orchestration essential to composition and did it themselves.

Gershwin resented the attacks and decided to prove himself to critics. The result was his Piano Concerto in F, which he fully orchestrated all by himself, thank you very much. The work premiered in December, 1926. Ira Gershwin later said that it was the bravest thing his brother had ever done. He certainly exposed himself to withering critique. One critic declared it not even good jazz—"conventional, trite, at its worst a little dull."

But George forged ahead with his concert career. After a 1928 trip to Europe, he composed *An American in Paris*, which premiered later that year and received the usual mix of reviews, from "nauseous clap trap . . . vulgar long-winded and inane" to "merrily, rollicking appealing music."

Opera Meets the Great White Way

The stock market crashed in 1929, taking Broadway along with it. Gershwin was able to live on royalties and concert tours, some of which took him beyond the usual big cities—in Sioux Falls, the audience wore overalls.

He also decided he wanted to write the first truly American opera. He took as his subject the book *Porgy* by DuBose Heyward, which tells the story of poor blacks living in the fictional Catfish Row in Charleston, South Carolina. Gershwin wanted to write a serious opera, not a musical: All the dialogue was to be sung, not spoken.

But Gershwin couldn't interest an opera house in the work, so it opened on October 10, 1935, at the Alvin Theater on Broadway. Critics and audiences left bewildered. Had they attended an opera or a musical? Gershwin didn't help matters by calling the work a "folk opera," although he always intended *Porgy* to be considered in the same category as *Aida*. Critics generally wrote off *Porgy* as pretentious Broadway fare.

Nice Work If You Can Get It

With Broadway still in the dumps, the sunny skies of Southern California beckoned to Gershwin. RKO lured both George and Ira with $55,000 and the chance to work with Fred Astaire and Ginger Rogers.

George left New York somewhat reluctantly. He would be leaving behind not only a city he loved but also his lover of ten years, Kay Swift. When Swift met Gershwin in 1925, she was married to a prominent banker and had three children. She and Gershwin fell hard for one another and conducted a highly public affair over the next ten years. Swift's husband tolerated the

MANY BELIEVED THAT GERSHWIN'S HEADACHES AND DIZZY SPELLS WERE THE RESULT OF BEING BONKED IN THE HEAD BY A GOLF BALL.

affair at first but the couple divorced in 1936. Gershwin and Swift were now free to marry, but instead they put their relationship on hold while George went to Hollywood. The playboy Gershwin seemed reluctant to tie himself down. He once asked, "Why should I limit myself to only one woman when I can have as many women as I want?"

In Hollywood, George, Ira, and Ira's wife, Lee, moved together into a Spanish-style stucco house with a tennis court in the backyard. One of their neighbors was Modernist pioneer Arnold Schoenberg, who played tennis regularly with George. George and Ira's movie *Shall We Dance?* opened in 1937, but this was by now the seventh Astaire-Rogers vehicle, and both audiences and the stars were getting tired of the formula.

Meanwhile, Gershwin started experiencing blinding headaches and dizzy spells. Friends suggested the symptoms were the result of getting beamed on the head by a stray golf ball while on the green with comic writer P. G. Wodehouse. Others suggested he was simply unhappy in Hollywood, so

he sought out therapists for analysis rather than medical doctors. On July 10, Gershwin collapsed and fell into a coma. A spinal tap revealed cancer, and George was rushed into emergency surgery. Doctors discovered an inoperable tumor reaching deep into his brain. Gershwin died on July 11; he was only thirty-eight years old.

Today all the debates about George Gershwin as highbrow or lowbrow seem a distant memory. Time has proven he was both a talented popular songwriter and a serious composer. Anyone who can produce "Someone to Watch Over Me" and *Rhapsody in Blue*, "Embraceable You" and Piano Concerto in F, "Fascinating Rhythm" and *An American in Paris* could be nothing less.

WHAT'S IN A NAME?

George and Ira got so fed up with being dismissed by "serious" musicians that they retaliated in song. In "Mischa, Jascha, Toscha, Sascha," the brothers mock the Russian musicians who thrived in American concert halls while Russian-American immigrants were attacked for playing popular music. One verse goes: "Names like Sammy, Max or Moe / Never bring the heavy dough / Like Mischa, Jascha, Toscha, Sascha."

RACE MATTERS

Porgy and Bess had a particularly tortuous history. The work was revived in the 1940s on Broadway with spoken instead of sung dialogue and cuts that reduced the running time. This became the standard version, and it made it all the way to the silver screen in 1959. Directed by Otto Preminger, the movie featured an all-star, all-black cast including Sidney Portier, Dorothy Dandridge, Sammy Davis, Jr., and Pearl Bailey. Critics attacked the movie as patronizing and deplored how heavily the songs had been cut. The film was withdrawn after a short run and is not available on DVD.

Opera companies ignored *Porgy* until 1976, when the Houston Grand Opera staged Gershwin's original score. Opera experts began to reevaluate the work, and soon it was hailed as a landmark in American opera. Questions remained, however, over its attitude toward African-Americans. Many singers and critics have attacked *Porgy* for perpetuating stereotypes. Soloist Grace Bumbry, who played Bess in a famous 1985 Metropolitan Opera production, said of the part, "I thought it beneath me, I felt I had worked far too hard, that we had come far too far to have to retrogress to 1935." Bumbry decided to accept the part because "It was really a piece of Americana, of American history, whether we liked it or not."

GOOD NIGHT, OSCAR, WHEREVER YOU ARE

One of the most famous interpreters of Gershwin's music was pianist and composer Oscar Levant. Levant's career in some ways paralleled Gershwin's: Both were descendents of Russian Jewish immigrants; both were initially known for popular songs but also composed and played seriously. Levant met Gershwin in 1928, and the two bonded immediately. When Gershwin tried out new compositions on two pianos, he liked Levant to take one of the keyboards; he frequently suggested Levant play at concerts he couldn't handle himself.

After Gershwin's death, Levant played himself in the 1945 Gershwin biopic *Rhapsody in Blue*, although the film took such liberties with Gershwin's life that Levant complained, "Even the lies about George are being distorted." He also played a composer in the 1951 film *An American in Paris*, starring Gene Kelly and Leslie Caron, which featured Gershwin's songs.

Levant's reputation as a pianist and composer was nevertheless overshadowed by his fame as a neurotic, drug-addicted wit. Levant was a frequent guest on the radio quiz show *Information Please!* and a regular on *The Jack Paar Show*. (Paar often signed off with the line, "Good night, Oscar Levant, wherever you are.") Levant didn't hesitate to discuss his neuroses, phobias, obsessions, compulsions, addictions, therapies, and shock treatments in public, bringing humor and forthrightness to the once-taboo subject of mental illness. "There is a fine line between genius and insanity," said Levant. "I have erased this line."

Levant died of a heart attack in 1972. He is buried in Los Angeles under a marker that, despite years of rumors to the contrary, does *not* actually read, "I *told* them I was ill."

ONE-HIT WONDER

One evening at a party, Levant turned to Gershwin and asked, "George, if you had to do it all over, would you fall in love with yourself again?"

Gershwin simply smiled and said, "Oscar, why don't you play us a medley of your hit?"

THE GRASS IS ALWAYS GREENER . . .

Several stories have surfaced about Gershwin seeking advice from the great composers of his day, although none of them can be verified. In one tale, Gershwin asked Maurice Ravel if he might study with him. Ravel supposedly replied, "Why do you want to become a second-rate Ravel when you are already a first-rate Gershwin?"

In another story, Gershwin requested lessons from Igor Stravinsky. Stravinsky replied by asking how much Gershwin made a year. When Gershwin told him, Stravinsky answered, "Perhaps I should take lessons from you."

AARON COPLAND

NOVEMBER 14, 1900–DECEMBER 2, 1990

ASTROLOGICAL SIGN:
SCORPIO

NATIONALITY:
AMERICAN

MUSICAL STYLE:
MODERNIST

STANDOUT WORKS:
"HOEDOWN" FROM *RODEO*

WHERE YOU'VE HEARD IT:
IN THE NATIONAL BEEF COUNCIL'S "BEEF: IT'S WHAT'S FOR DINNER" AD CAMPAIGN

"I ADORE EXTRAVAGANCE BUT I ABHOR WASTE."   QUOTABLE

Many composers have egos to spare. They push themselves forward until they're the life of the party, the head of the crowd, or at least the center of attention. Think of the egomaniacal Beethoven, the scintillating Liszt, the bon vivant Strauss.

It's a list Aaron Copland will never join. The modest American composer held back, never making proclamations, announcing manifestos, or even jumping into the middle of things—yet he dominated the American music scene for decades. How did he do it? With a quiet sense of self-confidence. Copland knew who he was and what kind of music he wanted to write, and without making a scene or throwing a fit, he let and nothing get in his way.

From Crown Heights to Gay Pa-ree

Aaron was the fifth child of Harris and Sarah Copland (formerly Kaplan), Jewish immigrants from Russian-controlled Lithuania who settled in Crown Heights in Brooklyn. The Coplands owned a popular department store and lived above their shop. Harris had no interest in music, but Sarah played the piano, and their daughter Laurine loved opera. Laurine was Aaron's first piano teacher, although he exhausted her musical knowledge after six months of teaching. By age eight he was making up songs at the keyboard, and at age eleven he started an opera called *Zenatello*—although he had to quit when he realized an entire score would be beyond the two chords he had at his disposal. A few years later, he signed up for a mail-order harmony course to teach himself composition. This proved less than helpful, and he eventually convinced his family to pay for advanced composition and theory classes in Manhattan.

Copland played in dance bands in Brooklyn and the Catskills to make money, but he never seriously considered pursuing popular music like his contemporary George Gershwin. His attention was fixed firmly on the concert hall, not the Broadway stage. In 1921 Copland headed for France, where he could study modern music, which was at the time frowned upon by most American conservatories and colleges. In Paris, he worked with Nadia Boulanger, a remarkable teacher whose students eventually included Burt Bacharach, Charlie Parker, Leonard Bernstein, and Quincy Jones. Boulanger taught both the traditional counterpoint of Bach and the modern innovations of Ravel and Stravinsky. Copland returned to the United States in 1925, ready to compose full-time.

At first he struggled as a full-time composer, patching together a living from occasional fellowships and the odd commission. Fortunately, he was frugal by nature; he holed up in tiny studio apartments or slept on the sofas of friends. He made it all the way through the Great Depression without going into debt or suffering undue hardship.

Copland's friends were creative types: poets, composers, novelists, and artists. Many of his friends were homosexual and he made no secret that he, too, was gay. Friends remarked on his acceptance of his own sexuality—he was happily free of the guilt and self-rejection that many gay men endured in the early twentieth century. One friend said of Copland, "He made peace with himself and so could be at peace with the whole world."

A Diamond Among the Beans

Two important areas of composition opened up for Copland in the late 1930s. The first was movie music. His first film score was for *The City*, a high-profile documentary on urban issues. He didn't make much money on the deal, but it proved he could work within the medium. His next project was *Of Mice and Men*, a film adaptation of John Steinbeck's 1937 novel directed by Lewis Milestone. Milestone granted Copland remarkable control as a composer, unlike most directors who didn't hesitate to chop, reorganize, or rewrite a composer's music. When the film was released in 1939, Copland received two Academy Award nominations.

After this success, he was soon earning up to $15,000 per score. He went on to write the music for *Our Town* (1940), *The North Star* (1943), *The Red Pony* (1948), and *The Heiress* (1948). But not all of these projects were easy successes. For *The Heiress,* director William Wyler had a studio composer surround Copland's elegant theme with a maudlin arrangement of a popular song. Composer André Previn said the result was like "suddenly finding a diamond in a can of Heinz beans."

A second area of emphasis for Copland was ballet music. In 1938, the Ballet Caravan Company commissioned *Billy the Kid*, a ballet based on the life of the Western outlaw. Copland turned to folk tunes for inspiration, drawing on cowboy songs like "Whoopee Ti-Yi-Yo, Git Along Little Dogies." Then when the Ballets Russes ended up stranded in New York during World War II, their choreographer Agnes de Mille sought out Copland for another cowboy ballet called "Rodeo." Copland created a rousing score that includes an adaptation of the traditional fiddle tune "Bonaparte's Retreat" in the "Hoedown" section.

Innovative modern dancer Martha Graham then approached Copland for a ballet. She could pay him only $500, but they hit it off, and he accepted the offer. The ballet went through numerous permutations—at one point the story was supposed to be about the Greek murderess Medea—but eventually became a tale about a wedding of western Pennsylvanian settlers. Copland made heavy use of the Shaker hymn "Simple Gifts" without knowing anything about the Shaker sect. "Appalachian Spring" became his most famous composition.

> TESTIFYING BEFORE SENATOR JOSEPH MCCARTHY, COPLAND GRACIOUSLY REFUSED TO MENTION A SINGLE NAME. TO ALL HYPOTHETICAL QUESTIONS, HE SAID "I HAVEN'T GIVEN THE MATTER MUCH THOUGHT."

Red-Handed

When millions struggled against poverty in the 1930s, Copland embraced a number of left-leaning causes. He never joined the Communist Party, but he came awfully close. He joined a group called the Composers' Collective, an organization formally affiliated with the American Communist Party, and in 1934 he wrote a song to the lyrics of the poem "Into the Streets May First," which includes lines like "Up with the sickle and hammer, / Comrades, these are our tools!"

It seems a long way from a trite Communist poem to two great works of American music, but for Copland the journey wasn't far. Shortly after the bombing of Pearl Harbor, conductor André Kostelanetz commissioned orchestral works that would present a "musical portrait gallery of great Americans." Copland composed *Lincoln Portrait*, a stirring, solemn piece with spoken narration that includes quotes from many of Lincoln's great speeches. Not long after, another conductor commissioned a series of orchestral fanfares from several American composers. Whereas the other composers dedicated their fanfares to military units or U.S. allies, Copland wrote his "Fanfare for the Common Man," saying, "It was the common man, after all, who was doing all the dirty work in the war and the army. He deserved a fanfare."

Despite the enormous success of these two patriotic works, a contingent of anti-Communist government officials eyed him with suspicion. In 1949, Copland was shocked to find his name listed among the "most notorious 50"

communists and fellow-travelers in the country. In 1953 a planned perform-ance of the *Lincoln Portrait* at the inauguration of President Eisenhower was dropped after Illinois Representative Fred Busbey, a diehard Red-baiter, protested on the floor of the House.

That April, Copland received the dreaded telegram summoning him to appear before the Senate Permanent Committee on Investigations chaired by Senator Joseph McCarthy. Copland testified at a private hearing lasting two hours. The composer handled himself with aplomb and treated his questioners with such graciousness that their hostility came off as gauche. By exuding calm sociability, he gave all appearances of being a friendly witness without providing a single name. To all hypothetical questions, he answered, "I haven't given the matter much thought."

So smooth was Copland's testimony that he was never recalled for fur-ther hearings or even blacklisted. The FBI continued to monitor his activities through 1955, but on the whole, Copland survived McCarthyism unscathed and completely true to himself.

A Common Man

As he entered old age, Copland relied on the help of a series of young, tal-ented men who were his lovers, secretaries, and housekeepers. Copland enjoyed their vitality, although their open embrace of homosexuality went far beyond anything the Copland could have imagined for himself. When parties got out of hand or stories got particularly risqué, Copland would put his hand on his chest and exclaim in mock distress, "And I thought this was a *respectable* household!"

In the mid-1970s, Copland started forgetting things—names, dates, why he picked up the phone to call someone. These were the first signs of Alzheimer's disease. By the mid-1980s he lived at home with round-the-clock nursing care. Copland died of pneumonia on December 2, 1990, a few weeks after his ninetieth birthday.

Copland's music has never lost its appeal. When ad agencies, Olympic organizing committees, or political parties need music that sounds "American," they reach for Copland. And the one-time accused communist sympathizer never lets them down.

WHAT DO YOU MEAN IT'S 1987?

Copland treated signs of his advancing Alzheimer's with characteristic humor. If he forgot the current year and had to be reminded, he would laugh and say, "Why it was *just* 1926 the other day!"

HISTORY TAKES NOTES

When Copland's *Lincoln Portrait* was dropped from an inaugural concert for Eisenhower because of anti-communist protests, journalist and historian Bruce Catton noted, "If this was in the end something less than a fatal blow to the evil designs of the men in the Kremlin, it at least saved the assembled Republicans from being compelled to listen to Lincoln's brooding words [quoted in the *Portrait*]: 'Fellow-citizens, we cannot escape history. We of this Congress and this Administration will be remembered in spite of ourselves.'"

THE ROAR OF THE CROWD

Although he came to it late in life, Copland thoroughly enjoyed conducting. He once said of the experience, "It's fun. It's well-paying. And you get applauded at the end. The orchestra does all the work and you turn around a take a bow. If you want to be nice, you ask the musicians to stand up, too, the poor dears."

PALLING AROUND WITH A DIFFERENT SORT OF MARX

Many critics said Copland demonstrated a "split personality" in his compositions. He wrote popular, hummable pieces like *Appalachian Spring*, but he also created challenging compositions such as the dodecaphonic *Connotations*. Copland was well aware of the criticism and liked to joke about it.

While he was working with the Samuel Goldwyn studio on *The North Star*, Copland gave a recital that included his Modernist Piano Sonata. During the intermission, he was introduced to the comedian Groucho Marx, who commented on the piece's modern style. "Well, you see, I have a split personality," exclaimed Copland. "It's okay, Copland," replied Marx, "as long as you split it with Samuel Goldwyn."

AND JUST WHERE *IS* THIS APPALACHIA?

The title of Copland's most famous composition wasn't settled until well after it was composed. He called the ballet that he wrote for Martha Graham "A Ballet for Martha." Here's Copland's story of what happened next:

> The first thing I said to her when I came down to the rehearsal here in Washington was, "Martha, whatdya call the ballet?" She said, "Appalachian Spring." "Oh," I said. "What a nice name. Where'd d'ya get it?" She said, "It's the title of a poem by Hart Crane." "Oh," I said. "Does the poem have anything to do with the ballet?" She said, "No, I just liked the title and I took it." And over and over again, nowadays people come up to me after seeing the ballet on stage and say, "Mr. Copland, when I see that ballet and when I hear your music I can just *see* the Appalachians and *feel* spring." I've begun to see the Appalachians myself a little bit.

Jazz

Antonín Dvořák was remarkably prescient when he called for American composers to base their work on the folk music of African-Americans. The music of slaves and their descendants became, in time, America's most significant contribution to world music.

Jazz started in New Orleans, where Dixieland brass bands played ragtime tunes with a rambunctious spirit. Jazz can be extremely difficult to define, but even at the start, improvisation, syncopation, blue notes, and polyrhythms contributed to its distinctive sound. In the 1910s, African-Americans brought it north to Chicago and New York, and from there it spread across the United States. Dixieland transformed into swing in the 1930s (think Count Basie and Tommy Dorsey), bebop in the 1940s (Charlie Parker, Dizzie Gillespie, and Thelonius Monk), and cool jazz in the 1950s (Miles Davis, Dave Brubeck, and Chet Baker). Latin jazz of the '60s incorporated Brazilian and Afro-Cuban instruments and melodies, and jazz fusion incorporated rock-and-roll rhythms and electronic instruments in the '70s.

From the start, classically trained musicians adopted jazz elements. Today it can be hard to hear the jazz influences in works like Ravel's *Boléro*, but his audiences certainly heard it—and they didn't always approve. Gershwin was the composer most closely allied with jazz—*Rhapsody in Blue* was intended as a jazz concerto—but Copland and Bernstein also wrote jazz-influenced music.

Some jazz artists repaid the favor by incorporating traditional European elements in their music. Duke Ellington moved beyond jazz into what he called simply "American music," with extended compositions such as "Black, Brown, and Beige," a jazz suite that tells the story of African-Americans. And the Modern Jazz Quartet combined jazz with a thorough understanding of Baroque counterpoint; they wrote dazzling fugues of bop- and swing-era standards.

Somewhere up there, Dvořák is smiling—and maybe tapping his foot to the beat.

DMITRY SHOSTAKOVICH

SEPTEMBER 25, 1906–AUGUST 9, 1975

ASTROLOGICAL SIGN:
LIBRA

NATIONALITY:
SOVIET RUSSIAN

MUSICAL STYLE:
MODERN

STANDOUT WORKS:
WALTZ NO. 2 FROM *SUITE FOR VARIETY STAGE ORCHESTRA*

WHERE YOU'VE HEARD IT:
AS THE CREDIT MUSIC FOR THE 1999 MOVIE *EYES WIDE SHUT*

"IF THEY CUT OFF BOTH HANDS, I WILL COMPOSE MUSIC ANYWAY HOLDING THE PEN IN MY TEETH."

QUOTABL

I magine playing a game in which no one tells you the rules, yet the price for breaking the rules is death.

This was the life of composer Dmitry Shostakovich. Hailed as a remarkable talent, he spent his life playing the dangerous game of life as a public figure in the Soviet Union. Sometimes crowds praised his brilliance and rejoiced in his compositions; other times *Pravda* attacked his works, performances of his music were banned, and his own ten-year-old son was forced to denounce him.

Many of his friends and colleagues died or ended up in the brutal gulags—but Shostakovich survived. He played the terrifying game and poured all his anguish into powerful, profound music that still has things to teach about the toll totalitarianism takes on the soul.

No Laughing Matter

When Revolution first shook Russia, the Shostakovich family were professionals living in St. Petersburg, nurturing their clearly brilliant son Dmitry. In later years, official biographers said Shostakovich was among the crowd that met Lenin at the St. Petersburg train station on his return from exile. Nice story, but completely unbelievable—Shostakovich was only ten years old at the time. The reality is that although the Shostakoviches weren't diehard Communists; they celebrated the revolution as the end of a corrupt and repressive regime.

Shostakovich entered the Petrograd Conservatory in 1919. The 1920s were grim years. At the unheated Conservatory, students wore coats, hats, and heavy gloves to classes, only taking off their gloves to write exercises. Nevertheless, Shostakovich dazzled teachers and fellow students with his First Symphony, which premiered to general acclaim on May 12, 1926.

Not long afterward, he was selected to represent the Soviet Union at the Chopin piano competition in Warsaw, but before he could go, he was required to pass a course in Marxist methodology. Shostakovich seems to have not taken this class very seriously. When another student was asked to explain the difference between the music of Liszt and Chopin on sociological and economic grounds, Shostakovich burst out laughing. He failed the exam. Fortunately, he was able appeal the decision and re-take the test with a straight face. In the future, he would learn not to be so glib about politics.

Stalin Is Not Amused

In 1932, Shostakovich married the physicist Nina Varzar. Their daughter, Galina, was born in 1936 and their son, Maxim, in 1938. Meanwhile, pressure had begun to build on Soviet artists to embrace social realism, a Leninist movement that claimed art should expose the crimes of capitalism and praise the benefits of socialism. Formalist "art for art's sake" was to be firmly stamped out, as well as complicated, confusing modernism; factory workers and farmers needed to be able to understand and appreciate art, not just the intelligentsia.

Around 1930, Shostakovich tried to marry these demands with the inclinations of his own creativity. The resulting opera, *Lady Macbeth of the Mtsensk District*, tells the tale of a nineteenth-century provincial merchant's wife who becomes so unhinged by her repressive capitalist life that she starts murdering her neighbors. The opera opened in January 1934 and was a huge hit.

On January 26, 1936, the opera hosted its most esteemed guest when Joseph Stalin and his entourage arrived. Ominously, the Supreme Leader walked out before the end. Two days later, Shostakovich opened *Pravda* to see an unsigned editorial titled "Muddle Instead of Music." It denounced *Lady Macbeth* as consisting of a "deliberately dissonant, muddled stream of sounds." Rather than being "genuine" music the Soviet masses could understand, this was "formalism" designed to appeal to the unwholesome tastes of the bourgeoisie. Lest Shostakovich miss the threat, the editorial concluded, "This is a game . . . that may end very badly."

Shostakovich quickly realized how precarious his position was as like-minded friends and colleagues were imprisoned, questioned, and sent to the gulags. Shoskakovich's mother-in-law was sent to a labor camp and his sister was exiled to Central Asia. Writer Maxim Gorky died under suspicious circumstances while enduring house arrest. It was all part of Stalin's Great Terror, during which nearly two million people died.

But Shostakovich survived. He kept his head down and his mouth shut. He had been at work on his Fourth Symphony when the *Pravda* article came out. When it became clear in rehearsal that the work's dark and dissonant ending failed to celebrate a glorious socialist future, Shostakovich withdrew it from performance.

He began his rehabilitation with his Fifth Symphony, which premiered on November 21, 1937. It's not an exaggeration to say that his life was at stake. But Shostakovich had transformed his style from dense and dissonant to accessible and harmonic. Described as depicting "a lengthy spiritual battle, crowed by victory," the work was an immediate triumph. Some observers—particularly those in the West—saw the symphony as capitulation. But the response of most Russians was identification with the work's assertion of will in the face of absolute terror.

Take That, Germany!

When Hitler marched his troops across the Soviet border in June, 1941, Shostakovich immediately volunteered for the army. Appallingly nearsighted, he was of no use to the military, so he joined the Home Guard and dug ditches around Leningrad. As German troops came closer, friends urged him to leave, but he stubbornly stayed put until he was ordered to evacuate to remote Kuybïshev.

He began his Seventh Symphony while still in Leningrad, and as the siege dragged on, he poured all his anxieties into the score. The symphony had its premiere in Kuybïshev, followed by performances across the U.S.S.R., all of which were celebrated as Russia's defiant response to the Nazi threat. Russia's allies also clamored to hear the work, so the score was transferred to microfilm and sent to New York by a circuitous route through Tehran, Cairo, and South America. Toscanini conducted the Western premiere on July 19, 1942, and *Time* magazine ran a photo of Shostakovich on its cover.

The people of Leningrad wanted to hear "their" symphony, too, so military aircraft slipped the score into the besieged city. The Leningrad Radio Orchestra assembled to rehearse the work, but only fifteen musicians showed up for the first session. A call went out to the front lines for anyone who could play an instrument. So desperate were conditions in the city that three members of the orchestra died of starvation before the premiere. To forestall German disruption of the performance, a Soviet bombardment was scheduled shortly beforehand. Russian soldiers rigged loudspeakers to broadcast the symphony into the no-man's-land between enemy lines. Music was an act of war, and Shostakovich was a wartime hero.

OK, I Take It Back

During the war, government attention was distracted by more pressing matters such as defeating Hitler, so for a time Shostakovich had some creative

breathing space. It was during this interlude that he wrote somber, melan-choly works such as his Eighth Symphony. This short-lived period of relative freedom ended in January, 1948. Leningrad party chief and Stalin favorite Andrei Zhdanov summoned composers for a three-day session of attacks on "formalism."

Long gone were the days when Shostakovich could laugh at Marxist methodology. He publicly apologized for his composing errors, saying, "When . . . the Party and all of our country condemn this direction in my creative work, I know that the Party is right." Nevertheless, the Central Committee banned many of his works and fired him from his job at the Conservatory. Ten-year-old Maxim Shostakovich was forced to denounce his father at school, and Shostakovich spent his nights sitting in the elevator landing out-side his apartment, so that if he were to be arrested, at least his family wouldn't be harmed.

HEART ATTACKS, KIDNEY STONES, AND LUNG CANCER WERE ONLY A FEW OF SHOSTAKOVICH'S PROBLEMS. NOTHING HELPED—NOT EVEN A LENINGRAD "SORCERESS" WHO PRACTICED LAYING ON OF HANDS.

A year later, the disgraced composer received a strange order: He was told he would represent the Soviet Union at the Cultural and Scientific Congress for World Peace in New York. Shostakovich resisted until he got a phone call from Stalin himself. Shostakovich summoned all his courage to ask how he could rep-resent his country when his country banned his music. It was one of the most courageous actions of Shostakovich's life, and Stalin promptly rescinded the order forbidding Shostakovich's compositions.

Nevertheless, the trip to New York was a nightmare. Every time Shostakovich opened his mouth, he made headlines. Soviet minders fol-lowed him wherever he went, demonstrators walked in front of his hotel room shouting for him to defect, and American conference participants tried to prompt candid confessions. When composer Morton Gould managed some-how to get him alone, he muttered, "It's hot in here," and walked away.

When Stalin died in 1953, political tensions finally began to ease across the Soviet Union. Within months, Shostakovich was able to premiere works completed years before but never performed. But he never really recovered from the blows of the Stalin years.

If You Can't Beat Them, Join Them

Nina Shostakovich had become a respected physicist in the field of cosmic radiation. While working at a remote research station in Armenia, she fell suddenly ill in December, 1954. She was diagnosed with colon cancer and died. The intelligent and pragmatic Nina had been Shostakovich's best supporter, and he was devastated by her loss and overwhelmed with the care of his two teenage children.

His friends knew the depth of his devotion to Nina, so they were surprised when he abruptly remarried in the summer of 1956. Margarita Kainova was a thirty-two-year-old Komonsol (Communist Youth) instructor; she restored order to the Shostakovich household but seemed to have little interest in her husband's music. They divorced in less than three years. In 1962, Shostakovich married for the third time. His new wife was Irina Supinskaya, a charming, intelligent twenty-seven-year-old who proved a much better match.

In 1960, Shostakovich joined the Community Party, a move that mystified friends and colleagues. His wife later said he had been blackmailed, and other sources report his saying, "I am scared to death of them." Now when young composers spoke of stretching their wings and testing the limits of authority, he told them, "Don't waste your efforts. Work, play. You're living here, in this country, and you must see everything as it really is."

Starting in the late 1950s, Shostakovich suffered ill-health, including weakness in his right hand that made it impossible to play the piano and difficult to write. He was diagnosed with polio, but is now believed to have suffered from ALS, or Lou Gehrig's disease. His condition made it difficult to get around—he fell frequently, and broke both of his legs. In the 1970s, his whole body seemed to be failing. He suffered repeated heart attacks, endured kidney stones, and was diagnosed with lung cancer. Shostakovich turned to all available sources for help, including a Leningrad "sorceress" who practiced laying on of hands. Nothing worked. He died on August 9, 1975.

Assessment of Shostakovich's legacy has shifted over the years. Many in the West—and a few in the Soviet Union—once condemned him as a propagandist who gave in to political pressure at the cost of his art; others searched his music for anti-Stalinist themes and depicted him as a closet dissident. Neither portrayal really fits. In the words of a recent critic, "Black-and-white categories make no sense in the shadowland of dictatorship."

COMPOSER TO THE STARS

On April 12, 1961, Yuri Gagarin, the first cosmonaut, sang the Shostakovich song, "My homeland hears, my homeland knows where in the skies her son soars on." Shostakovich was the first composer to have his work performed extraterrestrially.

HAPPINESS IS A COLD GLASS OF VODKA

Mstislav Rostropovich, widely considered to be one of the best cellists of the twentieth century, tells the following story about Shostakovich:

> He gave me the manuscript of the First Cello Concerto on 2 August 1958. On the sixth I played it to him from memory, three times. After the first time he was *so* excited, and of course we drank a little bit of vodka. The second time I played not so perfect, and afterwards we drank even more vodka. The third time I *think* I played the Saint-Saëns concerto, but he still accompanied *his* concerto. We were enormously happy.

SAMUEL BARBER

MARCH 9, 1910–JANUARY 23, 1981

ASTROLOGICAL SIGN:
PISCES

NATIONALITY:
AMERICAN

MUSICAL STYLE:
NEO-ROMANTIC

STANDOUT WORKS:
ADAGIO FOR STRINGS

WHERE YOU'VE HEARD IT:
AS SGT. ELIAS IS SHOT DOWN BY THE VIET CONG IN THE 1986
ACADEMY AWARD-WINNING FILM *PLATOON*

"HOW AWFUL THAT THE ARTIST HAS
BECOME NOTHING BUT THE AFTER-DINNER
MINT OF SOCIETY."

QUOTABL

*I*t takes a certain kind of personality to go against the flow, and in mid-twentieth-century America, modern music had the force of a riptide. At conservatories from California to Maine, aspiring composers embraced the innovations of Schoenberg and Stravinsky and rejected the earlier musical traditions as outdated, hackneyed, even anachronistic.

Faced with this kind of peer pressure, most people would give in and start writing tone rows. But not Samuel Barber. He didn't argue or protest—he just went his own way. Music critics were appalled and conservatories were outraged, but audiences ate it up. Barber wrote music they understood. How radical!

Please God, Don't Make Me Play Football

The Barber family of West Chester, Pennsylvania, lived a comfortable life. Roy Barber was a doctor who served on the board of trustees of the First Presbyterian Church. The family found eldest son Sam's passion for music baffling and encouraged him to enjoy the normal activities of an American kid—but even at age nine, Sam knew his own mind. He wrote his mother:

> Dear Mother: I have written this to tell you my worrying secret. Now don't cry when you read it, because it is neither yours nor my fault. I suppose I will have to tell it now without any nonsense. To begin with I was not meant to be an athlet. I was meant to be a composer, and will be I'm sure. I'll ask you one more thing.—Don't ask me to try to forget this unpleasant thing and go play football.—*Please*— Sometimes I've been worrying about this so much that it makes me very mad (not very).

There was no more talk about football. The Barbers arranged for their son to have advanced lessons at the Curtis Institute of Music in Philadelphia while he was still in high school.

Once Barber started at Curtis full-time, he also began regular summer trips to Europe. He fell in love with the Old World, particularly Italy—where it helped that he had a ready-made translator in fellow Curtis student and Italian native Gian Carlo Menotti. In Menotti, Barber also found a close friend and life partner. Although the stigma against homosexuality remained strong in the 1930s, Barber and Menotti lived together in peace by keeping a low profile.

Barber began composing seriously at Curtis and pursued his own path with confidence and dedication. He found inspiration in the old masters and paid little attention to the harmonic experiments of Stravinsky, the twelve-tone innovations of Schoenberg, or the jazz-inspired stylings of Gershwin. If sonatas and fugues were good enough Brahms, they were good enough for Barber.

Meet the Maestro

Barber owed his greatest success in part to the Italian conductor Arturo Toscanini. In 1933, he and Menotti visited Toscanini at his summer villa, and Barber so impressed the maestro that he offered to perform one of Barber's works. A consummate perfectionist, Barber worked for several years before he produced a work he thought worthy of Toscanini's attention, but in 1937 he finally sent the conductor the scores for two pieces, *Essay for Orchestra* and *Adagio for Strings*. A few months later Toscanini returned the scores without comment.

SAMUEL BARBER'S LAVISH OPERA ADAPTATION OF SHAKESPEARE'S *ANTONY AND CLEOPATRA* WAS A FLOP.

Barber and Menotti had planned to visit Toscanini later that summer, but Barber was so hurt, he sent Menotti alone. The conductor met Menotti and asked him about his friend. "Well, he's not feeling very well," Menotti replied, tactfully. Toscanini laughed. "I don't believe that," he said, "He's mad at me. Tell him not to be mad. I'm not going to play *one* of his pieces. I'm going to play *both*." In fact, Toscanini had returned the scores because he had them memorized. Barber's works had their premiere under Toscanini's baton with the NBC Symphony Orchestra, on a nationwide radio broadcast on November 5, 1938.

The *Adagio* received mixed reviews. Some found it refreshing that Barber had ignored modernist innovations: "Must a work be cacophonous in order to be of today?" wrote one critic. Others deplored the composition as hackneyed and stale. Audiences, on the other hand, loved *Adagio for Strings*.

Gone to Texas

The bombing of Pearl Harbor brought Barber's composing to an abrupt end. His poor eyesight made combat duty out of the question, so he enlisted in noncombatant service, hoping that once he joined the military he could find a way to combine service to his country with making music.

His first assignment was a desk job in New York. The work was boring and he had hours of free time, but his supervisor refused to let him compose in a vacant office because it would set a bad precedent. He managed, finally, to interest higher-ups in a project to compose a symphony dedicated to the Army Air Corps. So in 1943, Private First Class Barber was transferred to air corps headquarters in Fort Worth, Texas, and ordered to report to General Barton K. Yount. No one was expecting him and few understood why Washington had sent them a composer. But when General Yount finally saw Barber's orders, he decided that the bigwigs in Washington were behind the proposed symphony. He gave the composer his full backing and allowed him to do most of the work from home.

The delighted Barber went to work on his Second Symphony, nicknamed the *Flight Symphony*. Serge Koussevitsky and the Boston Symphony Orchestra premiered the symphony on March 3, 1944, just a few days before Barber's thirty-fourth birthday.

Puttin' on the Glitz

The postwar years saw Barber's reputation as a composer continue to grow. He wrote numerous orchestral and chamber works. He also wanted to write an opera, but he had a terrible time finding a libretto. Finally Menotti, an experienced librettist as well as composer, agreed to write one. The result was *Vanessa*, which premiered at the Met on January 15, 1958, and was an immediate success.

The Met invited Barber to compose a new opera for the opening of their new opera house in 1966. Barber decided the work would be based on Shakespeare's *Antony and Cleopatra*, his favorite play. Friends tried to dissuade him, pointing out that Shakespeare's plots rarely translated well to the opera stage. Even Menotti objected, and the resulting dispute was, Menotti later said, the most tenuous period of their relationship. Barber forged head, joined by Franco Zeffirelli, who had been brought on board by the Met as the director and librettist. Zeffirelli delighted in spectacle and wrote an extravagant libretto for an elaborate, lush opera.

Preparations took years. Soprano Leontyne Price went into near-seclusion for a year to prepare for the part of Cleopatra. Zeffirelli designed massive sets that included a huge sphinx and massive pyramids. A 57-foot turntable constructed to change scenes quit working a week before the performance and had to be turned by a stage crew in Egyptian costume. The live animals, including three horses, two camels, and an elephant, made so much noise backstage that they drowned out the orchestra. The premiere consisted of one disaster after another. Lighting cues misfired, so Price made her first entrance on a pitch-black stage. Later she was supposed to emerge from a pyramid, but the pyramid wouldn't open, so she sang an entire aria out of the audience's sight. Worst of all, Zeffirelli's extravaganza overwhelmed Barber's spare, elegant music.

It was a disaster.

Cue the Strings

Barber wasn't prepared for failure. He had received some negative reviews and the occasional snub, but his career had been one success after another. Now the *Antony and Cleopatra* fiasco made headlines around the world. He was humiliated.

He had other worries, too. Menotti had decided to spend less time in the United States, which meant that the couple had to sell their beloved house, Capricorn, north of New York City. Even after Barber bought an apartment in Manhattan, he still mourned the house's loss: "I really feel as if I have no home," he wrote. Friends worried about how much time he spent alone and how much he was drinking. He tried yoga and studied Buddhism, but nothing seemed to lift his depression.

In 1978, Barber was diagnosed with multiple myeloma, a cancer of the lymphatic system; he received chemotherapy treatments, but the disease took its toll. He died on January 23, 1981.

In his lifetime, Samuel Barber saw his *Adagio for Strings* become one of the most popular pieces of classical music in the world. Its aching sadness portrayed the sorrow of millions at the funeral of Franklin Delano Roosevelt and after John F. Kennedy's assassination. It's a piece that resonates to this day, forever immortalized in the score of Oliver Stone's Vietnam film *Platoon*. Former PFC Barber, who never saw combat, might have been surprised to know that his work would accompany some of the most gut-wrenching war scenes ever filmed.

THAT'S ONE SMASHING CELLO SOLO

In 1950, Barber was invited to record his Cello Concerto with Decca Records in England. The esteemed Zara Nelsova played the solo cello, amazing everyone with her mastery of the difficult score—particularly the orchestra cellists, who understood how truly challenging the piece was.

When Nelsova finished a particularly stunning passage, one of the orchestra's cellists suddenly leapt to his feet and shouted that he was giving up the instrument after hearing her play. He swung up his cello and smashed it on the side of stage. Splintered wood and strings flew everywhere.

The orchestra gasped, and Nelsova turned deathly pale. Then the entire cello section burst out laughing. The whole thing was a joke. The orchestra members had purchased a cheap cello in a pawn shop, to be smashed on cue. Nelsova accepted this tribute to her skill from her peers, and the recording session continued.

MUSIC FOR SHREDDER AND STRINGS

After the momentous premiere of his Second Symphony during World War II, Barber began to fret over imperfections in the score. He went to work on revisions as early as 1946, with the revised symphony debuting in 1949. Barber seemed satisfied by the new version, writing, "At last it is right."

But his evaluation of the score didn't last. In 1964, he decided that the reason the symphony was rarely performed was that it wasn't any good. So convinced was he that the work shouldn't be played that he went to the music library of his publisher, Schirmer's, and personally ripped all of the scores to shreds.

Barber believed he had eliminated all copies of the symphony, but in 1984 a full set of orchestra parts turned up in a Schirmer warehouse in England. The New Zealand Symphony Orchestra recorded the work, and in 1990 Schirmer re-released the score. So much for the composer's wishes.

JOHN CAGE

SEPTEMBER 5, 1912–AUGUST 12, 1992

ASTROLOGICAL SIGN:
VIRGO

NATIONALITY:
AMERICAN

MUSICAL STYLE:
EXPERIMENTAL

STANDOUT WORKS:
4'33"

WHERE YOU'VE HEARD IT:
YOU PROBABLY HAVEN'T

"I AM GOING TOWARD VIOLENCE RATHER THAN
TENDERNESS, HELL RATHER THAN HEAVEN, UGLY
RATHER THAN BEAUTIFUL, IMPURE RATHER THAN
PURE—BECAUSE BY DOING THESE THINGS THEY
BECOME TRANSFORMED, AND WE BECOME TRANSFORMED."

QUOTABLE

Big egos and great composers go hand in hand. Wagner certainly had ego to spare, as did everyone from Beethoven to Bernstein. The tendency of most composers is to indulge their will, even to celebrate it.

Not John Cage. He wanted to eliminate his ego altogether. A dedicated practitioner of Zen Buddhism, Cage believed that he could truly create only when he got his intentions and desires out of the way. The resulting compositions transformed the history of music and challenged audiences to wrestle with what was and was not music.

Don't Fence Me In

John Milton Cage Senior made his living as an inventor, developing such innovations as an early submarine, a radio powered by alternating current, and a color television. Unfortunately, Cage failed to patent his inventions properly, so the Cage family had little money and moved frequently in search of cheap housing. Their only child, John Milton Cage II, lived in half a dozen houses in his childhood, spending his middle- and high-school years in and around Los Angeles.

Cage was the valedictorian of his class at Los Angeles High School in 1928. He had considered becoming a Methodist minister, but by the time he entered Pomona College he wanted to write. His free spirit wasn't cut out for standardized education, so he dropped out of college. Music was his passion, but traditional composing had no appeal for him. Then he attended some concerts of work by Stravinsky, and he realized that music didn't have to be Bach or Beethoven. It could be something far more modern.

Cage sought out avant-garde teachers and eventually achieved his ultimate goal and met Arnold Schoenberg. He begged Schoenberg for lessons, but Schoenberg dismissed him, saying, "You probably can't afford my price." Cage replied that he couldn't afford any price, because he had no money at all. Schoenberg took him on anyway, figuring someone so bold had to have talent to match.

Both teacher and student soon realized they had entirely different ideas about music. Schoenberg might have been a modernist pioneer, but he believed in rules and structure, whereas Cage thought rules existed only to be broken. Matters came to a head when Schoenberg told Cage he would never succeed because he had no sense of harmony. Harmony, Schoenberg decreed, would be the wall through which Cage could not pass. "In that case I will devote my life to beating my head against that wall," countered Cage.

In Love and War

Cage was married to a tall, elegant young woman named Xenia Kashevaroff in 1935, and a few years later the couple moved to Seattle so that Cage could work at the Cornish School as a dance accompanist. There he met Mercier (later Merce) Cunningham, a talented young male dancer, and the two became good friends. Cage worked on composing percussion-only pieces, making instruments out of everything from pipes to Chinese gongs suspended in water. One experiment led to another, and soon he tried changing a piano's tone by adding metal plates, screws, strips of rubber, and sheets of paper behind or on top of the strings. The resulting instrument became known as "prepared piano." He also became interested in the potential of recorded sound in music; *Imaginary Landscape no. 1* of 1939 calls for two variable speed turntables on which single-frequency radio test records are played at various speeds.

In 1942, Cage and Xenia moved to New York City, although they often had to sleep on the floors of friends' apartments. Even after they got their own place, Cage's life was unsettled. There was the war, for one thing. Cage's parents had moved to New Jersey, and his father was at work on submarine sonar detection systems. Cage Senior hired his son to do library research for him, and since the work contributed to the war effort, Cage Junior was exempted from the draft.

But more disruptive was Cage's realization that he was in love with Merce Cunningham. Cage never discussed this topic, so no one knows the exact process by which he divorced Xenia and became Merce's lover, but he later admitted in what has to be an understatement that it was a "disturbing time."

This Is Your Brain on Silence

What rescued Cage from chaos was a series of lectures on Zen that he attended in the late 1940s. He had once wanted to be a Methodist minister, but he embraced Zen teachings on accepting the flow of life and also saw their applications for music. He began to describe his music as "purposeless play": "This play is an affirmation of life—not an attempt to bring order out of chaos, nor to suggest improvements in creation, but simply to wake up to the very life we are living."

Cage decided the problem with Western music was that the ego of the composer got in the way. He decided that music should be purposeless—but composing without purpose was a challenge. Cage's solution was to turn to the I Ching, an ancient Chinese text used as an oracular guide. Cage discovered he could use the I Ching to "write" music without inserting his own will into the process. He created charts containing blocks of music—various sounds, instruments, and/or tempos—and then assembled music from the blocks by flipping coins and consulting the I Ching. He would later employ other randomizers such as star charts and computer-generated numbers.

Zen emphasizes the incorporation of opposites (yin and yang), so Cage became as interested in silences as in sounds. While visiting Harvard, he spent time in an anechoic chamber, a space designed to be as soundproof as possible. He entered the room expecting to hear absolute nothingness, but was annoyed to find that two sounds persisted: a singing high tone and a low pulse. Assuming something was wrong with the room, he went in search of the engineer in charge. No, the engineer said, there's nothing wrong with the room; what Cage heard was his own body, the high hum of his nervous system and the low throb of his heart and circulation.

Cage decided to experiment with the idea that silence is never really

ON AN ITALIAN TV SHOW, CAGE BEWILDERED AUDIENCES BY PERFORMING "WATER WALK," IN WHICH HE PLAYED INSTRUMENTS SUCH AS A BLENDER, A GOOSE WHISTLE, AND A BOTTLE OF CAMPARI.

silent. And so, on August 29, 1952, at a concert in Woodstock, New York, pianist David Tudor premiered Cage's *4'33"*. Tudor walked onstage, put the score on the piano, and set a stopwatch. The he sat in silence. Periodically, Tudor got up and opened or closed the lid of the piano to mark the end of the three different movements. When his time was up, he walked off the stage.

Skeptics dismissed the piece as a stunt and noted that anyone could have written it. Yes, Cage responded, but no one else did. With *4'33"*, he had entered music history by *composing* four minutes and thirty-three seconds of silence.

At One with Modernity

As the years went on, Cage continued to innovate with new sounds, new technologies, and new critiques of traditional music. His five *Europeras*, composed between 1987 and 1990, deconstruct the genre by combining operatic elements such as plot, characters, settings, and songs via chance.

In the 1970s Cage adopted a macrobiotic diet and gave up smoking and drinking, so he approached his late seventies in excellent health. Plans were made for a major eightieth birthday celebration, but a week before the event his assistant found him unconscious in his apartment; he had had a massive stroke. Cage died on August 12, 1992.

You rarely hear the works of John Cage performed in concert halls—his innovations never caught on with the general public. But it would be wrong to think that he didn't change music. He essentially invented experimental music, electronic music, and art music. He influenced figures such as Philip Glass, Laurie Anderson, and Brian Eno. It's not surprising for composers today to include recorded sounds, an invented instrument, or a prepared piano in an orchestral piece.

That's a lot of impact for a guy who just wanted to go with the flow.

A REAL FUNGI

In 1954, Cage moved to a sort of commune in rural Rockland County about an hour outside of New York City. He loved taking long walks in the woods where, invariably, he happened upon prolific growths of mushrooms. Cage got curious about fungi. He befriended a leader of a local 4-H Club who taught him about mushroom identification, and before long, mushrooms were his passion. The members of Merce Cunningham's traveling dance company got used to stopping at odd moments on the side of the road so that Cage could forage for morels.

WHO WANTS TO BE A MILLIONAIRE, ITALIAN STYLE

His mushroom fixation paid off on a trip to Italy in 1959 when Cage appeared on a popular television quiz show, *Lascia o Raddoppia*. Each contestant was asked questions on a topic of his or her choice; as the weeks went on, the questions got increasingly difficult. If you got every question right for five weeks, you won five million lire— about eight thousand dollars. Cage convinced the show to let him perform his music before he answered the questions. After bewildering Italians with new pieces such as *Water Walk*, in which he played a Waring blender, a goose whistle, and a bottle of Campari, Cage blew them away by answering every single mushroom question correctly, week after week.

On the last show, Cage was sequestered in a glass isolation booth and asked to name every type of white-spored mushroom. He started to recite them slowly in alphabetical order, only to realize that the crowd was frantically pointing above his head: There was a time limit, and the clock was ticking (albeit out of his sight). Cage simply kept reciting and finished with only a fraction of a second to spare. He won the jackpot. After taxes and exchange transactions, Cage returned to the United States with $6,000—the most money he had ever made in his life—certainly more than he had ever made for his music.

In 1964, Cage was given the North American Mycological Association's Award for Contributions to Amateur Mycology: "Given annually to recognize a person who has contributed extraordinarily to the advancement of amateur mycology." He is the only musician to ever receive the award.

PLAY, REPEAT. PLAY, REPEAT. PLAY, REPEAT . . .

Cage didn't have much use for earlier composers, but he appreciated Frenchman Eric Satie. A contemporary of Debussy, Satie outdid even Cage in his eccentricities: He had an entire wardrobe of identical gray velvet suits and owned more than one hundred umbrellas. His music included such piano compositions as *Embryons desséchés* ("Dried-up Embryos") and *Sonatine Bureucratique*; his instructions to performers recommend playing "light as an egg" or "dry as a cuckoo."

Cage became enamored of Satie on his first trip to Europe, and in 1963 he decided to premiere Satie's composition *Vexations*: a simple, short piano piece that contains the instruction "to be repeated 840 times."

At six o'clock on the evening of September 9, Cage's friend Viola Farber sat down and started *Vexations*. At eight o'clock, another friend, Robert Wood, slid onto the piano bench and picked up where Farber left off. Eleven people in all took two-hour shifts. Audience members came and went; the *New York Times* staff writer fell asleep. The event finally wrapped up at 12:40 on September 11—the longest piano concert in history.

LEONARD BERNSTEIN

AUGUST 25, 1918–OCTOBER 14, 1990

ASTROLOGICAL SIGN:
VIRGO

NATIONALITY:
AMERICAN

MUSICAL STYLE:
NEO-ROMANTIC

STANDOUT WORK:
"I FEEL PRETTY" FROM *WEST SIDE STORY*

WHERE YOU'VE HEARD IT:
IN THE 2002 DARK COMEDY *DEATH TO SMOOCHY*

"TO ACHIEVE GREAT THINGS, TWO THINGS ARE
NEEDED: A PLAN, AND NOT QUITE ENOUGH TIME."

QUOTABLE

*T*here seemed to be nothing musical Leonard Bernstein couldn't do. Conduct? He brought out the best in orchestras. Compose classical music? Symphonies, operas—you name it, you got it. Write popular hits? Move over, Cole Porter, make room for *West Side Story*.

In fact, the only thing Bernstein couldn't do was control himself. So much talent, so much energy, so much personality—and so little discipline to keep it all in check.

Portrait of a Prodigy

Sam Bernstein arrived in America in 1908 at age sixteen, fleeing a life of misery and persecution in the Ukraine. He and his wife, Jennie, had a miserable marriage, and some of eldest son Leonard's earliest memories were of hiding with his sister Shirley while their parents fought. At Sam's insistence, Lenny attended the prestigious prep school Boston Latin and went to Harvard. His musical skills amazed friends and professors alike; he could sight-read anything and seemed to know theory by instinct. His compositions ranged from songs to symphonic overtures.

Bernstein said his future was decided when he met the conductor Dmitry Mitropolous, who half-promised him a job as assistant at the Minneapolis Symphony Orchestra if he trained in conducting. Bernstein enrolled at the Curtis Institute of Music in Philadelphia, where he was taught conducting by Fritz Reiner. Reiner pushed his students to know every note of a score before conducting it. When students practiced with a record player, Reiner would suddenly lift up the record needle and ask, "What note is the second clarinet supposed to be playing?" Bernstein could handle it— he was the only student Reiner ever gave an "A."

Breaking into the Big Time

Mitropoulos blew off Bernstein in the summer of 1939, leaving him at loose ends until he learned Boston Symphony conductor Serge Koussevitzky would teach conducting at the newly formed Tanglewood Music Festival. Koussevitzky's teaching little resembled Reiner's—he brought in a ballet master to teach pirouettes—but the combination of Reiner's rigor and Koussevitzky's body sense gave Bernstein an unmatched combination of skills.

Nevertheless, when he graduated from Curtis, Bernstein couldn't find a job. Mitropoulos had blown him off again, and no other orchestras were interested. World War II broke out, but Bernstein's asthma meant he was designated 4-F and exempted from service. In 1943 Artur Rodzinski, the new musical director of the New York Philharmonic, offered Bernstein a job as assistant conductor. Although it was enormously gratifying for the twenty-five-year-old, the job didn't promise much public exposure—Bernstein expected to lead rehearsals at most.

However, on the morning of November 14, Bernstein got a phone call. Bruno Walter, the Philharmonic's guest conductor, had the flu. Bernstein would have to conduct the Sunday afternoon program, which would be broadcast nationwide by CBS. Without rehearsing, Bernstein stepped in front of the New York Philharmonic and completely blew them all away. It was the most amazing conducting premiere in generations.

Broadway Will Have to Wait

Bernstein had always composed in his spare time. In 1942, he completed his Symphony no. 1, *Jeremiah*, based on the story of the Hebrew prophet. Observing his friend Aaron Copland's success with ballet music, Bernstein composed *Fancy Free* with Jerome Robbins in 1944. The ballet tells the story of three sailors with one day's shore leave in New York City. The ballet was a big hit, so Bernstein and Robbins teamed up with Betty Comden and Adolph Green to write a Broadway musical based on the same story. Bernstein had to have surgery to repair a deviated septum and Green needed his tonsils removed, so they had their surgeries at the same time and shared a hospital room. Nurses came and went as creative collaboration forged ahead. *On the Town* premiered on Broadway on December 28, 1944—and ran for 483 performances.

On opening night, Koussevitzky came backstage and raked Bernstein over the coals for squandering his talents. Koussevitzky wanted him to take over at the Boston Philharmonic when he retired, but that wouldn't happen if Bernstein got sucked into what the Russian Koussevitzky called "jezz."

Bernstein took his mentor's advice seriously—he seemed to want classical recognition more than popular fame. So he built up his conducting resume by touring concert halls and opera houses around Europe, becoming music director of the New York Symphony Orchestra, and serving as musical advisor to the Israel Philharmonic Orchestra.

Switch-Hitting

Some aspects of Bernstein's life were less likely to appeal to the Boston Philharmonic. His politics leaned so far left they often seemed in danger of tipping over, and the rumors about his homosexuality spread far and wide. Bernstein's secretary routinely jotted down the names and phone numbers of the men who wandered out of Bernstein's bedroom in the morning, because he tended to forget who they were. Nevertheless, women found Bernstein irresistible, and more than a few tried to get him to change teams. One, Felicia Montealegre, a Chilean-born actress, actually got him to propose. But he broke the engagement in just a few months.

Meanwhile, Koussevitzky's health was failing. He had schemed for years to have Bernstein as his replacement, but in 1948 he sensed that the philharmonic's board of directors wasn't on board. "If you don't want Bernstein," he told them, "I'll retire right now." The board promptly accepted his resignation.

> A SECRETARY JOTTED DOWN THE NAMES AND TELEPHONE NUMBERS OF THE MEN WHO WANDERED OUT OF BERNSTEIN'S BEDROOM IN THE MORNING; HE HAD A TENDENCY TO FORGET WHO THEY WERE.

Koussevitzky died in June 1951. Bernstein seemed stunned by the loss of his mentor. He got back in touch with Felicia, and the two married on September 9, 1951. They started a family right away. Their daughter, Jamie, was born in 1952.

Red-Side Story

If Bernstein hoped marriage would improve his reputation, he hadn't counted on Joseph McCarthy. In the early 1950s, his long association with liberal causes caught up with him, and he was named in the book *Red Channels* as an agent of Communist influence. Bernstein was never called for questioning by Joseph McCarthy (like Copland) or the House Un-American Activities Committee (like Jerome Robbins), but he was blacklisted in Hollywood.

One positive result of the scandal was that it got Bernstein back to Broadway—Koussevitzky was dead, and the Boston Philharmonic job had gone to someone else, so why not? He teamed up with Lillian Hellman, her-

self a victim of the blacklist, to write an operetta based on the classic French satire *Candide*. Hellman saw the work as an opportunity to expose the dark workings of McCarthyism; Bernstein saw it as a chance to write lilting, charming music. The result was a confused mish-mash, and the show closed soon after opening.

Better luck accompanied another project. For several years, Bernstein and Robbins had kicked around the idea of a modern *Romeo and Juliet*, and in 1955, the show went forward with Arthur Laurents writing the story and young Stephen Sondheim writing the lyrics. Bernstein's music contained innovative transformations and adaptations of both traditional and modern styles. The main theme of Beethoven's *Emperor* Concerto became the love song "Somewhere," and the song "Cool" contains a Schoenbergian twelve-note series in a bebop fugue. *West Side Story* opened in September 1957 and ran for 732 performances.

West Side Story vaulted Bernstein's reputation to stratospheric heights. And just as the show opened, Bernstein got the kind of job offer he'd been waiting for his entire life: the music director of the New York Philharmonic.

No Longer Living a Lie

Bernstein raised the profile of what was already one of the most famous orchestras in the world. He promoted the music of American conductors including Ives, Gershwin, and Copland, and recorded eight of Mahler's nine symphonies. He also returned to his own serious music. He wrote Symphony no. 3, *Kaddish*, in 1963 and dedicated it to the recently assassinated President Kennedy. His *Chichester Psalms*, setting three Biblical psalms in Hebrew, debuted in May 1965; simple and beautiful, the *Psalms* are among Bernstein's most popular orchestral works. He led the philharmonic for ten triumphant years.

Yet at the height of his fame, cracks appeared on the surface of his outwardly conventional personal life. Bernstein couldn't keep away from men. Felicia kept a stiff upper lip; she decorated the couple's homes with elegant furniture and tasteful flower arrangements and threw a hell of a party. As the years went on, however, those parties usually ended with her husband alone in a back bedroom with another man. One day, when Bernstein's youngest daughter, Nina, was walking to school, she passed a copy of the New York *Daily News* with the blaring headline "BERNSTEIN & WIFE SPLIT!" Bernstein held a press conference, at which he announced, "There comes a time in life when a man must be what he really is." In the coming years, he embraced the gay rights movement and had a succession of boyfriends.

Bernstein seemed to be casting off all the old-fashioned restraints on his behavior. His *Mass* of 1971, commissioned by Jacqueline Kennedy Onassis for the opening of the Opera House at Kennedy Center in Washington, was anti-war, anti-Nixon, anti-established religion, and basically, in Bernstein's own words, a "Fuck you!" to society. Although the work ends with a hymn for universal peace, scenes include a priest hurling consecrated bread and wine to the ground in a deliberate act of sacrilege. General consensus was that the work was a gross indulgence of the composer's notorious ego.

Last Hurrahs

Bernstein, however, remained the most popular composer in the world. On December 15, 1989, he conducted Beethoven's Ninth Symphony in East Germany as part of a live broadcast to more than twenty countries and an audience of 100 million, celebrating the fall of the Berlin Wall.

In the summer of 1990 Bernstein went to Tanglewood, as he had almost every year for fifty years. His health had suffered in recent years; heavy smoking had exacerbated his asthma and he often had to take oxygen. He mounted the podium to conduct Beethoven's Seventh Symphony, even though he could barely lift his arms for the first movement and took the tempo for the second movement far too slow. During the third movement he was consumed by a coughing fit. For the fourth, however, he seemed to gather all his energy and conducted with the ferocity of the Bernstein of old. It was his last appearance on stage. He left Tanglewood for Lenox Hill Hospital and died there on October 14.

At the time of his death, Bernstein's reputation was at a low point. Many critics, biographers, and musicians believed he had frittered away his talent by spreading his gifts too thin, allowing himself to be too distracted by fame and failures to impose any discipline on his life or his composing. Today that assessment is starting to shift—a recent critic said of Bernstein that "his failure outweighed many others' successes."

THE TROUBLE WITH TENORS

Bernstein had his share of problems with musicians. When rehearsing a choir in Vienna, the conductor exploded, "I know it's the historical prerogative of the tenor to be stupid, but you, sir, have abused that privilege!"

OTHER THAN THAT, EVERYTHING'S GREAT

Bernstein felt a special bond with the musicians of Israel, and in 1947 he began an affiliation with the Israel Philharmonic that would last for decades. On his first trip to the fledging nation, he wrote of the extraordinary atmosphere in which he conducted:

> I gave a downbeat at this morning's rehearsal. It coincided with a perfectly timed explosion outside the hall. We picked ourselves up and calmly resumed our labors. We've had four incidents in two days: a kidnapping at this hotel, a train demolished, a police station blown up, a military truck bombed. But the care sitters don't put down their newspapers, the children continue to jump rope. The Arab goatherd in the square adjusts another milking bag, and I give the next downbeat. The orchestra's fine.

On his second tour in 1948, Bernstein gave concerts in Jerusalem, Tel Aviv, and Haifa, but he wanted to go farther. He set out with volunteers from the orchestra, traveling across dangerous roads and treacherous deserts to reach towns such as battle-scarred Beersheba, where he conducted the first symphony in the town's history to an audience of soldiers. In Israel, he remains a hero to this day.

GIVE HIM TIME . . .

Bernstein had his own assessment of his problems. To composer Ned Rorem, he once said, "The trouble with you and me, Ned, is that we want everyone in the world to personally love us, and of course that's impossible: You just don't *meet* everyone in the world."

TOMATO, TOMAHTO

Bernstein's name has given lots of people fits over the years: Is the last syllable pronounced "stine" or "steen?" In fact, Bernstein himself changed the pronunciation over the years. In his youth, he went by the Yiddish-sounding "Bern*steen*," but around the time he got the New York Philharmonic appointment, he switched to the more Germanic "Bern*stine*." Today "stine" is the preferred pronunciation, but neither, really, is incorrect if you allow for Bernstein's own inconsistencies.

PHILIP GLASS

JANUARY 31, 1937–

ASTROLOGICAL SIGN:
AQUARIUS

NATIONALITY:
AMERICAN

MUSICAL STYLE:
MINIMALIST/POST-MINIMALIST

STANDOUT WORK:
KOYAANISQATSI

WHERE YOU'VE HEARD IT:
IN A 2006 EPISODE OF THE SITCOM *SCRUBS*

"TRADITIONS ARE IMPLODING AND EXPLODING EVERYWHERE—EVERYTHING IS COMING TOGETHER, FOR BETTER OR WORSE, AND WE CAN NO LONGER PRETEND WE'RE ALL LIVING IN DIF- FERENT WORLDS BECAUSE WE'RE ON DIFFERENT CONTINENTS."

QUOTABL

Philip Glass entered music at a time of transition. Schoenberg's dodecaphonics had dominated American conservatories for decades, but composers had begun to feel they had reached an impasse—twelve-tone music could only get you so far, and besides, audiences hated it.

Glass tried to find a new path, one that embraced harmonies and melodies people could understand but still broke new ground. For inspiration, he turned to a variety of sources: Indian rhythms, Cage-like electronic experimentation, and progressive rock-and-roll. In the end, he would create a new style for a new era and become the most famous composer of his generation.

Fascinating Rhythm

Ben Glass, an immigrant from Lithuania, had great entrepreneurial instincts, and in the 1930s he opened a popular record store in Baltimore. Glass sold a wide range of music and was fascinated by what *didn't* sell even more than what did. His son Philip grew up listening to the unsold albums his father brought home: Bartók, Hindemith, Shostakovich. Without any planning, Philip Glass absorbed a wide range of modern and avant-garde music as well as blues, jazz, and bebop.

Young Glass excelled in music and at school. He enrolled at the Peabody Conservatory of Music as a child, an accelerated program at the University of Chicago at fifteen, and Julliard at nineteen. However, Glass was frustrated with what he was taught—composition in the states was dominated by dense Schoenbergian twelve-tone music. He decided to concentrate on the basics of harmony and counterpoint, and so headed for Paris to study with Nadia Boulanger, the esteemed music educator who had taught Aaron Copland more than forty years earlier.

In Paris, Glass befriended a wide range of intellectuals and artists including musicians, filmmakers, and actors. He married avant-garde theater director JoAnne Akalaitis in 1965. One day some buddies asked him to help out with a film project: Music for the movie *Chappaqua* was going to be based on the compositions of Indian sitar-player Ravi Shankar, but Shankar didn't know how to write a score for Western musicians. Glass's job was to listen to Shankar's music and come up with a score—but he immediately ran into trouble. The rhythms of Indian music were like nothing he had heard before, and Western notation failed to capture their essential character. Gradually, Glass realized that Indian musicians understood harmony in a completely different way. Rather than breaking rhythm down into smaller and smaller increments, Indian music built up rhythms in recurring cycles. Glass was inspired.

OK, I'll Talk! Just Make It Stop!

Glass and Akalaitis returned to New York City and soon afterward heard the music of composer Steve Reich. Inspired by the work of John Cage, Reich played with recorded music, creating fascinating effects by playing the same snippet of tape on two machines at the same time but at slightly different speeds. In compositions such as *It's Gonna Rain* (1965), recorded sounds repeat over and over, going in and out of phase with one another and creating unexpected rhythms and harmonies.

A PASSENGER ONCE READ GLASS'S TAXI-DRIVER I.D. CARD AND EXCLAIMED, "YOUNG MAN, DO YOU REALIZE YOU HAVE THE SAME NAME AS A VERY FAMOUS COMPOSER?"

Glass combined Indian-inspired rhythms and Reich-inspired repetition to create his first signature compositions. In *Two Pages for Steve Reich*, for example, Glass composed music in which a phrase or segment of a phrase repeats itself in constantly changing multiples. When downtown Manhattan audiences heard this music, they quickly saw its parallels to contemporary visual art and labeled the style "minimalism." Some critics reacted to minimalism with delight at a genuine new American sound; others expressed horror at its "mind-numbing" repetition. At a Reich concert in the 1970s, one audience member stood up and announced that he was ready to confess.

Of course, none of this paid the bills, so Glass patched together a number of jobs. He and Reich briefly formed a company called Chelsea Light Moving, carrying furniture up and down Manhattan apartment staircases. He also worked as a plumber and cab driver and generally did whatever he could to make ends meet.

The Symphony Is Not Dead Yet

In 1975, Glass's involvement with theater took a leap forward with his avant-garde opera *Einstein on the Beach.* Developed with theater producer Robert Wilson, *Einstein* deconstructs traditional theater by presenting an opera without a plot, a story without characters, and an event without momentum. Singers chant numbers and "do re mi" while icons related to Einstein's work—a train, a trial, a spaceship—appear and disappear. With the work running five hours, the audience was invited to wander in and out at will. It premiered in July 1976 in Avignon, France, and reached the United States a few months later with a two-night run at the Metropolitan Opera.

Glass hadn't originally intended *Einstein* as the beginning of a cycle, but it turned out to be the first in a trilogy of operas about visionary historical figures. *Satyagraha,* based on the early life of Mahatma Gandhi, premiered in 1980, and *Akhnaten*, based on the life of a fourteenth-century BCE Egyptian pharaoh, opened in 1983 (all the lyrics are in ancient Egyptian). In both of these works, Glass's music moved away from pure minimalism into a more melodic style.

In 1987, Glass transformed his style even further when he set out to write accessible music—in Glass's words, music that his father, who had died in 1971, would have liked. The result was his Violin Concerto, which was his first composition for traditional orchestra and soloist. In it, he employed such traditional elements as a three-movement structure and an old-fashioned counterpoint form called *passacaglia*—critics labeled it "neo-baroque."

It was the start of a streak of symphonic compositions for Glass. Most composers of his generation saw the symphony as a dying form—killed off by the social and economic transformations of World War II. A few conductors, including Dennis Russell Davies, disagreed. He pestered Glass to write a symphony for years, finally commissioning one in 1992. Glass decided to approach the composition by turning to popular music, specifically the 1977 album *Low* by David Bowie and Brian Eno. They claimed to have been inspired by Glass, so Glass flipped the tables. He adapted themes from three of the album's instrumental pieces as the basis for the symphony's three movements. *Low* was followed by seven more symphonic works, with Symphony no. 4, *Heroes,* also drawing upon a Bowie-Eno album.

Clive Barker, Meet the Dalai Lama

The 1980s and '90s saw an increasing number of moviemakers turning to Glass for soundtracks. Several early projects were low-budget art flicks, such as filmmaker Godfrey Reggio's Qatsi trilogy. In 1990, he went to work on what he thought would be a similar project: a sophisticated psychological drama based on a short story by Clive Barker. Glass created a gothic-sounding score for chorus and pipe organ. However, along the way the studio fired the original writer and transformed the movie into a run-of-the-mill Hollywood slasher flick. And so it was that audiences at *Candyman* in 1992 were treated to a first-class score for a distinctly second-class movie.

More prestigious commissions started arriving in the late 1990s such as Martin Scorcese's 1997 film *Kundun* about the Dalai Lama. This was followed by *The Truman Show* (1998), *The Hours* (2002), and *Notes on a Scandal* (2006). He received Academy Award and Golden Globe award nominations for these scores, winning a Golden Globe award in 1999 for *The Truman Show*.

Glass generally keeps his private life private. He and Akalaitis had two children, Zachary and Juliet. Akalaitis and Glass divorced in 1980, and Glass married Luba Burtyk, a doctor. They too, divorced, and Glass married a collage artist named Candy Jernigan. Jernigan died tragically in 1991 at age thirty-nine of liver cancer; the disease was diagnosed only six or seven weeks before her death. In 2001, Glass married Holly Critchlow, a restaurant manager thirty years his junior, and the couple have two children, Marlowe and Cameron. According to media reports they are now separated.

Glass remains remarkably prolific in his seventies. Along with film scores for *The Illusionist* and *Cassandra's Dream*, he recently collaborated with songwriter and poet Leonard Cohen on an adaptation of Cohen's poetry collection *Book of Longing*. And he premiered a new opera, *Appomattox*, set at the end of the Civil War.

Glass no longer considers himself a minimalist—he prefers "classicist." Whatever you call him, he has undisputedly contributed to the transformation of American classical music. He helped prove that traditional harmonies and melodies still have life in them and can be approached in new, innovative ways. His work also points to a number of trends shaping music today: incorporation of non-Western traditions, integration of electronic music with the traditional orchestra, and a breakdown of the barriers between high and low music.

PHIL THE PLUMBER

Glass had to take on a lot of odd jobs to support himself in the 1960s and '70s. One day he was installing a dishwasher in a loft in SoHo when he looked up to see *Time* magazine art critic Robert Hughes staring at him. "But you're Philip Glass!" he said. "What are you doing here?" Glass replied that it was obvious that he was installing Hughes's new dishwasher. "But you're an artist!" Hughes shouted. Glass answered that he was also a plumber and could Hughes please go away so he could get back to work.

YOU TALKIN' TO ME?

Shortly after the New York premiere of *Einstein on the Beach*, Glass was driving a taxi. A well-dressed woman got into the cab, looked at his name, and said in some surprise, "Young man, do you realize you have the same name as a very famous composer?"

RATED NV FOR NONVIOLENCE

Glass's music has not always attracted praise. After the opening of *Satyagraha*, Glass's opera about Mahatma Gandhi's life promoting passive nonviolence, opera critic Henry Heidt noted, "This opera is well named as a deeply felt commitment to passive nonviolence on the part of the audience is required to sit through a full performance."

HARD KNOCKS

The repetitive tendencies in Philip Glass's music have prompted a number of jokes about the composer. Here's one:

> Knock, knock.
> Who's there?
> Knock, knock.
> Who's there?
> Knock, knock.
> Who's there?
> Philip Glass.
>
> You get the idea.

Video Game Music

Just when you think classical music is dead, it pops up in a new, unexpected form.

One recent manifestation of serious orchestral music is now a mainstay of pop culture: video games. Game music once consisted of simple little beeps and boops or tinny chirping melodies that drove you insane until you turned down the volume. Not anymore—the increasing sophistication of gaming has seen a corresponding increase in the sophistication of gaming music.

The undisputed pioneer in this field is Japanese composer Nabuo Uematsu, who has been composing music for the company Square-Enix and its *Final Fantasy* series since 1986. Game composers face unique challenges: They never know how long a gamer will engage in a particular setting, so they must allow for music to change in mood and duration depending on what the player does. Despite these challenges, game music has become rhythmically complex and harmonically advanced.

Furthermore, it has a huge audience—an audience that isn't necessarily attracted to the concert hall. Savvy symphony orchestras have teamed up with game companies and composers in recent years to present concerts that feature music from games such as *Final Fantasy, Super Mario Bros.*, and *The Legend of Zelda*, often in combination with laser light shows and video projections of memorable scenes. Orchestras hope gamers will like what they hear and come back when the program features Mozart and Beethoven instead of Hideo Kojima (composer for *Metal Gear Solid*) and Dave Perry (*Enter the Matrix.*)

So have faith, music lovers—there's a brave new world of composers' lives poised to take center stage on a small screen near you.

Selected Bibliography

Bailie, John. *The Da Capo History of Western Classical Music*. New York: Da Capo Press, 1999.

Carr, Jonathan. *The Wagner Clan: The Saga of Germany's Most Illustrious and Infamous Family*. New York: Atlantic Monthly Press, 2007.

Gammond, Peter. *Classical Composers*. Godalming, Surrey: CLB Publishing, 1995.

Gutman, Robert W. *Mozart: A Cultural Biography*. New York: Harcourt & Brace, 1999.

Hyland, William G. *George Gershwin: A New Biography*. Westport, Conn.: Praeger, 2003.

LeBrecht, Norman. *The Book of Musical Anecdotes*. New York: The Free Press, 1985.

Levison, Brian and Frances Farrer. *Classical Music's Strangest Concerts and Characters: Extraordinary But True Stories from Over Five Centuries of Harmony and Discord*. London: Robson Books, 2007.

Martin, Russell. *Beethoven's Hair: An Extraordinary Odyssey and a Scientific Mystery Solved*. New York: Broadway Books, 2000.

Mordden, Ethan. *Opera Anecdotes*. New York: Oxford University Press, 1985.

Phillips-Matz, Mary Jane. *Puccini: A Biography*. Boston: Northeastern University Press, 2002.

Revill, David. *The Roaring Silence: John Cage: A Life*. New York: Arcade Publishing, 1992.

Ross, Alex. *The Rest Is Noise: Listening to the Twentieth Century*. New York: Farrar, Straus and Giroux, 2007.

Slonimsky, Nicolas. *Lexicon of Musical Invective: Critical Assaults on Composers Since Beethoven's Time*. New York: W. W. Norton, 2000.

Slonimsky, Nicolas. *Slonimsky's Book of Musical Anecdotes*. New York: Schirmer Book, 1998.

Swafford, Jan. *Charles Ives: A Life with Music*. New York: W. W. Norton & Company, 1996.

Swafford, Jan. *The Vintage Guide to Classical Music*. New York: Vintage, 1992.

Index

Acknowledgments

Thanks so much to the great folks at Quirk Books for offering me another fantastic project, particularly Mindy Brown, for guiding me through the writing and first round of edits, and Margaret McGuire, for managing the draft through production and improving it in so many ways. Thanks also to Mario Zucca for his fantastic illustrations.

Enormous help was provided, as always, by the staff of the Texas Christian University Mary Coutts Burnett Library, although I would appreciate it if the person who keeps moving my—er, the—step stools from the music section would knock it off.

Another big thank you goes to Adam Chromy for guiding me through the business end of things, because contracts make me twitchy.

On a personal level, so many people helped me to get this book written: my friends, my family, and my church. But I must give special thanks to the two great musicians who introduced me to music in the first place: my parents, Tom and Martha Lunday. I am sorry that the years of piano and flute lessons never "took," but perhaps with this book you'll know that even if I can't play a note, you taught me to listen—and to love great music.